The Power
of Procedure

The Power of Procedure

The Litigation of Jones v. Clinton

Nan D. Hunter
Professor of Law
Brooklyn Law School

ASPEN LAW & BUSINESS
A Division of Aspen Publishers, Inc.
New York   Gaithersburg

1 2 3 4 5 6 7 8 9 0

ISBN 0-7355-2825-x

Library of Congress Cataloging-in-Publication Data

Hunter, Nan D.
    The power of procedure : the litigation of Jones v. Clinton / Nan D. Hunter.
        p. cm.
    ISBN 0-7355-2825-X (alk. paper)
    1. Jones, Paula—Trials, litigation, etc.   2. Clinton, Bill—Trials, litigation,
etc.   3. Sexual harassment—Law and legislation—United States.   I. Title.

    KF228.J66 H86 2002
    347.73'5—dc21   2002022500

About Aspen Law & Business
Legal Education Division

With a dedication to preserving and strengthening the long-standing tradition of publishing excellence in legal education, Aspen Law & Business continues to provide the highest quality teaching and learning resources for today's law school community. Careful development, meticulous editing, and an unmatched responsiveness to the evolving needs of today's discerning educators combine in the creation of our outstanding casebooks, coursebooks, textbooks, and study aids.

ASPEN LAW & BUSINESS
A Division of Aspen Publishers, Inc.
A Wolters Kluwer Company
www.aspenpublishers.com

Summary of Contents

Contents

CHAPTER SEVEN

Discovery: Relevance and Privacy

CHAPTER EIGHT
Discovery: Sanctions   123

CHAPTER NINE
Joinder and Intervention   137

Preface

What led to the impeachment of President Clinton?
The Federal Rules of Civil Procedure.

This book documents how that improbable statement came to be true. The first in the chain of events that ultimately led to President Clinton's impeachment was the filing of a civil action, *Jones v. Clinton.* This book shows how the procedural steps in the litigation of this case, especially during what President Clinton called the "dragnet of discovery," created what became one of the great political crises in U.S. history. The Articles of Impeachment, included in the Appendix, demonstrate by their repeated references to the case how directly that event flowed from the litigation of *Jones v. Clinton.*

The structure and design of this book reflect its intended use as a supplementary text in civil procedure and related courses. During the portions of a procedure course that focus on litigation, professors can use it to guide students through an actual case from beginning to end and from a new and different perspective: that of an attorney. As students read each document, they should imagine themselves as the lawyer whose job it was to draft the document, or as Judge Wright's law clerk, analyzing the legal issues raised in that stage of the lawsuit. It will challenge students to "think like a lawyer" and to look past politics and scandal to the operations of law.

Along the way, professors and students alike will see that the evolution of *Jones v. Clinton* incorporates most of the major litigation issues that arise in civil procedure and similar upper-level courses. By tracking these issues through a single case, professors can better illustrate, and students can better understand, the inter-relationships among the rules and their strategic uses. The book teaches students to identify and analyze issues of procedure from the ground up, an approach that students can add to the set of analytical tools which they learn to use for judicial opinions, statutes, and rules.

To put these procedural steps and documents in context, the book includes a narrative beginning to each chapter. Within the documents themselves, explanations and questions appear in a running commentary alongside the text, to prompt students into thinking critically as they read. At the end of each chapter are additional notes and comments that elaborate on the major issues raised during each stage in the litigation.

An additional pedagogical feature consists of the 16 exercises distributed throughout the book. To deepen their students' understanding of the core principles, professors may choose to assign any or all of them. Students may benefit from completing these exercises alone or in a study group as part of the process of studying for an exam.

The students who have used these materials in the past have said that they "bring procedure to life" in a way that demystifies what often seemed initially like a collection of technical and sometimes strange rules. Hopefully, students using this book will also find it clarifying and enriching. If nothing else, its readers will learn the power of procedure.

Nan Hunter

April 2002

Acknowledgments

Five classes of civil procedure students enabled me by their feedback and engagement with these materials to shape and refine what began as a set of sample litigation documents. Several students contributed greatly to the project by also working as my research assistants. Emma Gilmore did a superb job of bringing sense, completeness, and a finer level of analysis to the discovery materials. Others whose work was important were Dina Levy, Walter Naeder, Deirdre Sheridan, Thomas Wittig, and Rachel Wrightson. Vicki Turner of the clerk's office of the Eastern District of Arkansas provided generous assistance when questions arose that the documents could not answer.

Although pro forma acknowledgment of secretarial support staff is standard, in this case the thanks are profoundly heartfelt. Golda Lawrence patiently and without complaint unscrambled and/or retyped countless documents that arrived via downloading software that defied any attempt at basic word processing. As always, her work was of the highest quality. For his assistance in mining previously unknown zones of the cyberworld, I thank Francis Chin, also of the law school staff.

The book benefitted immeasurably from the comments of readers, including those recruited by Aspen whose identities are unknown to me. For their non-anonymous help, I thank Claire Kelly, Minna Kotkin, Nancy Polikoff, and Jennifer Rosato. Carol McGeehan and Richard Mixter of Aspen bear most of the blame for the fact that the book is actually being published. Jessica Barmack, Susan Boulanger, Paul Sobel, and Cathi Reinfelder nursed the text through various stages of manuscript production. And Lisa Duggan persuaded me that it was worth the effort.

The Power
of Procedure

CHAPTER ONE

The Complaint

INTRODUCTION

The *American Spectator,* a magazine specializing in conservative political commentary, published an article attacking President Bill Clinton in its January 1994 issue. The article, titled "His Cheatin' Heart," asserted that the President, while Governor of Arkansas, had affairs with numerous women. One paragraph stated:

> One of the [state] troopers told the story of how Clinton had eyed a woman at a reception in downtown Little Rock. According to the trooper, . . . Clinton asked him to approach the woman, whom the trooper remembered only as Paula, tell her how attractive the governor thought she was, and take her to a room in the hotel where Clinton would be waiting . . . On this particular evening, after her encounter with Clinton, which lasted no more than an hour as the trooper stood by in the hall, the trooper said Paula told him she was available to be Clinton's regular girlfriend if he so desired.

Paula Corbin Jones, a young woman who had once worked for the Arkansas Industrial Development Commission (AIDC), read the article, and especially that paragraph, with alarm. She believed that she was the "Paula" referred to and that others, possibly including her husband, might believe that as well. She told friends that the article misreported an incident that had occurred on May 8, 1991, at a conference being held at the Excelsior Hotel in Little Rock. She asked a recently divorced friend—Debbie Ballantine—for advice. Ballantine called the lawyer who had represented her in her divorce, Daniel Traylor. Jones met with Traylor, signed a retainer agreement, and the saga of *Jones v. Clinton* began.

Traylor was a solo practitioner with a practice focused on divorce, commercial matters, and real estate. He researched the possibility of a suit against the *American Spectator,* but the combination of the difficult standards that exist for recovering for libel against the press (the plaintiff must show that the defendant knew the story was false or was reckless as to its truth or falsity), and the fact that Jones's last name had not been in the article, made hers a very weak libel case. He concluded, however, that it could be worth it to bring a case against President Clinton, if only to induce a settlement in return for a waiver by Jones of all her claims. Traylor first consulted a local real estate developer, George Cook, who had been a supporter and friend to Governor Clinton, seeking a channel of communication with the White House. Cook contacted Bruce Lindsey, special counsel to the President, who told Cook to ignore the Jones story. Rebuffed, Traylor then turned to an old political enemy of Clinton's, local attorney Cliff Jackson.

Jackson had been contacted months before by the state troopers, who were seeking help in selling their story to the press. Jackson represented them, and arranged for the financing of the investigation that resulted in the *American Spectator* article. After Traylor described the Jones case to him, Jackson scheduled a press conference featuring Jones for February 11, 1994, at the upcoming Conservative Political Action Conference (C-PAC) in Washington. During the press conference, Jones told her story. Traylor said, "We've got Bosnia. We've got a health care crisis. We've got 18 children living in a room without a father. Mr. President, this is something that shouldn't occupy your energy and your attention. I would encourage you to come forward and . . . tell the American people what the truth of this matter is. If you made a mistake, the American people will forgive you." Most reporters discounted Jones's story because it appeared to be merely part of C-PAC's political crusade against Clinton. There was little coverage of her allegations, and, despite that free advice from Mr. Traylor, no offer to settle from the White House.

Meanwhile, Jackson was also seeking to arrange new counsel for Jones. He contacted Peter Smith, a wealthy businessman in Chicago who had provided the money to pay for the investigation of Clinton's past affairs. Smith in turn contacted Richard Porter, an attorney in the Chicago office of Kirkland and Ellis, who had worked on Vice President Quayle's staff after graduating from the University of Chicago Law School and clerking for Judge Richard Posner of the Seventh Circuit. Porter contacted a friend from law school, Jerome Marcus, an attorney with the Philadelphia firm of Berger and Montague. Porter and Marcus became actively, but secretly, involved in the case, drafting many of the most important memoranda of law filed on Jones's behalf. They were later joined in that effort by George Conway, an attorney with Wachtell, Lipton, Rosen and Katz in New York City. The trio eventually began referring to themselves as "the elves." However, none of the three—Porter, Marcus, or Conway—wanted to undertake direct or open representation of Jones.

The next inquiry in the search for a lawyer to represent Jones went to Professor Nelson Lund of the George Mason Law School, another law school friend of Porter and Marcus. Lund referred them to an attorney in northern Virginia named Gilbert Davis.

Gilbert Davis and his partner Joseph Cammarata became lead counsel. Most accounts of the case have described Davis and Cammarata as moderate Republicans, not admirers of the President, but not extreme Clinton-haters. Davis was older than the lawyers in the University of Chicago Law School friendship group. He had worked as a prosecutor and become a successful personal injury lawyer. Cammarata's specialty was tax law, but he also had trial experience.

Davis's and Cammarata's biggest problem was time. They were first consulted in late April 1994—almost three years after the encounter between Jones and Clinton. The statute of limitations had already expired on a claim for sexual harassment under Title VII of the Civil Rights Act of 1964, which prohibits sex discrimination in employment. The statute of limitations for most torts was three years; thus, for events occurring on the date of the alleged harassment, it expired on May 6, 1994.

Davis and Cammarata flew to Little Rock on May 4 and spent the day interviewing first Jones and then several witnesses who said that Jones had told them of then-Governor Clinton's crude actions shortly after they had occurred, three years earlier. That same day, the *Washington Post* reported that President Clinton had hired as his attorney Robert Bennett, a partner in Skadden, Arps, Slate, Meagher & Flom. The next day, Davis and Bennett spoke by telephone and discussed settlement. Davis told Bennett that Jones wanted no money, merely a statement clearing her name.

Davis and Bennett negotiated the following statement to be read by President Clinton:

> I have no recollection of meeting Paula Jones on May 8, 1991, in a room at the Excelsior Hotel. However, I do not challenge the claim that we met there and I may very well have met her in the past. She did not engage in any improper or sexual conduct. I regret the untrue assertions which have been made about her conduct which may have adversely challenged her character and good name. I have no further comment on my previous statements about my own conduct. Neither I nor my staff will have any further comment on this matter.

The deal fell through, however, in what seems in retrospect to have been a gigantic miscalculation by all parties. Davis said that he also wanted an agreement to toll the statute of limitations for six months, meaning that Clinton would waive that defense if Jones filed the case up to six months later. The reason, he said, was that he could not trust the White House not to leak or use slanderous material about Jones after the settlement was announced. Bennett refused, telling Davis that his request was a deal breaker. According to some reports, Jones's husband insisted that a settlement include money as well as an apology, and persuaded Jones to reject the proposed settlement on those grounds. For whatever reasons, the case did not settle. The complaint was filed on May 6, 1994.

CASE PLANNING

Before we examine the complaint in *Jones v. Clinton*, let us consider the case from the perspective of the attorneys at the outset of a lawsuit. For the remainder of the book, we will follow the case through the stages of litigation that compose the bulk of most law school procedure courses. Typically, however, casebooks omit activities that are critically important to lawyers but seldom result in reported opinions.

First, for both plaintiff's and defendant's counsel, extensive fact investigation starts immediately. It does not wait for discovery to begin (which was three years later in *Jones v. Clinton*). Most facts are gathered independently, by attorneys and other staff who are not limited by either the timing or the scope of discovery. Lawyers immediately begin to identify sources of proof—witnesses, documents, scientific evidence—that will support each element of their claims or defenses. In this investigation process, interviewing skill is essential. Although it usually cannot be included in a procedure course, interviewing experience is something that you should seek opportunities to acquire.

In this case, counsel on both sides had to engage in potentially tricky client interviews with conflicting goals. Jones's lawyers, for example, needed to elicit from her all the facts that could form the basis for viable legal claims, including facts that might have seemed insignificant to her. For example, she might have been focused on framing her story as solely about the alleged encounter between her and then-Governor Clinton. For her lawyers, however, it was important to also learn about the actions of the state trooper, whose presence was essential to what became their theory of the case: that Clinton illegitimately used his official authority as Governor in harassing her. In addition, they needed to test her story, both by asking her challenging questions and by assessing the reliability of what, if any, corroborative evidence existed. In essence, they had to both win her trust and try to determine whether she could be tripped up.

President Clinton's lawyers had their own fact development headaches. Aside from the media pressure created by his client's status as President, Bennett also must have felt the tension between needing to draw out a full version of what Clinton knew and wondering how hard to push him in testing the story. For defense counsel, the problem lay in using a style that was both aggressive and appropriate with an extremely powerful individual client. Bennett surely knew that too much deference could lead to his being blindsided later on, as indeed he was.

Exercise 1—Interviewing

Consider how you would prepare to interview either of these clients or a client in a similar case. You may imagine that lawyers simply look up from their desks in time for an appointment, ask a new client what happened, and then say something like, "I'll look into that." But good interviewing requires preparation. What (in addition to the type of fee you will charge) do you want your client to know about you? What other than his or her version of the facts will you seek to elicit in an initial interview? How will you approach the task of testing the client's story? Write a brief memorandum to the file in preparation for a client interview of Jones or Clinton.

Beyond fact investigation, Jones's lawyers had a lot to do at the outset of the suit, and not much time in which to do it. Their biggest hurdle was the statute of limitations. Given the infamy of the case, you already know that Jones's lawyers succeeded in alleging sexual harassment against President Clinton despite the expiration of the statute of limitations for Title VII. How did they do that? They recognized that because Clinton and the trooper were both officers of the state, their actions could be characterized as having been taken "under color of law." As a result, the same acts that would have given rise to a Title VII claim became the basis for a claim arising under the Constitution. Claims of constitutional violations carry the same statutes of limitations as the closest analogous state law personal injury claims.[1] Under Arkansas law, the tort of intentional infliction of emotional distress, the state law claim that most closely fitted the alleged facts, carries a three-year statute of

---

1. *Owens v. Okure*, 488 U.S. 235 (1989); *Wilson v. Garcia*, 471 U.S. 261 (1985).

limitations. By this creative lawyering, they were able to fold what otherwise would have been a statutory sexual harassment claim into a claim that Clinton violated the Due Process and Equal Protection Clauses of the Constitution by engaging in harassing acts.[2] The Arkansas state law claims were joined under the umbrella of supplemental federal court jurisdiction.

Thus emerged plaintiff's theory of the case: that Governor Clinton (and the trooper) abused the power of public office, using it to discriminate against Jones, a woman government employee, by treating her in a way that a male employee would not have been treated and by engaging in acts that were tortious as well as discriminatory. Even though they will almost certainly modify their theory of the case as the lawsuit moves forward, lawyers representing a plaintiff should always be able to summarize the central points of their case, usually in a paragraph or two, before even filing the complaint. You can think of it as writing a summary of what you want to be saying at closing argument.

Lastly, in almost all cases a parallel track begins at the same time that the lawsuit begins. Typically, the dominant concern in litigation is the preparation for and conduct of a trial. On the parallel track the dominant concern is resolution without trial, usually by settlement. As occurred in *Jones v. Clinton*, settlement discussions often begin before the lawsuit is filed. Acquiring greater leverage for negotiation may be as much the purpose behind litigation moves as is preparing for trial. Statistically, this seems wise; approximately 50 percent of cases filed in federal courts are settled.[3] Therefore, counsel need to develop strategies with both tracks in mind.

However, a lawyer's primary goal should be neither litigation nor settlement per se, but solving the client's problems. Lawyers can sometimes develop creative settlement arrangements that are win-win solutions to disputes. Rather than simply negotiating about how many dollars a settlement should be worth, for example, lawyers may be able to identify things that their clients want even more than money and work out a proposal that gives each side at least some significant portion of what they value most.[4]

At the prefiling stage in *Jones v. Clinton*, settlement negotiations centered on the wording of a statement by the President—not an apology, but also not a denial or an accusation that Jones's story was false. The parties reached agreement on the

2. They did not originate this approach. *See, e.g., Bohen v. City of East Chicago, Ind.,* 799 F.2d 1180, 1185 (7th Cir. 1986). *See generally,* Mark M. Hager, Harassment and Constitutional Tort: The Other Jurisprudence, 16 Hofstra Lab. & Employment L.J. 279 (1999).

3. No data are recorded as to settlement per se. Of the civil cases terminated in federal court from March 2000 to March 2001, only 2 percent reached trial (5,782 of 249,138 terminated cases). Administrative Office of the U.S. Courts, *2001 Annual Report of the Director* 53, Table C-4. For about 17 percent of the terminations (42,051 cases), there was no judicial involvement, *id.,* and one can assume that virtually all of those were settled. For the remaining approximately 83 percent (207,087 cases), some judicial action, including settlement conferences, occurred prior to termination. *Id.* Although it is not possible to be precise, a reasonable estimate would probably be that half of those cases settled as well. Other estimates of settlement rates have clustered in the range of 50 percent. Steven Flanders, *Blind Umpires—A Response to Professor Resnik,* 35 Hastings L.J. 505, 517 n.56 (1984) (settlement rate approximately 60 percent); Michael Newman, *In-House Court Mediation in the U.S. District Courts,* 48 Fed. Law. 4 (Oct. 2001) (settlement rate approximately 40 percent).

4. *See, e.g.,* Robert Mnookin, et al., Beyond Winning: Negotiation to Create Value in Deals and Disputes (2000); Carrie Menkel-Meadow, When Winning Isn't Everything: The Lawyer as Problem Solver, 28 Hofstra L. Rev. 905 (2000); Paul Brest and Linda Hamilton Krieger, Lawyers as Problem Solvers, 72 Temple L.J. 811 (1999).

wording, but not on whether Jones would receive a six-month suspension of the statute of limitations as insurance against further accusations. First, note that compliance with the statute of limitations is not essential to a court's jurisdiction; the defendant can waive it, and thus it can be used as a bargaining chip in prefiling negotiations. Second, imagine the concerns that each side brought to this question. Jones's lawyers wanted to ensure that Clinton could not simply turn around and disparage Jones after reaching a settlement, with the knowledge that she had forfeited all further recourse. Clinton's lawyers wanted protection against Jones using press coverage that the White House couldn't control as a pretext for filing later, or perhaps they wanted an airtight guarantee that the case would go away if they issued this statement. Can you suggest how lawyers negotiating in good faith might have addressed these concerns? Because the lawyers in this case were unable to resolve those issues, the following complaint was filed on the day after the negotiations broke down.

IN THE UNITED STATES DISTRICT COURT
FOR THE EASTERN DISTRICT OF ARKANSAS
WESTERN DIVISION

PAULA CORBIN JONES
                    Plaintiff,   NO. LR-C- 94-290

        v.   JURY TRIAL DEMANDED

WILLIAM JEFFERSON CLINTON and
DANNY FERGUSON
                    Defendants

COMPLAINT

Plaintiff Paula Corbin Jones, by counsel, brings this action to obtain redress for the deprivation and conspiracy to deprive Plaintiff of her federally protected rights as hereafter alleged, and for intentional infliction of emotional distress, and for defamation.

JURISDICTION

1. This Court has subject matter jurisdiction pursuant to (a) 28 U.S.C. §1331, because the case arises under the Constitution and laws of the United States; (b) 28 U.S.C. §1343, because this action seeks redress and damages for violation of 42 U.S.C. §§1983 and 1985 and, in particular, the due process and equal protection provisions of the United States Constitution, including the rights protected in the Fifth and Fourteenth Amendments thereof; and (c) 26 U.S.C. §1332 since there is diversity of citizenship and this is a civil action involving, exclusive of interest and costs, a sum in excess of $50,000. This Court also has jurisdiction over the causes of action alleged in Counts III and IV pursuant to federal pendant jurisdiction.

2. Venue is appropriate in this judicial district under 28 U.S.C. §1391(b), because Defendants William Jefferson Clinton and Danny Ferguson reside here, and a substantial part of the events giving rise to this Complaint occurred here.

THE PARTIES

3. Plaintiff Paula Corbin Jones (hereafter "Jones") is a citizen of the State of California. Prior to her marriage on December 28, 1991, Plaintiff was known as Paula Rosalee Corbin.

4. Defendant William Jefferson Clinton (hereafter "Clinton") is a citizen of the State of Arkansas or alternatively of the District of Columbia.

Introductory Paragraph Although not required, counsel often write a paragraph summarizing the claims and framing the case, especially if they know that the complaint is likely to be read by nonlawyers. Do you think this is an effective one?

Jurisdiction This is a case with multiple bases for subject matter jurisdiction: federal question, diversity, and supplemental jurisdiction. Note that the federal court system's cover sheet requires that a plaintiff indicate the primary basis. (See Appendix 3.) Why do you think he picked the one he did? Why would he then have pled facts to support both? (See Paragraphs 3 and 4.)

Venue Note that Jones alleges that defendants "reside" in Arkansas, not that they are citizens, tracking the language of the venue statute. Even if President Clinton retained his Arkansas citizenship, did he continue to reside there? Does it matter?

Diversity of Citizenship Jones, Clinton, and Ferguson were all Arkansas citizens when the relevant events occurred. How can there be diversity? Had Jones remained in Arkansas, could there have been diversity? Did President Clinton retain his Arkansas citizenship after becoming President? If so, would there be any effect on subject matter jurisdiction in this case?

5. Defendant Danny Ferguson (hereafter "Ferguson") is a citizen of the State of Arkansas.

FACTS

6. On or about March 11, 1991, Jones began work as an Arkansas State employee for the Arkansas Industrial Development Commission (hereafter "AIDC"), an agency within the executive branch of the state of Arkansas. The Governor of Arkansas is the chief executive officer of the executive branch of the State of Arkansas.

7. On May 8, 1991, the AIDC sponsored the Third Annual Governor's Quality Management Conference (hereafter "Conference"), which was held at the Excelsior Hotel in Little Rock, Arkansas. Clinton, then Governor of Arkansas, delivered a speech at the Conference on that day.

8. Also on that day, Jones worked at the registration desk at the Conference along with Pamela Blackard (hereafter "Blackard"), another AIDC employee.

9. A man approached the registration desk and informed Jones and Blackard that he was Trooper Danny Ferguson, Bill Clinton's bodyguard. Defendant Ferguson was at that time a law enforcement officer within the ranks of the Arkansas State Police and assigned to the Governor's Security Detail. He was in street clothes and displayed a firearm on his person. He made small talk with Jones and Blackard and then left.

10. At approximately 2:30 P.M. on that day, Ferguson reappeared at the registration desk, delivered a piece of paper to Jones with a four-digit number written on it and said: "The Governor would like to meet with you" in this suite number. Plaintiff had never met Defendant Clinton and saw him in person for the first time at the Conference.

11. A three-way conversation followed between Ferguson, Blackard and Jones about what the Governor could want. Jones, who was then a rank-and-file Arkansas state employee being paid approximately $6.35 an hour, thought it was an honor to be asked to meet the Governor. Ferguson stated during the conversation: "It's okay, we do this all the time for the Governor."

12. Jones agreed to meet with the Governor because she thought it might lead to an enhanced employment opportunity with the State. Blackard told Jones that she would assume Plaintiff's duties at the registration desk.

13. Trooper Ferguson then escorted Jones to the floor of the hotel suite whose number had been written on the slip of paper Trooper Ferguson had given to Jones. The door was slightly ajar when she arrived at the suite.

14. Jones knocked on the door frame and Clinton answered. Plaintiff entered. Ferguson remained outside.

How to Read the Facts
What follows is a lengthy recitation of the facts as Jones alleges them. If you were an associate working for Clinton's lawyer and were asked to analyze this complaint for its legal sufficiency, how would you do so? You would probably just read the complaint straight through initially. On your second reading, however, you might jump from this point to the counts alleged and note the bases in law that Jones alleges for her claims. You would then research the elements of each claim or count. Next, you would read the facts again, and see how they match up against the required elements. If you want to do that now, skip ahead to the last sections of the complaint, and read the notes outlining the elements of each claim. Then read the facts.

15. The room was furnished as a business suite, not for an overnight hotel guest. It contained a couch and chairs, but no bed.

16. Clinton shook Jones's hand, invited her in, and closed the door.

17. A few minutes of small talk ensued, which included asking Jones about her job; Clinton told Jones that Dave Harrington is "my good friend." On May 8, 1991, David Harrington was Director of the AIDC, having been appointed to that post by Governor Clinton. Harrington was Jones's ultimate superior within the AIDC.

18. Clinton then took Jones's hand and pulled her toward him, so that their bodies were in close proximity.

19. Jones removed her hand from his and retreated several feet.

20. However, Clinton approached Jones again. He said: "I love the way your hair flows down your back" and "I love your curves." While saying these things, Clinton put his hand on Plaintiff's leg and started sliding it toward the hem of Plaintiff's culottes. Clinton also bent down to attempt to kiss Jones on the neck.

21. Jones exclaimed, "What are you doing?" and escaped from Clinton's physical proximity by walking away from him. Jones tried to distract Clinton by chatting with him about his wife. Jones later took a seat at the end of the sofa nearest the door. Clinton asked Jones: "Are you married?" She responded that she had a regular boyfriend. Clinton then approached the sofa and as he sat down he lowered his trousers and underwear exposing his erect penis and asked Jones to "kiss it."

22. There were distinguishing characteristics in Clinton's genital area that were obvious to Jones.

23. Jones became horrified, jumped up from the couch, stated that she was "not that kind of girl" and said: "Look, I've got to go." She attempted to explain that she would get in trouble for being away from the registration desk.

24. Clinton, while fondling his penis said: "Well, I don't want to make you do anything you don't want to do." Clinton then stood up and pulled up his pants and said: "If you get in trouble for leaving work, have Dave call me immediately and I'll take care of it." As Jones left the room Clinton looked sternly at Jones and said: "You are smart. Let's keep this between ourselves."

25. Jones believed "Dave" to be the same David Harrington, of whom Clinton previously referred. Clinton, by his comments about Harrington to Jones, affirmed that he had control over Jones's employment, and that he was willing to use that power. Jones became fearful that her refusal to succumb to Clinton's advances could damage her in her job and even jeopardize her employment.

26. At no time, nor in any manner, did Jones encourage Clinton to turn the meeting toward a sexual liaison. To the contrary, the unwanted sexual advances made by Clinton were repugnant and abhorrent to Jones who took all reasonable steps she could think to do to terminate Clinton's perverse attention and actions toward her.

27. Jones left the hotel suite and came into the presence of Trooper Ferguson in the hallway. Ferguson did not escort Plaintiff back to the registration desk. Jones said nothing to Ferguson and he said nothing to her during her departure from the suite.

28. Jones was visibly shaken and upset when she returned to the registration desk. Pamela Blackard immediately asked her what was wrong. After a moment, during which Jones attempted to collect herself, she told Blackard much of what had happened. Blackard attempted to comfort Plaintiff.

29. Jones thereafter left the Conference and went to the work place of her friend, Debra Ballantine.

30. When Ballantine met Plaintiff at the reception area, she immediately asked Jones what was wrong because Jones was visibly upset and nervous. Plaintiff wanted to talk about something that just happened and wanted to discuss it someplace privately. Ballantine and Jones went to a private area in the office, and later outside. Jones then told Ballantine what had happened with Clinton in the hotel suite. According to Ballantine, Jones told her that Clinton said as she left the room, "I know you're a smart girl and I'm sure you'll keep this to yourself."

31. Ballantine urged Jones to report the incident. Plaintiff refused, fearing that, if she did so, no one would believe her account, that she would lose her job, and that the incident would endanger her relationship with her then-fiancé (now husband), Stephen Jones.

32. Later, on the same day, Plaintiff also described the substance of her encounter with Clinton to her sister, Charlotte Corbin Brown.

33. Within two days of May 8, 1991, Plaintiff also informed her sister, Lydia Corbin Cathey, and her mother, Delmar Lee Corbin, [about] the substance of her encounter with Clinton.

34. Plaintiff also told her fiancé, Stephen Jones, that "Bill Clinton made a pass at me but I said 'no.'" She, however, did not at that time tell him the lurid details of her horrific encounter with Clinton in the hotel suite, which she feared, if disclosed, might ruin her relationship with Mr. Jones.

35. Plaintiff continued to work at AIDC. One of her duties was to deliver documents to and from the Office of the Governor, as well as other offices within the Arkansas State Capitol complex. In or about June, 1991, while Jones was performing this duty, Ferguson saw her at the Governor's office and said: "Bill wants your phone number. Hillary's out of town often and Bill would like to see you." Plaintiff refused to provide her telephone number.

36. On another occasion, Ferguson approached Jones and asked: "How's Steve?" This frightened Plaintiff and made her feel as if she was being watched and was not safe. She had never told Ferguson or Clinton the name of her fiancé.

37. Plaintiff and Stephen Jones later married. She gave birth to her child and returned to work, after which she encountered Ferguson at Governor Clinton's office. Ferguson told her: "I've told Bill how good looking you are since you've had the baby." This, too, frightened Plaintiff and made her feel that her activities were being monitored.

38. On one occasion, Plaintiff was accosted by Clinton in the Rotunda of the Arkansas State Capitol. Clinton draped his arm over Plaintiff, pulled her close and tightly to his body and said: "Don't we make a beautiful couple—beauty and the beast?" Clinton directed this remark to his bodyguard, Trooper Larry Patterson, an officer of the Arkansas State Police and also a member of the Governor's Security Detail.

39. Jones continued to work at AIDC even though she was in constant fear that Governor Clinton might take retaliatory action against her because of her rejection of his abhorrent sexual advances. Her enjoyment of her work was severely diminished. In fact, she was treated in a hostile and rude manner by certain superiors in AIDC. This rude conduct had not happened prior to her encounter with Clinton. Further, after her maternity leave she was transferred to a position which had no responsible duties for which she could be adequately evaluated to earn advancement. The reason given to her by her superiors for the transfer was that her previous position had been eliminated. This reason was untrue since her former position was not abolished. It was a pretext for the real reason which was that she was being punished for her rejection of the various advances made by Clinton described above. In addition, the job in which she was placed called for a higher grade and pay, yet she was not paid more money than she received in her previous position. Although other employees received merit increases, Jones never received a raise beyond a cost of living increase.

Inartful Pleading?
Paragraph 39 does not seem to meet the model of "simple, concise, and direct" pleading that Rule 8 calls for. How would you redraft this paragraph? Consult Rule 10(b). How would you rewrite the sentence that begins, "It was a pretext . . ."? What Rule permits a form of factual allegation that cannot be stated with certainty?

40. Jones terminated her employment and separated from AIDC service on February 20, 1993. On May 4, 1993, Plaintiff, her husband and child moved to California.

41. In January, 1994, Plaintiff visited her family and friends in Arkansas. While Jones was in Arkansas, Ms. Ballantine telephoned Jones to arrange a meeting for lunch. During the telephone conversation, Ballantine read to Plaintiff a paragraph from an article published in the January, 1994 issue of the *American Spectator* magazine regarding Plaintiff's hotel suite encounter with Clinton. [A copy of the *American Spectator* article was attached to the complaint.]

42. The *American Spectator* account asserts that a woman by the name of "Paula" told an unnamed trooper (obviously Defendant Ferguson), who had escorted "Paula" to Clinton's hotel room, that "she was available to be Clinton's regular girlfriend if he so desired," thus implying

a consummated and satisfying sexual encounter with Clinton, as well as a willingness to continue a sexual relationship with him. These assertions are untrue. The article, using information apparently derived from Ferguson, also incorrectly asserts that the encounter took place in the evening.

43. The *American Spectator* account also asserted that the troopers' "'official' duties included facilitating Clinton's cheating on his wife. This meant that, on the State payroll, and using State time, vehicles, and resources, they were instructed by Clinton on a regular basis to approach women and to solicit their telephone numbers for the Governor, to drive him in State vehicles to rendezvous points and guard him during sexual encounters; to secure hotel rooms and other meeting places for sex: . . ." and various other things to facilitate Clinton's sex life including "to help Clinton cover-up his activities by keeping tabs on Hillary's whereabouts and lying to Hillary about her husband's whereabouts." Although this pattern of conduct by Clinton may be true, the magazine article concluded, evidently from interviews with troopers from Clinton's Security Detail, including Ferguson, that "all of the women appear to have been willing participants in the affairs and liaisons."

Conclusory Pleading?
What factual assertions are contained in Paragraph 44? Consider how this paragraph relates to the claims for relief. Is it too speculative? Or may inferences be pled along with facts?

44. Since Jones ("Paula") was one of the women preyed upon by Clinton and his troopers, including by Defendant Ferguson, in the manner described above, those who read this magazine account could conclude falsely that Jones ("Paula") had a sexual relationship and affair with Clinton. Jones's reputation within her community was thus seriously damaged.

45. Jones realized that those persons who already knew about the hotel room encounter could identify her as the "Paula" mentioned in the *American Spectator* article. She became extremely upset because, inter alia, she feared that the statements in the magazine would damage her relationship with her husband, her family, and her friends and acquaintances, some of whom might have believed that she had agreed to be Clinton's "girlfriend" at a time when she was engaged to Mr. Jones.

46. On January 8, 1994, at approximately 12:00 noon, Jones and Ballantine were dining at the Golden Corral Steakhouse in North Little Rock, Arkansas. Trooper Ferguson, who happened to be dining with his wife at this restaurant, came over to their table to talk to Jones. Since Jones believed that the ultimate source of the report in the *American Spectator* of the hotel suite encounter was Trooper Ferguson, she confronted him on this matter. Trooper Ferguson stated that he was sorry that Jones's first name had appeared in the magazine article but that he had purposely concealed her last name and place of employment from those to whom he recounted the incident. Trooper Ferguson also said that he knew Jones had rebuffed Mr. Clinton's sexual advances because, "Clinton told me you wouldn't do anything anyway, Paula."

47. Because the false statements appearing in the *American Spectator* article that Jones was willing to have sex with Clinton (and the innuendo that she had already done so when she left the hotel suite)

threatened her marriage, her friendships, and her family relationships, Plaintiff spoke publicly on February 11, 1994, that she was the "Paula" mentioned in the *American Spectator* article, that she had rebuffed Clinton's sexual advances, and that she had not expressed a willingness to be his girlfriend. Jones and her lawyer asked that Clinton acknowledge the incident, state that Jones had rejected Clinton's advances, and apologize to Jones.

48. Clinton, who is now President of the United States of America, responded to Jones's request for an apology by having his press spokespersons deliver a statement on his behalf that the incident never happened, and that he never met Plaintiff. Thus, by innuendo and effect, Clinton publicly branded Plaintiff a liar. Moreover, as recently as the week this Complaint was filed, Clinton, through his White House aides, stated that Plaintiff's account of the hotel room incident was untrue and a "cheap political trick."

49. Clinton hired an attorney, who, as Clinton's agent, said that Jones's account "is really just another effort to rewrite the results of the election [i.e., for President of the United States] and . . . distract the President from his agenda." The attorney further asked the question: "Why are these claims being brought now, three years after the fact?" The attorney also asked how Jones's allegations could be taken "seriously." These comments by Clinton's counsel, on behalf of Clinton, imply that Jones is a liar.

50. Dee Dee Meyers, White House Spokeswoman, said of Jones's allegations: "It's just not true." Thus, the pattern of defaming Jones continues to this date.

51. Clinton knows that Jones's allegations are true and that his, and his attorney's, spokespersons', and agents' denials are false.

52. The outrageous nature of Clinton's branding of Jones as a liar is aggravated in that a greater stigma and reputation loss is suffered by Jones by the statements of the President of the United States in whom the general public reposes trust and confidence in the integrity of the holder of that office.

53. Clinton, a member of the Arkansas State Bar, knew or should have known on May 8, 1991, and thereafter, that Arkansas law provides that harassment, including the touching or attempt or threat to do so which subjects the victim to offensive or potentially offensive physical contact, is a criminal violation of Arkansas Code Annotated 5-71-208.

54. While Jones was in Clinton's hotel suite, Jones was falsely imprisoned by Clinton's intentional restriction of her personal freedom of movement without legal right. Clinton's use of force in pulling Jones toward him, his words and acts, and the armed police guard outside the door, in conjunction with the impressive atmosphere of her being alone with the Governor of the State who was also her superior's boss, caused her to be initially and temporarily afraid to terminate the meeting.

55. The statements, acts, and omissions of Clinton's agents, servants, and employees who acted under his explicit and implicit instructions and supervision, during the pertinent periods herein when he was Governor of Arkansas, and after he became President, bind Clinton under the doctrines of agency, joint conduct, master-servant, respondent superior, and conspiracy.

56. The actions of the Arkansas state employees, including Defendant Ferguson and other agents of Clinton were taken under color of state law.

57. Clinton's actions and omissions above stated caused Jones embarrassment, humiliation, fear, emotional distress, horror, grief, shame, marital discord, and loss of reputation.

COUNT I: DEPRIVATION OF CONSTITUTIONAL RIGHTS AND PRIVILEGES (42 U.S.C. §1983)

58. Plaintiff incorporates by reference paragraphs 1 through 57.

Elements of Count I
Count I contains a number of claims. The primary claim is one of sexual harassment, which normally arises under Title VII of the Civil Rights Act. Here, however, the statute of limitations for that claim had expired. Because Clinton was a public official, plaintiff's counsel essentially merged a sexual harassment claim into a claim that he violated the equal protection and due process clauses of the Constitution. As a result of alleging a constitutional violation, one element of the claim is that Clinton was acting under color of state law. The other elements are the same as in all sexual harassment claims: either that plaintiff was subjected to unwelcome sexual advances, based on his/her sex, that were linked to a tangible job benefit; or that plaintiff was subjected to unwelcome "hostile environment" sexual harassment that materially affected the conditions of employment.

59. Plaintiff is entitled to the equal protection of the laws under the Fourteenth Amendment of the United States Constitution, and due process of law under the Fifth and Fourteenth Amendments of the United States Constitution.

60. Defendant Clinton, as Governor of Arkansas, acting under color of state law, discriminated against Plaintiff because of her gender by sexually harassing and assaulting her on May 8, 1991, and thereafter, and this deprived Jones of her right to equal protection of the law.

61. Further, he continued personally, and through agents, to impose a hostile work environment on Plaintiff in which she feared the loss of her employment and the possible adverse employment actions against her, including job discrimination and monitoring of her personal life. As described above, she was placed in a category separate from other public employees in that she was actually subjected to hostility by her superiors, which deprived her of an opportunity for advancement and she suffered an economic deprivation.

62. Plaintiff, as a citizen and Arkansas state employee, was entitled to due process protection of freedom from arbitrary action which jeopardized her property interest in her public employee job in that she should not have been subjected arbitrarily to the fear of losing that job or of having to provide sex to the Governor as a quid pro quo for keeping the job. Further, she should not have been subjected arbitrarily to the fear of losing the enjoyment of a proper and pleasant work environment, or to other adverse actions which she feared and which deprived her of the proper enjoyment and efficiency of her work. Clinton's actions deprived Jones of her due process liberty and property interests guaranteed to her by the Constitution of the United States.

63. Plaintiff also was entitled to a due process liberty interest in her reputation as an honest public employee. Clinton's actions and statements deprived Jones of these rights.

64. Plaintiff, for a brief period of time, was held against her will by the oppressive atmosphere of intimidation caused by the presence of the highest official of the State of Arkansas and an armed guard at the door. Not only was she subjected to unwelcome sexual advances, but also was personally restrained and imprisoned by the seizing of her person, against her will, by Clinton and his agent.

65. The above-described actions of Clinton were undertaken when he was acting under the color of state law, as Governor of Arkansas, and said actions deprived Jones of federal equal protection and due process rights guaranteed by the Fifth and Fourteenth Amendments of the United States Constitution, and made actionable by 42 U.S.C. §1983 (The Civil Rights Act).

COUNT II: CONSPIRACY TO DEPRIVE PERSONS OF EQUAL PROTECTION OF THE LAWS (42 U.S.C. §1985)

66. Plaintiff incorporates by reference paragraphs 1 through 65.

67. Clinton conspired with his Security Detail, including with Defendant Ferguson, and perhaps with others currently unknown to this Plaintiff, to deprive Jones of equal protection of the laws and of equal privileges and immunities under the laws, as further set forth in Count I above.

68. The conspirators committed some acts in furtherance of the conspiracy which included contacting Jones and bringing her to Clinton on May 8, 1991 to permit him to attempt to entice her on to have a sexual liaison with him.

69. As a result of the conspiracy, Jones was injured by Defendants in her person and property and deprived of having and exercising her rights and privileges as a citizen of the United States, as is more fully set forth in Count I.

COUNT III: INTENTIONAL INFLICTION OF EMOTIONAL DISTRESS

70. Plaintiff incorporates by reference paragraphs 1 through 69.

71. The conduct of Clinton herein set forth was odious, perverse, and outrageous. Not only were the acts of sexual perversity unwelcome by Jones, but they were willful, wanton, reckless, intentional, persistent, and continuous in the hotel room.

72. Clinton's sexual advances, assaults upon and imprisonment of Jones's person, and his exposure of his erect penis and his requests of acts to be performed thereupon were extreme, intentional, and caused Jones severe emotional distress.

73. Not content with the events in the hotel on May 8, 1991, Clinton on subsequent occasions, acting himself and through his agents, as specified above, aggravated further the initial severe emotional damage to Jones.

Here, Plaintiff alleges that Clinton, acting under color of state law, deprived her of a property interest (in her job) and deprived her of a liberty interest both by harming her reputation and, in essence, falsely imprisoning her. This last claim would import the elements of the tort of false imprisonment, which Arkansas law defines as "detention without sufficient legal authority." *Grandiean v. Grandiean*, 869 S.W.2d 709 (Ark. 1994).

Elements of Count II
The elements of conspiracy law that apply here are that (1) defendants did conspire (2) for the purpose of depriving a person of equal protection of the laws; (3) that defendants acted to further that aim, which (4) resulted in a deprivation of equal protection of the law.

Elements of Count III
This is a state law claim. Under Arkansas law, plaintiff must prove (1) that the defendant intended to inflict emotional harm or should have known that it was a likely result; (2) that the conduct was "extreme and outrageous"; (3) that defendant caused plaintiff's distress; and (4) that plaintiff's distress was severe. *M.B.M. Co. v. Counce*, 268 Ark. 269, 596 S.W.2d 681 (1980).

74. These actions were so outrageous in character, and extreme in degree, as to go beyond all possible bounds of decency, and to be regarded as atrocious and utterly intolerable in a civilized society.

COUNT IV: DEFAMATION

75. Plaintiff incorporates by reference paragraphs 1 through 74.

Elements of Count IV
This is another state law claim. Defamation occurs when defendant communicates to a third person information that harms plaintiff's reputation in the community.

76. On several occasions on and after February 11, 1994, Clinton, and his agents and employees acting pursuant to his direction, maliciously and willfully, defamed Jones by making statements which Clinton knew to be false. These statements were made with the intent and certain knowledge that they would be reprinted in the print and other media.

77. Such statements by Clinton, his agents, and employees, characterized Jones as a liar and as being "pathetic," and damaged her good name, character, and reputation.

78. Defendant Ferguson's statements likewise maliciously and willfully defamed plaintiff and damaged her good name, character, and reputation. Ferguson's statement that Jones had agreed to be Clinton's girlfriend, and his innuendo that she had willingly participated in a sexual encounter, were knowingly false.

79. That Ferguson knew these statements were false is confirmed by Clinton's denial to Ferguson that anything happened of a sexual nature between Clinton and Jones.

RELIEF REQUESTED

WHEREFORE, Plaintiff requests the following relief:

"Jointly and Severally"
What does this term mean? It is used to allege that each defendant, individually, committed wrongs against plaintiff, as well as wrongs they committed together, so that plaintiff can collect damages from either or both. How might its inclusion in the complaint affect other procedural issues in the case?

a. Count I, judgment against Defendant Clinton for compensatory damages of $75,000; punitive damages for Defendant's willful, outrageous, and malicious conduct, of $100,000; the costs of her suit and attorneys' fees; nominal damages, and such other and further relief as the Court may deem proper.

b. Count II, judgment against Defendant Clinton and Defendant Ferguson, jointly and severally for compensatory damages of $75,000; punitive damages for Defendant's willful, outrageous, and malicious conduct, of $100,000; the costs of her suit and attorney's fees; nominal damages, and such other and further relief as the Court may deem proper.

Punitive Damages
What are the criteria for punitive damages? What is the importance of requesting this remedy? How will its inclusion in the complaint affect future litigation moves?

c. Count III, judgment against Defendant Clinton for compensatory damages of $75,000; punitive damages for Defendant's willful, outrageous, and malicious statements and conduct, of $100,000; the costs of her suit and attorneys' fees; nominal damages, and such other and further relief as the Court may deem proper.

d. Count IV, judgment against Defendant Clinton and Defendant Ferguson, jointly and severally for compensatory damages of $75,000; punitive damages for Defendant's willful, outrageous, and malicious statements and conduct, of $100,000; the costs of her suit and attorneys' fees; nominal damages, and such other and further relief as the Court may deem proper.

JURY TRIAL DEMANDED

Plaintiff demands a trial by jury on each of the counts.

Respectfully Submitted,
PAULA CORBIN JONES
By Her Counsel
Gilbert K. Davis
Joseph Cammarata
Attorneys for Plaintiff
9516-C Lee Highway
Fairfax, Virginia 22031
(703) 352-3850

VERIFICATION

I hereby certify under penalty of perjury that I am the Plaintiff in the above-captioned case; that I have read the foregoing Complaint; and, that the facts related therein are true and correct to the best of my knowledge, information, and belief.

Paula Corbin Jones

Verification Swearing to the complaint on penalty of perjury constitutes a verification. Rule 23.1. It is not required and seldom done. Its role here may have been to impress the public by emphasizing that Jones had read the complaint and would stand behind this set of facts. It will also enable the lawyers to later use the complaint as an affidavit if they desire to; *affidavits* are simply "sworn to" statements.

NOTES AND COMMENTS

1. The constitutional–statutory relationship.   Now that you have read the complaint, you have seen the way that Jones's lawyers pled the merged sexual harassment–Constitutional violation claim. You may have noticed that another statute was involved as well.

Plaintiff's claims in Counts I and II invoked both the Fourteenth Amendment and 42 U.S.C. §1983 (1994). The Fourteenth Amendment provides substantive law: Every citizen is entitled to "equal protection of the laws." But the Amendment does not create a private right of action to enforce that right. That function is performed by §1983, which provides

Every person who, under color of any statute, ordinance, regulation, custom, or usage, of any State or Territory or the District of Columbia, subjects, or causes to be subjected, any citizen of the United States or other person within the jurisdiction thereof to the deprivation of any rights, privileges, or immunities secured

by the Constitution and laws, shall be liable to the party injured in an action at
law, suit in equity, or other proper proceeding for redress . . . .

It is §1983 that uses the phrase "under color" of state law. Can you identify which
allegations in the complaint relate to the element of "under color" of state law?

2. Sui generis?   Consider the ways in which this was or was not a typical complaint. Its use of salacious detail, for example, was obviously meant to have a particular political impact. Yet many complaints contain more details than are necessary to
survive a motion to dismiss. How would you write a complaint in a case arising
from essentially the same factual assertions but which did not involve a prominent
political figure?

3. Two schools of thought.   Again, imagine that this were a less notorious case.
Often, the lawyer who drafts a complaint writes a short, succinct, minimalist complaint. (Remember that Form 9 of the Federal Rules of Civil Procedure [FRCP], for
example, is legally sufficient.) Alternatively, she could elect to put in more detail,
trying to convey the richness of the story from her client's point of view. Consider
the pros and cons of each choice. What tactical considerations will be most important? Keep in mind that complaints have multiple audiences: opposing counsel, the
opposing party, possibly the judge (judges do not read complaints as they are filed,
but will refer to them later if motions to dismiss or discovery disputes require), and
perhaps others for whom it could serve as an introductory summary of the case
(potential witnesses, the press, etc.).

Exercise 2—Ramifications of Pleading Decisions
Make a list of the strategic decisions that went into the drafting of the Jones
complaint. You might begin with the decisions whether to elaborate on details
and to include scandalous assertions. For each decision, write what you believe
will turn out to be the pros and cons of that decision as the lawsuit unfolds.
Include the items identified in the marginal notations in the complaint—for
example, the inclusion of joint and several liability and of punitive damages—
as well as other strategic issues that occur to you as you read these notes and
reexamine the complaint. Modify the list and reassess the ramifications as you
read each chapter on later stages of litigation.

4. Is this complaint sufficient?   Compare the elements of each claim with the
facts as alleged. How does a lawyer know which facts are essential and which are
not? That is determined by which facts plaintiff will need to prove at trial to support
each element of the claim. What are the essential facts in this case? Review the descriptions of the claims in the marginal notations. If there are essential facts missing
from the complaint, the judge may legitimately assume them not to be true. On first
reading, this complaint may seem to contain more facts than anyone would want
to know. Is it possible, however, that necessary facts are missing?

5. Are there Rule 11 problems with the complaint?   Were there grounds under
Rule 11(b) of the FRCP for Clinton's lawyers to file a motion for sanctions? Rule
11(b) provides three bases for a motion for sanctions: (1) improper purpose or harassment; (2) an inadequate basis in law; and (3) an absence of present or likely
evidentiary support for allegations of fact. Can you identify any portions of the com-

plaint that were vulnerable under those criteria? Were there specific paragraphs in the complaint that Jones's lawyers may have included as an anticipatory defense to a Rule 11 challenge? Should any facts have been designated as "likely to be established upon further investigation or discovery"?

6. *Procedure under Rule 11.*   If President Clinton's lawyers were to assert that the complaint had violated Rule 11 on any basis, how would they proceed? List the steps that they would be required to take before filing a motion. Do you think that the mechanics of pursuing a Rule 11 motion would affect the decision whether to proceed in the first place?

7. *Process policy and Rule 11.*   One might argue that this complaint is an example of a document that is not objectively without basis, but nonetheless one that was filed for an improper purpose, such as harassment, under Rule 11(b)(1). What should the standard be in such a situation? Should it matter whether the improper purpose, if there was one, was generated by the party or by her lawyers? Very little law exists on this question. The Ninth Circuit drew a distinction between complaints and motions, ruling that a complaint filed for an improper purpose, such as harassment, would not be sanctioned unless it was legally frivolous, but that motions or other documents filed for an improper purpose could be sanctioned under Rule 11 even if not frivolous. *Aetna Life Ins. Co. v. Alla Medical Services, Inc.,* 855 F.2d 1470 (9th Cir. 1988). The Fourth Circuit adopted this test:

> If a complaint is not filed to vindicate rights in court, its purpose must be improper. However, if a complaint is filed to vindicate rights in court, and also for some other purpose, a court should not sanction counsel for an intention that the court does not approve, so long as the added purpose is not undertaken in bad faith and is not so excessive as to eliminate a proper purpose. Thus, the purpose to vindicate rights in court must be central and sincere.

In re Kunstler, 914 F.2d 505, 518 (4th Cir. 1990).

More fundamentally, what deeper policy interests would be implicated by a Rule 11 challenge when the "central purpose" of a complaint is to harass or undermine a political figure? Should that be an acceptable use of litigation, so long as the complaint contains legally colorable claims? Or, should "improper purpose" alone be grounds for Rule 11 sanctions? Professor Carol Rice Andrews has argued that President Clinton could have filed a Rule 11 motion based solely on the evidence of political motives, and that improper motives alone violate Rule 11. However, she also concluded that imposition of Rule 11 sanctions in a political case such as this one would have violated the plaintiff's rights under the First Amendment. Carol Rice Andrews, *Jones v. Clinton: A Study in Politically Motivated Suits, Rule 11 and the First Amendment,* 2001 B.Y.U. L. Rev. 1. How do you think those concerns should be balanced?

8. *Counts, claims, and incorporation.*   In Paragraphs 58, 66, 70, and 75, the complaint is formatted such that a new "count" begins. What is the relationship between counts and claims? It is customary in complaints to formulate a separate count for "[e]ach claim founded upon a separate transaction or occurrence . . . whenever a separation facilitates the clear presentation of the matters set forth." Rule 10(b). This format more clearly places the defendant on notice of what legal claims

he must defend against. As the marginal notation at Paragraph 59 states, Count I in this case is a compound of several claims or theories for recovery under the same statute (42 U.S.C. §1983): quid pro quo sexual harassment, hostile environment sexual harassment, false imprisonment, and harm to plaintiff's reputation. Because each numbered paragraph of facts may be pled in support of one or more claims, each count uses the "incorporates by reference" assertion to invoke all facts in support of all claims. *See* Rule 10(c).

9. Prayer for relief.   In a simple case, attorneys might state the prayer for relief in one paragraph, rather than in a separate prayer for each count, as was done here. To some extent, it is a matter of style; what is essential is that the prayer put defendant on notice of the types of relief sought. *See* Rule 8(a). When there are multiple defendants, subdividing the prayer for relief by count serves to clarify which relief is sought as to which defendant. In this case, that is the difference between section (a) and sections (b), (c), and (d) of the prayer.

10. Trial by jury.   Plaintiff's demand for trial by jury follows the prayer for relief. Why is it logical for the specification of relief to precede the jury demand? It is the nature of relief that determines whether the Seventh Amendment right to trial by jury is triggered. (However, courts look beyond the mere recitation of a prayer for damages to see if the claim being asserted supports it.) If the jury demand is omitted from the complaint, has plaintiff waived her right to trial by jury? Could the defendant request a trial by jury? *See* Rule 38. The size of the jury may also be a strategic consideration. At a pretrial conference, Bennett requested twelve instead of six jurors, because he thought that Jones could not get a unanimous verdict against President Clinton from twelve people in Arkansas. *See* Rule 48. Consider how each party's strategy will be affected by the question of who—judge or jury—will ultimately decide the facts.

11. What about in personam jurisdiction?   If you have already studied the materials in civil procedure about personal jurisdiction, you may have noticed that there are no allegations in the complaint regarding that. Why would the complaint so carefully plead the basis for subject matter jurisdiction and contain no allegations as to personal jurisdiction? Note also how the two are treated differently in Rule 12(h)(1) and (3).

CHAPTER TWO

Motions Testing
the Complaint

INTRODUCTION

The primary mechanism that a defendant uses to test the legal sufficiency of a complaint is a motion under either Rule 12(b)(6) or 12(c). A motion to dismiss under Rule 12(b)(6) is almost always filed prior to the answer; a motion for judgment on the pleadings under Rule 12(c) is filed after or at the same time that the answer is filed.

Their function, however, is the same: to test whether the plaintiff has stated a claim (or claims) for which relief can be granted. In deciding on either motion, a judge must treat all factual allegations in the complaint as if they were true and draw all reasonable inferences in favor of the plaintiff. Judges do not consider evidence in deciding such motions; they are to look only at the pleadings as the source of facts. If the plaintiff has asserted a claim that could be the basis for legal relief if all the facts she has alleged are proven to be true, the motion should be denied.

In *Jones v. Clinton*, as you will see in the next chapter, President Clinton was able to bypass filing a motion to dismiss by first filing a special motion asserting presidential immunity. As a result, there was never a Rule 12(b)(6) motion as such, and the court's assessment of the sufficiency of Jones's complaint occurred pursuant to a Rule 12(c) motion. (You will consider in the next chapter whether President Clinton's strategy violated the timing aspects of Rule 12.) We consider the Rule 12(c) motion now, although out of order with the actual chronology of the lawsuit, because it was no different in content or analysis than if it had been litigated as a Rule 12(b)(6) motion. In most cases, the set of issues being argued in this chapter will be raised by a Rule 12(b)(6) motion, filed prior to the answer.

What follows are excerpts from the parts of the motion papers that address the sexual harassment claims. (Only the memoranda of law are excerpted because the motion itself is typically quite short; it usually states only the relief sought and the Rule under which it is brought. The heart of the argument goes into the accompanying memorandum of law.) Following these excerpts is Judge Wright's opinion analyzing the sufficiency of each count in the complaint.[1] Compare the parties' arguments and the judge's analysis to your answer to Note 4 at the end of Chapter 1.

---

1. Case caption and signatures are omitted for the remainder of the documents.

MEMORANDUM IN SUPPORT OF PRESIDENT CLINTON'S MOTION FOR JUDGMENT ON THE PLEADINGS AND DISMISSAL OF THE COMPLAINT

. . . In Count I, the Complaint asserts that when President Clinton was Governor of Arkansas, he subjected plaintiff to sexual harassment and thereby deprived her of her constitutional rights to equal protection and due process, in violation of 42 U.S.C. §1983. The President vehemently denies these allegations. However, even if they are accepted as true for purposes of this motion, plaintiff herself has alleged nothing more than private conduct—a single overture, abandoned as soon as she stated it was unwelcome. This alleged conduct is not a deprivation of her constitutional rights, and the Complaint fails to allege other crucial elements of a §1983 claim premised on sexual harassment.

Note that this brief is framed, not as a denial of any allegations, but as an argument that plaintiff "fails to plead facts to show" certain elements and that the complaint "lacks any allegation" as to other elements of the claim.

First, the Complaint fails to plead facts to show that the Governor's actions constituted state action taken under color of law. It lacks any allegation that the alleged personal conduct by the Governor was related to official authority, and the allegation that the defendant was a public official or that he used a member of his security detail to gain an introduction to plaintiff cannot satisfy this requirement. Similarly, the Complaint lacks any allegation that he acted with the specific intent to deprive plaintiff of any rights based on her gender.

Another of the Complaint's fatal flaws is the absence of allegations setting forth essential elements of a sexual harassment claim based either on quid pro quo harassment or a hostile workplace environment. With respect to quid pro quo harassment, the Complaint lacks a legally cognizable allegation of a threat made or benefit promised in connection with the alleged sexual approach, and does not allege any tangible adverse impact on plaintiff's job following her alleged rejection of that approach. Indeed, the Complaint fails on the most basic element of causation: it does not allege that Governor Clinton—who was not plaintiff's supervisor—communicated to plaintiff's employer about her or took or threatened to take any other action to cause any asserted adverse impact on plaintiff's working conditions.

Likewise, the Complaint fails to allege a hostile workplace. Aside from the supposed single incident at the Excelsior Hotel on May 8, 1991, the Complaint alleges only one other contact with Governor Clinton, only a few additional contacts with his co-defendant Trooper Ferguson, and conclusory claims that plaintiff's superiors were rude. Viewed objectively, as the law requires, none of these additional contacts alleges a hostile workplace. Taken individually or as a whole, these contacts do not in any way constitute the kind of pervasive, intimidating, abusive conduct that courts require to establish a hostile work environment claim. . . .

To establish a claim of quid pro quo sexual harassment, a plaintiff must assert, inter alia "that the employee's submission to the unwelcomed [sexual] advances was an express or implied condition for receiving job benefits or that the employee's refusal to submit to a supervisor's sexual demands resulted in a tangible job detriment." [citation omitted]. . . .

Plaintiff fails to allege either a benefit offered to her, or a threat made against her, or that she suffered any sort of tangible job detriment as a result of her alleged refusal of the defendant's purported advance. Most significantly, she fails to allege that Governor Clinton—who was not her immediate supervisor—communicated with her employer and thereby caused any adverse job consequences she allegedly suffered. Plaintiff's claim of quid pro quo harassment turns on her allegation that the Governor implicitly threatened her by twice mentioning his friendship with the head of the Arkansas Industrial Development Commission ("AIDC"), the agency at which plaintiff was employed as a clerk. (Compl. ¶¶17, 24.) These allegations, however, do not indicate that any threat was made. Nor does plaintiff allege that the Governor offered any job benefit if she complied with the alleged advances.

Moreover, even by plaintiff's own allegations, the Governor did not persist after she made it clear that she was not interested in a sexual relationship; explicitly told her that he did not want her to do anything she did not want to do; and did not in any way interfere with her leaving the room when she expressed a desire to do so. (Compl. ¶¶23-24.) These allegations fall far short of the typical scenario where quid pro quo harassment is found. . . .

Absent any threat or offer of benefit, plaintiff must allege that a "tangible job detriment" resulted from the defendant's conduct. The only job impacts alleged here, however, are at best subjective and intangible. Plaintiff alleges that following the alleged encounter with the Governor, she was in fear of losing her job, and that certain unnamed superiors were rude to her. She further alleges that following a subsequent maternity leave, she was assigned to a new position that had "no responsible duties for which she could be adequately evaluated to earn advancement." (Compl. ¶39.) Plaintiff fails, however, to allege that the grade, class, or pay rate of her post-maternity leave job was different from her old job.

Courts consistently have held that intangible harms of this nature cannot support a claim of quid pro quo harassment. . . .

Most critically, plaintiff fails to allege any facts which would give rise even to an inference that the Governor took steps to bring about any of these asserted changes in her working conditions. Indeed, the Complaint does not allege that he ever actually spoke about her or the alleged May 8 incident to anyone in a position to affect her job situation. Accordingly, the Complaint fails to plead quid pro quo harassment.

Again, note that the argument focuses on a "failure to allege" and "failure to plead." What is the difference between these two terms?

In *Meritor Sav. Bank v. Vinson,* 477 U.S. 57 (1986), the Supreme Court recognized that a sexual harassment claim could [also] be premised on a work environment characterized by conduct "sufficiently severe or pervasive 'to alter the conditions of [the victim's] employment and create an abusive working environment.'" 477 U.S. at 67. In *Harris v. Forklift Svs. Inc.*, 510 U.S. 17 (1993), the Court added that a plaintiff's subjective perception that a work environment was abusive is not enough: "Conduct that is not severe or pervasive enough to create an objectively hostile or abusive work environment—an environment that a reasonable person would find hostile or abusive—is beyond Title VII's purview." 510 U.S. at 21. Under these standards, the Complaint also fails to allege a hostile workplace claim. Plaintiff's attempt to cobble together allegations sufficient to make out a hostile environment claim stands in stark contrast to the facts that underlie legitimate hostile workplace claims. First, the alleged incident at the Excelsior Hotel on May 8,1991 fails to support a hostile environment claim because a single alleged advance and rejection is insufficient absent extreme coercion or physical abuse, which is not alleged here.

Plaintiff then alleges a few additional contacts—only one of which involved the Governor—over the course of her employment with AIDC, none of which on their face constitute harassment, much less harassment on the basis of sex. These also include three comments allegedly made by Trooper Ferguson, and a conclusory allegation that unnamed superiors were rude. (Compl. ¶¶35-39.)

Plaintiff alleges that these comments made her "feel" that she was being "monitored." (Compl. ¶37.) But as *Harris* makes clear, it is not plaintiff's subjective feelings that control, but whether a reasonable person would objectively view these comments as hostile and abusive. Even if these comments are read in the sinister light that plaintiff seeks to cast, and even if taken together with the alleged incident at the hotel, these contacts do not begin to meet the level of severe or pervasive hostile or abusive conduct required. . . .

Plaintiff also alleges that during this period, unnamed superiors at AIDC treated her in a hostile, rude manner and she allegedly was transferred to a position which had no responsible duties and called for a higher grade and pay which she allegedly did not receive. (Compl. ¶39.) Plaintiff simply fails to allege any objective on-the-job harassment of the type which has consistently characterized findings of hostile work environments.

Indeed, the incidents alleged here fail even to equal the allegations made in cases where courts rejected a hostile environment claim. Thus, any contention that this Complaint states a hostile workplace claim should be rejected. . . .

PLAINTIFF'S MEMORANDUM IN OPPOSITION TO THE MOTION OF DEFENDANT WILLIAM JEFFERSON CLINTON FOR JUDGMENT ON THE PLEADINGS

Having been thwarted in his first attempt to short-circuit this litigation before factual discovery, defendant William Jefferson Clinton

("Mr. Clinton") now takes a second bite at that apple. He seeks judgment on the pleadings, but without coming to terms with the heavy burden such a motion imposes. Mr. Clinton's memorandum of law ignores important allegations of the Complaint; places an interpretive spin on other allegations, contrary to the dictates of the Federal Rules of Civil Procedure, 12(c), while rewriting the Complaint to describe conduct very different from what is actually alleged; and ultimately argues for a misapplication of the law governing those allegations. . . .

In practice and effect, Mr. Clinton does not ask the Court to assess the legal sufficiency of the factual allegations under the notice pleading standard of Fed. R. Civ. P. 8, but rather to weigh the allegations as if they were evidence—instead of letting a jury do it. . . .

This is the core point of Plaintiff's brief.

The alleged actions of Mr. Clinton and his agents are not merely shocking: they are also clear abuses of power conferred upon Mr. Clinton as an official of the State of Arkansas. Simply put: if Mr. Clinton had not been backed by the power of the state, made manifest on more than one occasion by armed troopers and Mr. Clinton's power to take or make miserable plaintiff's job, this would be a commonplace claim of outrage.

Yet, having chosen to challenge the sufficiency of the Complaint, Mr. Clinton does not confront the allegations and argue that they are not actionable. He does not argue, for example, that a directive from a superior official to a subordinate, delivered by an armed law enforcement officer, is not "action under color of state law," or that the conduct actually alleged would not be actionable.

Rather, defendant's memorandum is an exercise in rewriting the allegations, placing emphasis on some, ignoring others, and rewriting plaintiff's claim. Whatever utility this exercise may have for closing argument to a jury, it is misplaced at the Rule 12(c) stage.

For example, the directive by an armed state trooper to a young female state employee that "the Governor wishes to see you" in a particular hotel room, during a government-sponsored conference, so that he can expose himself and ask for sex, is transformed into the mere claim that he "used a member of his security detail to gain an introduction to her." "Gain an introduction?" And nothing more? . . . Rewriting the Complaint to make it allege only that a man used his bodyguard to "gain an introduction" to a young woman makes the facts at issue here sound like a genteel romantic interlude lifted from the pages of a Jane Austen novel. Unfortunately for all concerned, it is far from what the Complaint alleges. . . .

Mr. Clinton has a mistaken view of the role of the Complaint in cases of this type. Ms. Jones does not allege fraud, or mistake, for which Fed. R. Civ. P. 9 sets forth a heightened pleading standard. Rather, the allegations here relate to a claim for a garden-variety Section 1983 claim based on outrageous, sexually-related misdeeds.

In such a case, all that is needed is a short and plain statement of the claim under Fed. R. Civ. P. 8. Ms. Jones has more than complied with the dictates of the Federal Rules, which "do not require a claimant to set out in detail the facts upon which he bases his claim." *Conley v. Gibson,* 355 U.S. 41, 47 (1957). . . .

Instead of recognizing these basic rules and framing his arguments accordingly, Mr. Clinton consistently attacks the Complaint only because it does not conform to some other, much higher, standard. For example, he contends there is no adequate causal link between plaintiff's refusal to have sex with him, and the subsequent adverse employment actions she experienced, because the Complaint "fails to allege any *facts*" . . . (emphasis added) to show *how* Mr. Clinton caused the adverse employment actions to come about. But that, of course, misapprehends the proper legal standard: the issue at this stage of the case is whether plaintiff has *simply alleged,* which she has, that the adverse employment actions were indeed the result of her refusal to do Mr. Clinton's bidding, in the hotel room on May 8, 1991, and later. See ¶39 ("the real reason [for adverse employment actions, including failure to obtain raises and *de facto* demotions] was that she was being punished for her rejection of the various advances made by Mr. Clinton described above."). At the Rule 12(c) stage, that is enough. . . .

The Complaint alleges that Mr. Clinton took the actions he did with respect to plaintiff "because of her gender." Complaint ¶60. This is—without more—sufficient under Rule 12(c).

Even if required to allege more, which she is not, plaintiff has alleged facts which demonstrate Mr. Clinton's intent to act because of Ms. Jones's gender. When he first met her, Mr. Clinton knew little about Ms. Jones. He knew her gender, her appearance, and the fact that she was a state employee. The Governor's admiration for plaintiff's "curves"; the attempted kiss in the hotel room; the pulling of plaintiff toward him; . . .—surely each suffice independently to permit a trier of fact to conclude the conduct was based on female gender. . . .

Under Section 1983, as under Title VII, it is unlawful to create a sexually hostile or abusive work environment. As the Eighth Circuit has recognized, "[s]exual harassment can take place in many different ways." [citation omitted] "The harassment need not be explicitly sexual in nature, though, nor have explicit sexual overtones." [citation omitted] "In assessing the hostility of an environment, a court must look to the totality of the circumstances." [citation omitted]

Factors relevant to the analysis include "the frequency of the discriminatory conduct; its severity; whether it is physically threatening or humiliating, or a mere offensive utterance; and whether it unreasonably interferes with an employee's work performance," but no single factor is dispositive. The nature of this analysis makes it "quintessentially" an exercise for the trier of fact, and courts have appropriately been reluctant to dispose of hostile environment claims on summary judgment, much less on Rule 12 motions.

Mr. Clinton argues that "a single alleged advance and rejection is insufficient absent extreme coercion or physical abuse." Not so: standing alone, a single serious episode of sexual harassment *can* create an actionable hostile environment. Moreover, Mr. Clinton's actions on May 8 constitute a series of distinct and escalating sexual advances each followed by a separate rebuff by Ms. Jones. In any event, defendant ignores many of the additional actions, on later dates, pled in the Complaint.

The events of May 8, whether considered one collective incident or multiple harassment events, created an actionable hostile environment. Even a single, isolated incident of severe harassment can state a claim under *Meritor* and *Harris;* defendant's "asser[tion] that a single incident of sexual harassment cannot amount to actionable sex discrimination" under Section 1983 "is a mistaken statement of the law." [citation omitted] . . .

A number of factors reinforce the conclusion that a trier of fact could reasonably conclude the May 8 incidents to have created a hostile environment. First, the harasser was not only Ms. Jones's ultimate superior, but also the most powerful political figure in the State. Second, the type of harassment was extreme and outrageous. . . .

Third, the harassment was effected, at least in substantial part, by Mr. Clinton's use of an armed bodyguard, a state law enforcement officer, who brought plaintiff to the room and then stood outside the door during Mr. Clinton's sexual advance.

Fourth, the venue of the conduct is noteworthy. Mr. Clinton's advances were not in the generally-benign location of an office, where a passer-by might intervene, interrupt, or at least witness. It was in a closed, guarded, and otherwise-vacant hotel room. . . .

A reasonable trier of fact could conclude that the May 8 events, in and of themselves, constituted a hostile environment—and, on these pleadings, Mr. Clinton cannot meet his burden under Rule 12(c) to convince the Court that a hostile environment is not legally and sufficiently well-pleaded.

Even assuming, *arguendo,* that the events of May 8 constitute "a single, un-actionable incident," [quoting President Clinton's Memorandum] the Complaint also alleges that Ms. Jones was subjected to a hostile environment after May 8. Among other things:

- Mr. Clinton communicated to Ms. Jones (through Mr. Ferguson) Mr. Clinton's desire to get Ms. Jones's phone number, and to see her, while Mr. Clinton's wife was out of town. Complaint ¶35.
- Mr. Ferguson indicated that he had obtained information, never communicated to him by her, about Ms. Jones's personal relationships. Complaint ¶36.

- Mr. Ferguson told Ms. Jones that he had commented to Mr. Clinton on her physical appearance following her pregnancy. Complaint ¶37.
- Without invitation, Mr. Clinton accosted Ms. Jones in the State Capitol, touched her in an inappropriate, familiar, and unwanted way, and made a sexual remark about the two of them in front of another person. Complaint ¶38.
- Following her rejection of Mr. Clinton's sexual advances, and—as the Complaint alleges—as a direct result thereof, Ms. Jones was treated in a hostile and rude manner by supervisors and eventually transferred to a dead-end job. Complaint ¶39. . . .

Contrary to Mr. Clinton's assertion, the Complaint also properly alleges a cause of action for quid pro quo sexual harassment. . . . As explained by the [Equal Employment Opportunity Commission] EEOC Guidelines, quid pro quo sexual harassment occurs when "submission to such conduct is made either explicitly or implicitly a term or condition of an individual's employment [or] submission to or rejection of such conduct by an individual is used as the basis for employment decisions affecting such individual." 29 C.F.R. §1604.11(a).

The unlawful offer to exchange favors for job action need not be explicit; an implicit threat is equally actionable. Indeed, an implied conditioning of job status upon sexual favors "is far more likely to take place than is the explicit variety."

Mr. Clinton argues that the Complaint is deficient for three reasons:

(i)   failure to allege that "a benefit [was] offered to [Ms. Jones], or a threat made against her,"
(ii) failure to allege that Ms. Jones "suffered any sort of tangible job detriment as a result of her" rejection of Mr. Clinton's sexual advance; and
(iii) failure to allege that Mr. Clinton "caused any adverse job consequences" she allegedly suffered.

Yet the Complaint alleges every one of these factors and, what is more, alleges facts from which a reasonable jury would readily infer these facts.

First, the fact that the Governor implicated the terms and conditions of Ms. Jones's job with the State leaps from the page. As the Complaint alleges, the first thing Mr. Clinton did in the hotel room was to make clear that he had ultimate power over her—as well as over her boss. Complaint ¶17. And after she rebuffed his advances Mr. Clinton made a crystal clear threat: "You are smart. Let's keep this between ourselves." Complaint ¶24; *see also* Complaint ¶30.

Ms. Jones reasonably perceived these comments as conveying the message that Mr. Clinton "had control over Ms. Jones's employment, and that he was willing to use that power." Complaint ¶25. Any thinking state employee would have perceived the same threat: "a reasonable person in [Ms. Jones's] position would have believed that [she] was the subject of quid pro quo sexual harassment," *Nichols v. Frank,* 42 F.3d at 512, from the state official possessed of the greatest power to confer benefits for compliance and punishment for refusal.

Second, Ms. Jones time and again alleges tangible job detriment as a consequence of her rejection of Mr. Clinton's sexual overture. For instance, Ms. Jones "was transferred to a position which had no responsible duties for which she could be adequately evaluated to earn advancement." Complaint ¶39. This is precisely the sort of job detriment often underlying a classic quid pro quo claim. Mr. Clinton is simply wrong when he says Ms. Jones must allege that "the grade, class, or pay rate of her post-maternity leave job was different from her old job." However, here too Ms. Jones claims an economic deprivation (Complaint ¶39).

Third, the Complaint also alleges the requisite causal relationship. Ms. Jones pleads explicitly that Mr. Clinton's conduct, and her refusal of his requests for sex, was the cause of the harm she suffered. Complaint ¶39 (Ms. Jones "was being punished for her rejection of the various advances made by Clinton"). At this stage, prior to discovery, Ms. Jones need allege no more than this. . . .

JUDGE WRIGHT'S DECISION

Paula Corbin Jones v. William Jefferson Clinton
974 F. Supp. 712 (E.D. Ark. 1997)

District Judge WRIGHT.

. . . Under Fed. R. Civ. P. 12(c), a motion for judgment on the pleadings . . . is to be analyzed under the same standards that would have been employed had the motion been brought as a motion to dismiss under Fed. R. Civ. P. 12(b)(6). In considering such a motion, all facts alleged in the complaint are assumed to be true. The complaint should be reviewed in the light most favorable to the plaintiff, and should not be dismissed unless it is clear beyond doubt that the plaintiff can prove no set of facts thereunder which would entitle him or her to relief. A motion to dismiss is not a device for testing the truth of what is asserted or for determining whether the plaintiff has any evidence to back up what is in the complaint. The issue is not whether the plaintiff will ultimately prevail but whether the plaintiff is entitled to offer evidence to support the claims, irrespective of a judge's disbelief of a complaint's factual allegations or a judge's belief that the plaintiff cannot prove what the complaint asserts. Thus, a motion to dismiss should be granted " 'as a practical matter . . . only in the unusual case in which a plaintiff includes allegations that show on the face of the complaint that there is some insuperable bar to relief.' "

1.

. . . The President argues that Count I fails to allege the basic elements of a civil rights claim: intent and action taken under color of state law. He argues that plaintiff has failed to allege facts showing that he acted against her with the intent to deprive her of constitutionally protected rights because of her membership in a protected class, and that plaintiff has alleged no nexus between the exercise of the Governor's authority and the conduct she alleges and no control by the state over the alleged conduct. The Court has considered the matter and concludes that plaintiff's allegations are sufficient to state an actionable claim under §1983. . . .

In this case, the nature of plaintiff's allegations are such that it can be fairly said that the alleged actions were based on plaintiff's status as a female. Among other things, plaintiff alleges that then-Governor Clinton expressed an admiration for her "curves," attempted to kiss her in the hotel room and pulled her towards him, placed his hand on her leg and slid it toward the hem of her culottes, exposed his penis and requested that she "kiss it," hugged her in the Rotunda of the Capitol and described them as a couple, and directed a state trooper to inform her that the Governor's wife was out of town often and that the Governor would like to see her. She notes that the Governor had never met her prior to the incident in the hotel suite and that all he knew about her was, in her words, "that she was a state employee and a woman—a woman with flowing hair and nice 'curves.' ". . .

This is not to say that the Governor's alleged actions would not also support a finding that such actions were because of characteristics personal to plaintiff. Indeed, the line between harassment because of gender and harassment based on factors personal to a plaintiff "becomes indistinct when those factors which are personal to an individual include attributes of sexual attraction." Nevertheless, . . . the Court finds that plaintiff has sufficiently alleged that the Governor's actions were based on an intent to harass because of her status as a woman as opposed to mere characteristics which were personal to her. . . .

There can be no doubt that plaintiff's allegations describe conduct that was under color of state law. Although it remains to be seen whether plaintiff will be able to sustain these allegations, she has sufficiently alleged that the President exercised power possessed by virtue of his being Governor of the State of Arkansas in committing the alleged acts and that she only came into contact with him due to his authority as Governor. Plaintiff's allegations thus satisfy §1983's color of law requirement.

The President also argues that Count I fails to set forth the essential elements of a §1983 sexual harassment claim. As a general matter, a claim of sexual harassment under §1983 must satisfy the contours of a sexual harassment claim under Title VII. In this regard, courts have generally separated sexual harassment claims into two categories—quid pro quo cases and hostile environment cases. The Court finds that Count I sufficiently alleges both categories of sexual harassment.

To make a prima facie case of quid pro quo sexual harassment, a plaintiff must show that (1) she was a member of a protected class; (2) she was subjected to unwelcome sexual harassment in the form of sexual advances or requests for sexual favors; (3) the harassment was based on sex; and (4) her submission to the unwelcome advances was an express or implied condition for receiving job benefits or her refusal to submit resulted in a tangible job detriment.

The Court finds that plaintiff has satisfied the first three factors. . . .

The primary focus of the President's argument for dismissal of plaintiff's claim of quid pro quo sexual harassment is directed to the fourth factor. He argues that this claim is fatally flawed because she fails to allege either a benefit offered to her or a threat made against her, fails to allege that she suffered any sort of tangible job detriment as a result of his alleged advance, and fails to allege that the Governor—who was not her immediate supervisor—communicated with her employer and thereby caused any adverse job consequences which she allegedly suffered.

The Court [notes] plaintiff's allegations regarding how then-Governor Clinton indicated that he had influence over her ultimate superior within the AIDC, how he, in effect, reminded her of his influence with her superior after she rejected his alleged sexual advances by instructing her to keep quiet, and how her rejection of the Governor's alleged advances caused her to suffer adverse employment actions, including being transferred to a position that had no responsible duties for which she could be adequately evaluated to earn advancement and failing to receive raises and merit increases. Contrary to the President's assertions, then, plaintiff has alleged that there was a threat, has alleged that she suffered a tangible job detriment, and has alleged that there was a causal relationship between her rejection of the Governor's alleged sexual advances and the harm she allegedly suffered. Whatever may become of these allegations, they suffice at this time to state a prima facie case of quid pro quo sexual harassment.

The Court also finds that plaintiff has sufficiently alleged a hostile work environment cause of action. Unlike quid pro quo sexual harassment, hostile work environment harassment arises when "sexual conduct has the purpose or effect of unreasonably interfering with an individual's work performance or creating an intimidating, hostile, or offensive working environment." . . . The behavior creating the hostile working environment need not be overtly sexual in nature, but it must be " 'unwelcome' in the sense that the employee did not solicit or invite it, and the employee regarded the conduct as undesirable or offensive." The harassment must also be sufficiently severe or pervasive "to alter the conditions of employment and create an abusive working environment." [citation omitted] . . .

The President's primary argument for dismissal of plaintiff's hostile work environment claim is that aside from the supposed single incident at the Excelsior Hotel, the complaint alleges only one other contact with him, alleges only a few additional contacts with Ferguson, and contains conclusory claims that plaintiff's supervisors were rude. He argues that taken individually or as a whole, these contacts do not in any way constitute the kind of pervasive, intimidating, abusive conduct that courts require to establish a hostile work environment claim.

In assessing the hostility of an environment, a court must look to the totality of the circumstances. Circumstances to be considered include "the frequency of the discriminatory conduct; its severity; whether it is physically threatening or humiliating, or a mere offensive utterance; and whether it unreasonably interferes with an employee's work performance." No single factor is determinative, and the court "should not carve the work environment into a series of discrete incidents and then measure the harm occurring in each episode." [citation omitted] Even a single incident of sexual harassment can in some circumstances suffice to state a claim of hostile work environment sexual harassment.

The Court finds that the totality of the actions alleged in this case are such that they can be said to have altered the conditions of plaintiff's employment and created an abusive work environment. In addition to what is alleged to have occurred in the hotel suite, plaintiff alleges that she was subjected to additional encounters with Ferguson and the Governor, including being "accosted" in the Rotunda of the State Capitol. She claims that following her rejection of the Governor's alleged sexual advances, her enjoyment of her work was "severely diminished," she was treated in a hostile and rude manner by supervisors, and, as previously noted, her rejection of the Governor's alleged advances caused her to suffer adverse employment actions, including being transferred to a position that had no responsible duties for which she could be adequately evaluated to earn advancement and failing to receive raises and merit increases. She further claims that these alleged actions and omissions caused her, among other things, embarrassment, humiliation, fear, emotional distress, horror, grief, and shame. Although the President's argument regarding the inadequacy of plaintiff's hostile work environment claim is not without some force, the question of whether alleged harassment is sufficiently severe or pervasive for purposes of establishing hostile work environment is "quintessentially a question of fact," and one the Court simply cannot resolve on this record. Plaintiff's allegations as they now stand state a hostile work environment claim.

For his final argument under Count I, the President argues that plaintiff fails to state an actionable due process claim as she has failed to allege a cognizable property loss, failed to allege deprivation of a protected liberty interest in reputation, and failed to allege a deprivation of a protected liberty interest arising from alleged false imprisonment. The Court agrees in all respects. [Judge Wright found that plaintiff failed to allege that she had been fired or forced out of her job, and thus had sustained no property damage in her employment; that there was no claim for a harm to reputation absent some property loss; and that the facts as she stated them did not amount to false imprisonment.]

2.

The Court next addresses the President's argument that Count II fails to state an actionable §1985(3) claim. . . . The President argues that Count II fails to allege intent to deprive plaintiff of equal protection based on gender and is based on what is at most an alleged violation of Title VII. The Court disagrees with both of these arguments. . . .

Plaintiff has satisfied the intent requirement of §1985(3) in this case as women are a protected class falling within the ambit of the protections afforded by §1985(3), and the Court has already determined that plaintiff sufficiently alleges that the Governor's alleged actions were based on an intent to harass because of her status as a woman as opposed to mere characteristics which were personal to her. As plaintiff has also alleged at least some facts which would suggest that the defendants "reached an understanding" to violate her equal protection rights, the Court finds that plaintiff states an actionable §1985(3) claim. . . .

3.

The Court next addresses the President's argument that Count III of plaintiff's complaint fails to state an actionable claim of intentional infliction of emotional distress. Arkansas recognizes a claim of intentional infliction of emotional distress based on sexual harassment. . . . The Court finds that plaintiff's allegations are sufficient to state an actionable claim for the tort of intentional infliction of emotional distress.

The President argues that plaintiff's factual allegations plainly purport to state claims for assault, battery, false imprisonment, spoken words, and harassment under state law, and that claims based on such conduct are governed by the one year statute of limitations set forth in Ark. Code Ann. §§16-56-104; 5-1-109. He argues that because the alleged actions of which plaintiff complains occurred no later than February 1993 and the complaint was not filed until May 1994, plaintiff's claim in Count III of the complaint is time-barred and she cannot evade the governing time-bar by labeling her claim "intentional infliction of emotional distress."

It is true that a complaint simply saying that the lawsuit is one for a particular cause of action does not make it so. In cases raising questions regarding the nature of the cause of action, the Court must look to the facts alleged in the complaint to determine the true nature of the cause of action and whether the action is time-barred. "If there is doubt as to which of two or more statutes of limitation applies to a particular action or proceeding, and it is necessary to resolve the doubt, it will generally be resolved in favor of the application of the statute having the longest limitation."

Although it may well be the case that the alleged conduct of which plaintiff complains could fall within the rubric of other legal theories, there can be no doubt that such conduct is also encompassed by the tort of intentional infliction of emotional distress. The Arkansas Supreme Court has held that one is subject to liability for the tort of outrage or intentional infliction of emotional distress if he or she wilfully or wantonly causes severe emotional distress to another by extreme and outrageous conduct. In *M.B.M. Co. v. Counce,* 268 Ark. 269, 596 S.W.2d 681 (1980), the Arkansas Supreme Court stated that "[b]y extreme and outrageous conduct, we mean conduct that is so outrageous in character, and so extreme in degree, as to go beyond all possible bounds of decency, and to be regarded as atrocious, and utterly intolerable in civilized society." The Court has previously detailed the alleged conduct on which plaintiff bases her lawsuit and will not repeat those allegations here. Suffice it to say that such conduct, if true, could well be regarded as atrocious and utterly intolerable for purposes of establishing a claim for the tort of intentional infliction of emotional distress. As this claim was also filed within the applicable three-year statute of limitations for such a claim, the Court denies the President's motion for dismissal of Count III.

4.

Lastly, the Court addresses the President's argument that plaintiff's defamation claim in Count IV fails because it is founded on statements that are absolutely privileged, not actionable as a matter of law, and fails to allege defamation with the requisite specificity. The Court agrees with the President that the statements at issue in this case are absolutely privileged as a matter of law and, therefore, grants the President's motion for dismissal of this claim on that basis.

Statements made prior to the commencement of judicial proceedings are absolutely privileged if made in connection with possible litigation. Arkansas recognizes this privilege, and it covers statements made by both attorneys and parties to the possible litigation. The privilege is narrowed closely by "relevancy" and "pertinency" requirements, however, and does not cover the publication of defamatory matter that has "no connection whatever" with the possible litigation. . . .

There can be no doubt that the statements at issue in this case were made prior to possible litigation as it was less than three months prior to the filing of the complaint that plaintiff and her attorney, at an event attended by the media, publically asked the President to acknowledge the alleged incident that is the subject of this lawsuit, to state that the plaintiff had rejected his advances, and to apologize to her. The President did in fact respond to the plaintiff's allegations and hired an attorney, and this lawsuit soon followed. Given these circumstances, the Court has no difficulty in concluding that the statements of both the White House aides and the President's attorney were made prior to possible litigation for purposes of the privilege. . . .

For the foregoing reasons, the Court finds that President Clinton's motion for judgment on the pleadings and to dismiss the complaint should be and hereby is granted in part and denied in part. The Court grants the President's motion with respect to plaintiff's due process claims in Count I of the complaint and with respect to her defamation claim against the President in Count IV. The Court denies the President's motion in all other respects. This case will go forward with respect to plaintiff's §1983 sexual harassment claim against the President in Count I, her §1985(3) conspiracy claim against the President and Ferguson in Count II, her state law claim for the tort of intentional infliction of emotional distress against the President in Count III, and her defamation claim against Ferguson in Count IV.

NOTES AND COMMENTS

1. Law, not facts.   As you see from the briefs of the parties, the question before the court at this stage is solely whether there is a basis in law for plaintiff's claims. The arguments in this case also illustrate the various kinds of approaches to making an argument that plaintiff has failed to state a claim. They include the following:

- That the complaint contains no allegations as to a particular element.
- That the allegations are insufficiently precise.
- That a claim is time-barred.
- That there is no substantive law that can serve as a basis for a claim.
- That the acts alleged could be the basis for a claim in other contexts, but not here.

2. The architecture of a lawsuit.   Imagine that you are Judge Wright's law clerk and that it is your job to draft an outline of the issues presented and how they should be resolved. Such an exercise would again illustrate the relationship between the structure of separate claims, as pled in the complaint, and the substantive law underlying (or not) each claim. If you wanted to chart this structure, including Judge Wright's ruling, you might produce something like the chart on the next page.

3. Claim by claim.   Don't fall into the common habit of referring to a "motion to dismiss the case." Motions to dismiss are directed to claims, not cases. If a case has only one claim, the two will be synonymous. If all claims are challenged, the motion will be to dismiss the complaint.

Most plaintiffs join several claims, as in *Jones v. Clinton,* and the judge's ruling will specify claim by claim which are to be dismissed and which are to go forward. When there are multiple parties, the analysis is both claim by claim and party by party. In this case, for example, the defamation claim against Clinton was dismissed, but the defamation claim against Ferguson went forward.

President Clinton's Motion for Judgment on the Pleadings (Rule 12(c))

COMPLAINT	DEFENDANT: COMPLAINT FAILS TO ALLEGE:	PLAINTIFF REBUTTAL:	JUDGE WRIGHT'S RULING:
Count I (42 U.S.C. §1983)	1. Under color of state law 2. Intent to deprive based on gender 3. Quid pro quo (a) Threat or benefit (b) Tangible adverse action (c) Causation 4. Hostile environment—pervasive hostility 5. Deprivation of constitutionally-protected right (a) No actual job loss (b) Harm to reputation w/o property loss not actionable (c) No true false imprisonment	1. Allegations re: "armed troopers," "directive from superior officer," etc. 2. Allegations re: Clinton's sexual interest and attraction 3. (a) Allegations of implied threat of retaliation (b) Allegation of transfer to inferior job (c) Allegation of cause suffices without factual "proof" 4. Allegations of series of advances, totality of circumstances 5. (a) Property interest in assurance of job implied by state law (b) Reputation linked to job status (c) Temporary restraint suffices	1. Adoption of Plaintiff's arguments 2. Adoption of Plaintiff's arguments 3. Adoption of Plaintiff's arguments 4. Adoption of Plaintiff's arguments 5. Adoption of Defendant's arguments; Count I (5) dismissed
Count II (42 U.S.C. §1985(3))	Intent to deprive based on gender	See #2 above	See #2 above
Count III (Intentional Infliction of Emotional Distress)	1. Statute of limitations, if claim were correctly labeled 2. Insufficient specificity	1. Allegations fall within scope of IIED; no time bar 2. Allegations clearly amount to extreme and outrageous conduct	1. Adoption of Plaintiff's arguments 2. Adoption of Plaintiff's arguments
Count IV (Defamation)	1. Privilege 2. Insufficient specificity	1. Waived; litigation privilege does not apply to press conference 2. Allegation of use of "liar"	1. Adoption of Defendant's arguments; Count IV dismissed 2. Issue not reached

CHAPTER THREE

Pre-Answer Motions

INTRODUCTION

In the previous chapter, we studied the most common kind of Rule 12 motion: one that challenges the legal sufficiency of a complaint. In this chapter, we will focus on the process policy principles behind the consolidation mandate for Rule 12 motions and discuss the possibility of pre-answer motions other than those specified in Rule 12.

The consolidation and timing principles in Rules 12(g) and 12(h) may strike you as rather dry and technical. If so, you may be surprised to read briefs by and against lawyers for the President of the United States arguing about their proper interpretation. The context for these arguments—whether the President should be granted immunity from civil suit while in office—raises a number of fascinating questions about the practical realities of contemporary litigation and the extent to which procedural rules should be the same for all parties, in all kinds of lawsuits.

To analyze those questions, we take a step backward in time from the motion we studied in Chapter 2, to the period immediately following the filing of the complaint. On June 16, 1994, about six weeks after the complaint was filed,[1] Judge Susan Webber Wright, to whom the case had been assigned, held a conference with the attorneys for all parties. Lawyers for President Clinton had requested the conference to alert the judge to the fact that they intended to file a "motion to set briefing schedule" requesting that further proceedings in the case be suspended. This motion would ask that all motions, answers, or other responses be delayed until after the court ruled on their first motion, which would be to freeze the case until the President left office, on the ground of presidential immunity from civil suit while in office.

Does Rule 12 permit such a procedure? The Rules do not answer that question directly; you must interpret how Rules 12(g) and 12(h) should apply to this situation.

---

1. Bennett had signed a waiver of service, which is a standard form in civil litigation. See Appendix 3. It establishes that defendant waives formal service of the papers after receiving them in fact, so that plaintiff does not have to formally certify that service occurred. In return, defendant is automatically granted 60 days (instead of the normal 20) in which to respond or answer. Rule 4(d).

Rule 12(g) permits only one pre-answer motion that raises a defense to a claim for relief. Rule 12(h)(2) explicitly preserves certain grounds—prominent among them, a motion to dismiss for failure to state a claim—but *only* for the answer or for a motion filed at the same time as the answer. At the time of this conference, Bennett could have filed a Rule 12(b)(6) motion that included the immunity defense, instead of the "motion to set briefing schedule." Instead, he sought to keep open his ability to file a second *pre-answer* motion if he lost the immunity argument. Bennett was in essence asking for a waiver of Rule 12(g).

As was apparent to everyone, the primary goal of the President's lawyers was delay. This is a common strategy employed by defense counsel in many kinds of cases. To a limited extent, the Rules enable delay, by allowing a pre-answer motion seeking dismissal before the defendant has to file an answer. The justification, of course, is that the efficiency gained by weeding out nonviable claims justifies the delay that results when motions to dismiss are denied. For defendants, the advantage of pre-answer motions is that they not only produce delay in general, but they specifically delay the moment when the defendant has to respond to each assertion of fact in the complaint.

In this case, the stakes were considerably higher than in most lawsuits. Shortly after the complaint was filed, then White House Counsel Lloyd Cutler said to Robert Bennett, Clinton's personal attorney in the *Jones* case, "The win is getting it beyond the [1996] election. Nothing else matters."

Bennett's first move in the lawsuit was this "special" motion. His theory of the motion was that if the President was immune from lawsuits over private matters while in office, he should not have to litigate anything, even a motion to dismiss for failure to state a claim. Prior law on presidential or executive branch immunity had not resolved this point. In the two most important precedents, the defendant had raised the immunity issue without seeking to carve out a special exception to Rule 12(g). *See Mitchell v. Forsyth*, 472 U.S. 511 (1985); *Nixon v. Fitzgerald*, 457 U.S. 731 (1982).

When Bennett apprised the judge and opposing counsel of his forthcoming motion, Jones's lawyers argued strenuously that it was impermissible to assert an immunity defense without having that "count" as the sole pre-answer motion permitted by the FRCP. Judge Wright allowed Bennett to file his motion, but advised counsel that she would consider arguments about Rule 12 as well as those concerning the substantive law of presidential immunity. In the excerpted motion papers that follow, only the portions addressing the Rule 12 and litigation policy issues are included. The arguments are a good explication of the process policy conflict between allowing fast-track consideration of a potentially dispositive motion and requiring that the defendant raise all grounds for an early dismissal in one bundle to avoid piecemeal adjudication.

At the conclusion of the materials on President Clinton's immunity motion, we will consider the procedures for filing other, more common pre-answer motions that do not come within the scope of Rule 12.

PRESIDENT CLINTON'S MOTION TO SET BRIEFING SCHEDULE

President Clinton, by and through counsel, hereby moves the Court to bifurcate the briefing schedule with respect to President Clinton's motions to dismiss, so as to permit him to file a motion to dismiss on the grounds of presidential immunity on or before August 5, 1994, and to defer and preserve all other pleadings and motions that must or may be filed under the Federal Rules of Civil Procedure until such time as the presidential immunity issue is finally resolved. The reasons for the President's request are explained more fully in the Memorandum that accompanies this Motion.

Note that the President's lawyers have given this motion a title that suggests that it raises only trivial issues of timing.

MEMORANDUM IN SUPPORT OF PRESIDENT CLINTON'S MOTION TO SET BRIEFING SCHEDULE

. . . President Clinton maintains that the complaint should be dismissed without prejudice to its reinstatement after he leaves office, on the grounds that incumbent Presidents are constitutionally immune from having to litigate private suits for civil damages. Although this is not the place to argue the merits of the immunity motion, it is necessary to understand the nature of that motion in order to appreciate why resolution of the immunity issues should precede all other pleading or briefing in this case. . . .

The Supreme Court has cautioned that immunity is an issue to be resolved "at the earliest possible stage of a litigation." *Anderson v. Creighton,* 483 U.S. 635, 646 n.6 (1987). In the present case, the "earliest possible stage" for resolving the immunity question is now, before joining any issue on the merits or the sufficiency of the complaint.

Immunity is a preliminary legal question as to whether a defendant has "an entitlement not to stand trial *or face the other burdens of litigation.*" *Mitchell v. Forsyth,* 472 U.S. 511, 526 (1985) (emphasis added). "The entitlement is an *immunity from suit* rather than a mere defense to liability . . . ." *Id.* "One of the purposes of immunity . . . is to spare a defendant not only unwarranted liability, but unwarranted demands customarily imposed upon those defending a long drawn out lawsuit." . . .

Nowhere does this principle have more force than where presidential immunity is asserted, inasmuch as the Supreme Court has recognized that presidential immunity serves two significant, constitutionally-based public interests: it prevents a President from becoming a target for numerous, vexatious lawsuits, and it assures that a President's energies and attention will not be diverted from the singular executive duties assigned to him by the Constitution. If President Clinton is required to file comprehensive pleadings or motions to dismiss before the immunity issue is resolved, he and the public as a whole will be substantially deprived of the very protections presidential immunity exists to provide.

The Court's interest in conserving its own resources also points to the conclusion that it should not ask the parties to brief, and it should not consider, motions to dismiss based on grounds other than presidential immunity. As the Court is well aware, regardless of how it rules on the immunity issue, its decision will be subject to immediate appeal.

Assuming the President's immunity motion is granted, there will not be any need to brief or resolve any other motions in this case. Should the immunity motion fail to persuade this Court, proceedings below should be stayed as the issue works its way through the appellate process. Either way, there will be no immediate need for the parties to brief, or this Court to undertake, the rigorous and time-consuming task of ruling upon what are likely to be lengthy and complex motions to dismiss in this case. . . .

Here Bennett is alluding to the kinds of issues raised in the motion in Chapter 2.

Without prejudging the basis for or appealability of any ruling of this Court, we simply observe that any motions under Rule 12(b) in this matter are likely to relate to issues substantially different from those raised by the immunity motion. Accordingly, there is no precedent to suggest that the Eighth Circuit would accept jurisdiction over appeals from Rule 12(b) motions at the same time that it must hear an appeal of the immunity issue in this case. It would therefore seem the better course to conserve the Court's and the parties' resources, and to limit the proceedings to the immunity issue until this fundamental consideration has been resolved. . . .

PLAINTIFF'S MEMORANDUM IN OPPOSITION TO THE MOTION OF DEFENDANT CLINTON TO SET BRIEFING SCHEDULE

William Clinton seeks extraordinary procedural and scheduling relief for his unique claim of immunity from suit involving pre-presidential acts. His pending motion asks nothing less than a categorical suspension of the Federal Rules of Civil Procedure. An American citizen, even one who happens to be president, is not above the normal processes established for the legal testing of a plaintiff's claims.

Federal Rule of Civil Procedure 12 expressly requires *every defendant* to either answer the complaint or file a single dispositive motion setting forth all Rule 12 defenses, including immunity. That rule binds *every litigant* sued in federal court—even sovereign U.S. states, asserting sovereign immunity under the Constitution's Eleventh Amendment.

Though no great affairs of state are at issue in this case, Mr. Clinton claims that his present office requires this Court to exempt him from the limited duty imposed by Federal Rules 8 and 12 to answer the complaint or file a dispositive motion. The law is clear that there is no such exemption accorded any party claiming immunity.

Mr. Clinton's request would delay this case for years. It is a transparent attempt to stay as far and as long as possible from the merits. Delay carries with it the risk that memories will fade, evidence will disappear, witnesses will die or become hard to locate, and, in short, the case will become stale. Each party is entitled to an expeditious resolution of all claims. . . .

The reasons for this simple and categorical duty—*i.e.,* to answer or file a single proper Rule 12 motion—are straightforward. First, Rule 12 and related case law expressly require it. Second, . . . the policies of judicial economy and the efficient administration of justice counsel against duplicative, piecemeal, protracted, and inefficient litigation. Indeed, the burden to be borne by Mr. Clinton, as well as by the courts and the plaintiff, will be substantially lower if the issues are briefed and argued once rather than seriatim. Third, judicial discretion counsels strongly against addressing the "complex" immunity question if, as Mr. Clinton vehemently insists, the complaint can be disposed of on other, less momentous, and nonconstitutional grounds. If some counts are stricken, the case is narrowed, and the potential for distractions, which Mr. Clinton so fears, is lessened. If all counts are stricken, the case is over. . . .

Again, this alludes to the kind of motion that President Clinton ultimately did file, which we read in Chapter 2.

Rules 8 and 12 of the Federal Rules of Civil Procedure expressly require litigants to respond to a complaint with either an answer or a single dispositive motion setting forth all existing legal bases for dismissing a complaint. Rule 12(g), which Mr. Clinton has not even mentioned, specifically prohibits the delaying tactic employed by his current motion. . . . Indeed, Rule 12(g) formerly allowed the tactic Mr. Clinton employs. Until 1948, successive motions to dismiss the complaint were permitted. The Advisory Committee concluded that the right to file motions seriatim "was unnecessary and promoted delay." 5A Wright & Miller, Federal Practice & Procedure §1384 at 725. Rule 12 was, therefore, modified to bar the practice.

The rules are designed to "eliminate unnecessary delay at the pleading stage," and they therefore "requir[e] the presentation of [either an answer or] an omnibus pre-answer motion in which defendant advances every available Rule 12 defense." 5 Wright & Miller, Federal Practice and Procedure, §1384 at 837 (footnote omitted). They are mandatory, and permit no exceptions under any circumstances relevant here.

Defendant Clinton seeks exactly what Rule 12 denies: which is the right to brief the immunity issue for as long as that takes, and then to come back to this Court and file other dispositive motions previewed in his memorandum. . . . Thereafter, his obligation to answer the complaint will be postponed for an additional period of time until the second set of motions is resolved. Because the Rules expressly bar this practice, defendant seeks an exemption no other litigant would be allowed. . . .

This common sense rule conforms to the logic implicit in the Federal Rules. A plaintiff's complaint comes before a defendant's answer and assertion of defenses. No answer or defense is needed when a complaint is facially flawed. Rule 12, for this reason, authorizes the filing of dispositive motions before the filing of an answer. Because immunity is a defense, the sensible approach is to reach it only if the complaint is facially valid. This approach makes even more sense here, because, by his own account, Mr. Clinton is not even asserting a full-

> blown defense; he only asserts a reason to delay the case. If defenses are not reached until the facial legal merits of the complaint are determined, *a fortiori* arguments about timing of discovery and trial must await determination that the complaint actually states a claim. . . .
>
> Defendant Clinton's effort to brief the immunity issue alone is a transparent attempt to "avoid joining issue." He would have this Court suspend the basic pleading rules that govern every litigant, even those asserting the sovereign immunity of U.S. states, which impose the duty to answer a complaint or file a proper dispositive motion as required by Rule 12. He would also require the Court to ignore a basic principle guiding its discretion which counsels against reaching unnecessary constitutional issues. Finally, granting Mr. Clinton's motion would assure that resolution of this case took as long as possible. . . .

RESOLUTION OF THE ISSUE

President Clinton won his argument to lift the strictures of Rule 12, but lost his motion to dismiss on grounds of presidential immunity, not only before Judge Wright but at every level of the federal judiciary. Judge Wright allowed the filing of and then denied the motion to dismiss. She ruled that discovery should go forward, but that any trial would be stayed until the end of his presidency. 869 F. Supp. 690 (E.D. Ark. 1994).

Following are excerpts from Judge Wright's ruling:

. . . [P]laintiff argues that the Federal Rules of Civil Procedure require every defendant, including the President of the United States, to either answer a complaint or file a single dispositive motion raising all available grounds for dismissal, including absolute immunity. Certainly, that is one way to handle a case, but it is not the only way it can be done. Plaintiff asserts, however, that the briefing schedule sought by the President is "nothing less than a categorical suspension of the Federal Rules of Civil Procedure." To the contrary, Rule 12 specifically allows for successive motions to dismiss for failure to state a claim. *Sharma v. Skaarup Ship Management Corp.*, 699 F. Supp. 440, 444 (S.D.N.Y. 1988), *aff'd*, 916 F.2d 820 (2d Cir. 1990), *cert. denied*, 499 U.S. 907 (1991). "Although defenses of lack of jurisdiction over the person, improper venue and insufficiency of process are waived if not raised in a party's first responsive pleading, 'A defense of failure to state a claim upon which relief can be granted . . . may be made in any pleading permitted or ordered under Rule 7(a), or by motion for judgment on the pleadings, or at the trial on the merits.'" *Id.* (citing Fed. R. Civ. P. 12(h)). See also 2A *Moore's Federal Practice* ¶12.07[3] at 12-102 (2d ed. 1994) (affirmative defenses not enumerated in Rule 12(b) may be made by motion under Rule 12(b)(6)); 5A Charles A. Wright & Arthur R. Miller, *Federal Practice and Procedure* §1361 at 447-48 (1990) (Rule 12(b)(6) motions are exempted by Rule 12(g) from the consolidation requirement). The briefing schedule sought by the President is in conformity with the Federal Rules of Civil Procedure and does not afford him privileges unavailable to other defendants.

To be sure, the plaintiff's interest in seeking prompt relief for the alleged violation of her rights is certainly legitimate and not to be minimized. The Court, however, finds that plaintiff's concern that the briefing schedule proposed by the President will entail undue delay is unfounded. Should the Court deny the President's claim of immunity, such order would be immediately appealable. This would be so regardless of the Court's ruling on any other Rule 12(b) motions.

Furthermore, it must be recognized that the relief plaintiff seeks is of a purely personal nature, the delay of which will affect but a single individual who waited two days short of three years in which to file her lawsuit. The President's claim to immunity from suits for civil damages, on the other hand, is equally legitimate and may affect "not only the President and his office but also the Nation that the Presidency was designed to serve." *Fitzgerald*, 457 U.S. at 753. Indeed, the amenability of a sitting President to suits for civil damages raises significant and important constitutional issues, the resolution of which will directly impact the institution of the Presidency. That being so, and because the President's constitutional responsibilities and status require this Court to exercise judicial deference and restraint, the Court finds that the President should be allowed to defer the filing of any other motions or pleadings until such time as the issue of immunity has been resolved by this Court. . . .

869 F. Supp. at 905-906.

The Eighth Circuit reversed Judge Wright's order staying trial, on the ground that the stay amounted to the functional equivalent of a grant of temporary immunity. 72 F.3d 1354 (8th Cir. 1996). It ruled that discovery would go forward, as Judge Wright had ruled, but with no delay of any stage of the proceeding, including trial.

On January 13, 1997, the Supreme Court heard argument in the case.

ORAL ARGUMENT OF ROBERT S. BENNETT ON BEHALF OF THE PETITIONER

MR. BENNETT: Mr. Chief Justice and may it please the Court: I am here this morning on behalf of the President of the United States, who has asked this Court to defer a private civil damage suit for money damages against him until he leaves office.

QUESTION: Is the request to totally dismiss the suit or to permit delay of the trial and any in-court appearance . . . or that sort of thing?
MR. BENNETT: It is to delay the trial of the case and to—

QUESTION: How about discovery?
MR. BENNETT: And the discovery of the case. There is—

QUESTION: How about discovery of people who are not the President, other witnesses and things like that?
MR. BENNETT: That is correct, Your Honor. We—as—

QUESTION: You—you want to delay that as well?
MR. BENNETT: I want to delay that as well. However—

QUESTION: Should that be a general rule if preservation of evidence becomes crucial in a case?
MR. BENNETT: As we discussed in the District Court below, Justice O'Connor, we have

agreed, and the District Court noted, that if there's a danger of the loss of any evidence, that we would cooperate to preserve it and make use of the Federal Rules of Civil Procedure. . . .

QUESTION: . . . I assume you're arguing that it is interference or the risk of interference with the actual presidential duties during the four-year term that is the source of whatever privilege you request; isn't that right?

MR. BENNETT: That's correct.

QUESTION: Right. Now, how does that take you from interference with the President himself, as—as a deponent or as a witness or simply as a party attending a trial, and—and go to the further extent of—of giving you some kind of a privilege to preclude discovery, which does not personally involve the President? How—how is the interference there enough for you?

MR. BENNETT: Well, Mr. Justice Souter, it's the realities of real-world litigation. . . .

QUESTION: Well, it's going to keep *you* busy. (Laughter.) I mean, the President isn't going to attend these depositions; you are.

MR. BENNETT: But in the real world of litigation, Mr. Justice Souter, do you think when Mr. Davis, as he—as he claims, that he's going to be deposing all of the troopers; and any time the President of the United States has come into contact with a member of the opposite sex, he intends to inquire of that; this is a conspiracy complaint; they talk about pattern of conduct—

QUESTION: Yes, but, Mr. Bennett—

MR. BENNETT: —don't you think I'm going to have to talk to the President of the United States about all those events? . . .

QUESTION: Mr. Bennett, do you think all those events are relevant to this case?

MR. BENNETT: I think some trial courts would say they are not and some trial courts might—might say they are. We haven't gotten to that question yet. . . .

ORAL ARGUMENT OF GILBERT K. DAVIS ON BEHALF OF THE RESPONDENT

. . . QUESTION: What in your view is an interference? That is, suppose, for example, that the lawyers are deposing non-White House witnesses and it turns out that every statement they made is in the newspaper and the President says, but I have to respond to each of these. They're saying I was in a certain place at a certain time, or I said something to somebody only a month ago. And then somebody else says something about what he didn't say, and then somebody says something about where there's a paper that somebody wrote it down, and then it goes into—we all know how those things work, and suppose the President says, look, I don't have time to go into all of these things. I don't have time to remember every single thing I said to everybody and anything that's tangentially related. It's interfering, right now. Now, what in your view—is that an interference, or is—

MR. DAVIS: I think that the rule here, Justice Breyer, is an actual, imminent interference with his job and a claim that he makes. . . .

QUESTION: . . . [W]hat is the lower court to do?

MR. DAVIS: Well, I think the lower court has its function and its duty to decide whether that is a good-faith claim. . . . And if it is not, then you may have a conflict between the person of the President and a judge. He would respond. He would just go to the—

QUESTION: So the trial court judge at the State court level is to determine whether the offer—the complaint made by the President's lawyer is made in good faith or not?

MR. DAVIS: I think he must make the claim of actual interference with his duties, that as another example, the torrent of litigation has come—is so much, that I am only responding now to civil complaints.

QUESTION: But don't we know that that's inevitable in a suit like this? This argument here today is taking an hour. All the counsel and all participants in the argument have thought about it for at least the weekend if not a week. (Laughter.) There's an anxiety component, there's an intellectual commitment—

MR. DAVIS: Yes, sir.

QUESTION: —there's an emotional commitment—

MR. DAVIS: Yes, sir.

QUESTION: —that's far more extensive than some time chart would indicate. And I think that's part of what the President is saying, is if he's going to defend this lawsuit it will absorb substantial energies.

MR. DAVIS: I don't believe, Justice Kennedy, that the Constitution protects him in his personal capacity. . . .

QUESTION: May I ask a question in that regard about third-party depositions, and we're concerned about their impact on the office of the President and so forth. Would it be permissible for the trial judge in trying to control the litigation and recognize the special problems of the President to narrow discovery to matters that relate to the particular incident involved in the trial and say, no, you can't ask about the history for the last 10 years, or 45 other police officers and so forth. Would that be a permissible use of the trial judge's discretion?

Make a note of this question about whether certain limits on discovery would be within the judge's discretion. We will return to this issue in Chapter 7.

MR. DAVIS: I think the trial judge always has the opportunity and the duty to balance the interests—

QUESTION: So it would be permissible to him to narrow discovery and the scope of inquiry—

QUESTION: Mr. Davis, I don't think you're answering some of the questions quite as frankly as we might hope you would. To say that the trial judge could consider it isn't to say whether he's bound by it.

MR. DAVIS: I don't think he is bound—. . .

QUESTION: Mr. Davis, what is at risk for you taking into account two things. Mr. Bennett said that it would be appropriate to take depositions to perpetuate testimony if there's a danger that the testimony won't be available later and, should you prevail, you get interest on any damage award, so what is at stake in a postponement?

MR. DAVIS: Well, what is at stake, and this is—these interests I think are substantial to the plaintiff. She can lose her cause of action if either she or the President dies. . . .

QUESTION: One of the major concerns, of course, is the extent to which you plan to go into collateral matters.

MR. DAVIS: I can't, and I wouldn't bind, because I'm not certain whether they are admissible. I'm not certain what they—if they would tend to show a fact that we need to prove I think I would be duty bound as counsel to pursue that.

QUESTION: Suppose, because there are other parties involved, that it were 10 days of trial, 2 working weeks, and—pick a number—15 depositions. Do you think that would be a substantial investment of the President's time?

MR. DAVIS: It could very well be. It could very well be, and—. . .

QUESTION: I mean, it's an exercise of the court's discretion in each instance. [Why can't we trust the court's discretion to decide that participating in a lawsuit would be too burdensome for a President,] assuming there's an evidentiary basis for it?

MR. DAVIS: Well, the court needs to have a factual basis on which to exercise discretion.

QUESTION: Okay, and let's assume that the President's lawyers come in and they provide one.

MR. DAVIS: If they do provide a factual basis that justifies a continuance, then certainly the court has authority to do it.

QUESTION: So the only thing . . . we're really arguing about, then, is whether there ought to be a blanket rule that can be invoked simply by saying, I want this deferral for four years.

MR. DAVIS: Exactly.

QUESTION: As distinct from a rule in which the President's lawyers are going to come in and say, these are the practical stakes involved, and they therefore justify a four-year continuance. That's all we're really arguing about.

MR. DAVIS: That's all we're arguing about, yes, sir. . . .

The Supreme Court unanimously affirmed the Eighth Circuit. In an opinion by Justice Stevens, the Court held that the President does not enjoy immunity from civil suit for actions allegedly taken prior to assuming office, if they are not official acts. *Clinton v. Jones,* 520 U.S. 681 (1997). The Court distinguished *Nixon v. Fitzgerald,* 457 U.S. 731 (1982), which held that a civil damages suit cannot be maintained against the President for action taken while in office, if the action was within even the "outside perimeter" of his official duties.

The Court was unswayed by Clinton's arguments that having to respond to the demands imposed by the litigation would impede the execution of his official responsibilities. The Court ruled that Judge Wright had abused her discretion in deferring the trial until after he left office. "[T]he case at hand, if properly managed by the District Court, [ ] appears to us highly unlikely to occupy any substantial amount of [the President's] time." 520 U.S. at 702.

Nor was the Court worried about future fallout for other presidents. As to "the risk that our decision will generate a large volume of politically motivated harassing and frivolous litigation . . . we are not persuaded that [this risk] is serious. Most frivolous and vexatious litigation is terminated at the pleading stage or on summary judgment, with little if any personal involvement by the defendant. Moreover, the availability of sanctions provides a significant deterrent to litigation directed at the President in his unofficial capacity for purposes of political gain or harassment." *Id.* at 708-709 [citing Rule 11].

NOTES AND COMMENTS

1. Unrealistic or prudent? The Supreme Court's decision has become a much-criticized ruling. Lawyer–journalist Jeffrey Toobin described it as evidence of the Court's "collective ignorance. It had been decades since any of them had tried a case as a lawyer."[2] U.S. Court of Appeals Judge (and former law professor) Richard Posner called it the product of "the ineptitude of an unpragmatic Supreme Court locked in a backward-looking jurisprudence."[3] Was the Court's willingness to rely on Rule 11 as protection against harassing litigation unrealistic? What did they ignore by focusing on early termination "at the pleading stage or on summary judgment"? (As you will see in Chapter 10, *summary judgment* is a mechanism that normally follows discovery, in which the judge examines whether there is enough evidence supporting a claim to amount at least to a genuine issue as to all material facts.)

Others have defended the result. Citing Justice Breyer's concurring opinion, in which he recommended that Congress address the problem, Professor Cass Sunstein wrote that "The Supreme Court rightly resisted the claim to build up from an ambiguous constitutional text an immunity that certainly is not there and that is not a necessary implication from it. . . . [T]he proper remedy to the policy problem . . . is statutory, not constitutional. Congress should, it seems to me, pass a law saying that while the President is in office, he or she cannot be subject to civil actions, but the statute of limitations is not going to bar suits that are brought the day after he or she leaves office."[4]

Moreover, the author of the opinion is adamant that the decision was correct. Speaking at the Seventh Circuit Judicial Conference in 1999, Justice Stevens acknowledged that the decision had been widely regarded as "one of the dumbest opinions ever written." Notwithstanding that, in his view, "I don't think anyone on the Court would change a word in the opinion if they had to do it over again."[5]

What do you think? Do the Rules make it too easy for parties in high-stakes cases to engage in excessive litigation or to use litigation to achieve aims other than those related to the actual claims in the case? Should high government officials be insulated from litigation over private matters while they remain in office?

2. Claim-specific procedure?   Judge Posner proposed a different basis for resolving the immunity issue:

> Missing from [the] opinion is any consideration of the significance of the fact that the Paula Jones case was about sex. . . . [I]t should have been apparent to the Justices that public exposure of the details of the President's sex life could undermine the President's authority and effectiveness. It would, though, have required great skill to write an opinion that gave the President immunity from being sued over sex without making the plaintiffs in sexual harassment suits seem like second-class legal citizens.[6]

One of the signal characteristics of the Federal Rules of Civil Procedure is their transsubstantive character; that is, the same procedures apply to all kinds of cases.

2. Jeffrey Toobin, A Vast Conspiracy: The Real Story of the Sex Scandal That Nearly Brought Down a President 117 (1999).

3. Richard A. Posner, An Affair of State: The Investigation, Impeachment and Trial of President Clinton 14-15 (1999).

4. Cass R. Sunstein, Lessons From a Debacle: From Impeachment to Reform, 51 Fla. L. Rev. 599, 611 (1999).

5. Tony Mauro, "A Look Back at *Clinton v. Jones,*" The American Lawyer, July 5, 1999.

6. Posner, *supra* note 3 at 227.

For example, when the Rules were adopted in 1938, the abolition of separate procedures for law and equity was considered an important step to modernize and streamline the legal system. Judge Posner's suggestion goes to a temporary immunity defense, which would suspend a case, rather than to pleadings. However, it would represent a move away from the transsubstantive model. What do you think of the idea? A step backward, or a pragmatic revision to deal with the realities of modern politics? Should litigation over sexual matters be subject to unique rules of procedure? What are the advantages and disadvantages of such an approach?

3. Much ado about nothing?   You might wonder at the motions strategy of the President's lawyers. Since they won on the Rule 12 point, after losing the immunity argument in the Supreme Court they still could have filed a pre-answer motion to dismiss for failure to state a claim. Instead, they filed the Rule 12(c) motion for judgment on the pleadings that we read in Chapter 2, and filed the answer on the same day as the Rule 12(c) motion. Why? Didn't that render all the debate about the purpose and meaning of Rule 12 a waste of time? If the President's motion to suspend the case on the ground of presidential immunity had been filed as a Rule 12(b)(6) motion, as Jones's lawyers insisted that it should have been, President Clinton's lawyers could have done exactly what they ended up doing anyway—filing a Rule 12(c) motion with the answer. The only grounds that would have been waived by omission from a Rule 12(b)(6) motion would have been those relating to service, venue, and other issues that never appeared to pertain to this case.

Perhaps it was much ado about nothing. But consider two factors. By the time of the Supreme Court's ruling, public commentary was starting to build around the fact that, although the case was three years old, the President had not yet formally admitted or denied any of the factual allegations. His lawyers could have delayed that moment further, but he was beginning to pay a political price for doing so. On the other hand, his lawyers may have concluded that they had already achieved their most important goal for the early stages of the case: the 1996 election was over.

OTHER PRE-ANSWER MOTIONS

Students often form the impression that motions based on Rule 12 are the only proper motions for filing prior to an answer. That is not the case, however. A *motion* is any "application to the court for an order." Rule 7(b)(1). Rule 12 concerns only responses or objections to the complaint. There is no rule that forbids other motions from being filed at the outset of a case. In general, unless the FRCP or the local rules in a particular district provide otherwise, a motion can be filed whenever it is "timely," and timeliness depends on the circumstances surrounding the specific motion.

Let us consider a hypothetical motion that could have been, but was not, made in the Clinton case. When a complaint is filed in the clerk of court's office, the case is assigned to a judge, who is selected at random from among the judges in that district. In this instance, the case was assigned to Judge Susan Webber Wright. What if one of the parties believes that the judge who draws the case might be biased? Any action to transfer the case to another judge should be made as soon as the identity of the judge is learned. How would that party proceed? The proper response would be to file a motion to recuse the judge, which would be a separate pre-answer motion entirely independent of any Rule 12 motions. The Rules do not refer specifically to a motion to recuse, but it, like any number of other possible motions, would fall within the general rubric of Rule 7.

Exercise 3—Motion to Recuse Judge

Consider the following facts and then draft a motion to recuse Judge Wright. When Judge Wright was a student at the University of Arkansas Law School, she took a course from then-Professor Bill Clinton. Clinton lost some of the students' exams at the end of the semester; one of the lost exams was hers. He offered to give a B to each student whose exam he lost, but Judge Wright (then Susan Webber), one of the top students in the school (and the first woman to edit the *Arkansas Law Review*), declined the offer and asked to take a second exam. She got an A. Immediately after graduation, she became a volunteer in the campaign of Clinton's Republican opponent in that year's (1974) congressional election. (The Republican won.) She later returned to the law school as a professor herself, and, in 1988, chaired the Arkansas "Lawyers for Bush" committee. In 1990, the first President Bush appointed her to the federal bench.

The legal standard for recusal is set by two statutes: 28 U.S.C. §§144 and 455. Section 144 sets out the process for a party seeking recusal:

> Whenever a party . . . makes and files a timely and sufficient affidavit that the judge before whom the matter is pending has a personal bias or prejudice either against him or in favor of any adverse party, such judge shall proceed no further therein, but another judge shall be assigned to hear such proceeding.
>
> The affidavit shall state the facts and the reasons for the belief that bias or prejudice exists . . . A party may file only one such affidavit in any case. It shall be accompanied by a certificate of counsel of record stating that it is made in good faith.

Section 455(a) addresses self-disqualification by a judge:

> Any . . . judge . . . of the United States shall disqualify himself in any proceeding in which his impartiality might reasonably be questioned.

Courts have interpreted each provision to include the grounds stated in the other. *In re Kansas Public Employees Retirement System,* 85 F.3d 1353 (8th Cir. 1996). Although it may sound like §144 requires that the challenged judge step aside as soon as an affidavit is filed, the practice is that the judge being challenged rules on whether to grant the recusal motion. On appeal, that judge's ruling is reviewed under an abuse of discretion standard. *Id.*

How would you frame the argument that these facts required Judge Wright to recuse herself? What would be the strongest arguments against recusal? For each party, which process values would you rely on most heavily?

CHAPTER FOUR

The Answer

After the immunity question was decided by the Supreme Court in May, 1997, the case returned to Judge Wright's docket in Little Rock. On July 3, 1997, President Clinton filed the motion for judgment on the pleadings that you read in Chapter 2. On the same day, he also filed the following answer:

ANSWER OF PRESIDENT WILLIAM JEFFERSON CLINTON

President William Jefferson Clinton, through his undersigned attorneys, answers the Complaint in the above-captioned matter as follows:

GENERAL DENIAL

The President adamantly denies the false allegations advanced in the Complaint. Specifically, at no time did the President make sexual advances toward the plaintiff, or otherwise act improperly in her presence. At no time did the President conspire to or sexually harass the plaintiff. At no time did the President deprive plaintiff of her constitutional rights. At no time did the President act in a manner intended to, or which could, inflict emotional distress upon the plaintiff. At no time did the President act in a manner intended to or which could defame the plaintiff.

Plaintiff has suffered no damages which properly may be attributed to President Clinton. As Governor of Arkansas, Mr. Clinton never took any action or made any request of any state employee to interfere with or otherwise detract from plaintiff's advancement, promotion, or job responsibilities.

Plaintiff's allegations against the President first were announced at a political event sponsored by vigorous opponents of the President while plaintiff was seated next to an attorney with whom she

Introductory Statement
This section is not required in an answer, but provides an opportunity to summarize the contents in what amounts to a statement to the public.

had agreed to share the proceeds from any resultant book or film deal. Thus, plaintiff thrust herself into the public limelight by bringing to the attention of the world that she believed she was the "Paula" referred to in the *American Spectator* article, which did not identify her by last name, and by joining with long-time political opponents of the President who sought to discredit him and his Presidency. This, we believe, was done to maximize plaintiff's potential to derive economic benefit and simultaneously to harm the President politically. In responding to the plaintiff's public charges and defending himself against these unfounded allegations, the President, through his agents, did not defame plaintiff.

SPECIFIC DENIALS—JURISDICTION

1. Paragraph 1 of the Complaint states legal conclusions as to which no response is required.

VENUE

2. Paragraph 2 of the Complaint states legal conclusions as to which no response is required.

THE PARTIES

3. President Clinton is without knowledge or information sufficient to form a belief as to the truth of the allegations set forth in paragraph 3, and therefore denies the same.

4. President Clinton admits he is a resident of Arkansas.

5. President Clinton is without knowledge or information sufficient to form a belief as to the truth of the allegations set forth in paragraph 5, and therefore denies the same.

FACTS

6. President Clinton admits that the Governor of Arkansas serves in the executive branch. Based on information and belief, he also admits that at some point in time plaintiff was an employee of the Arkansas Industrial Development Commission. President Clinton is without knowledge or information sufficient to form a belief as to the truth of the remaining allegations set forth in paragraph 6, and therefore denies the same.

7. Admitted.

8. President Clinton is without knowledge or information sufficient to form a belief as to the truth of the allegations set forth in paragraph 8, and therefore denies the same.

9. Based on information and belief, President Clinton admits that Danny Ferguson was a state trooper assigned to the Governor's security detail on or about May 8, 1991. He is without knowledge or information sufficient to form a belief as to the truth of the remaining allegations set forth in paragraph 9, and therefore denies the same.

10. President Clinton denies the allegations set forth in paragraph 10 to the extent they purport to allege that he requested to meet plaintiff in a suite at the Excelsior Hotel. He is without knowledge or information sufficient to form a belief as to the truth of the remaining allegations set forth in paragraph 10, and therefore denies the same.

11. President Clinton is without knowledge or information sufficient to form a belief as to the truth of the allegations set forth in paragraph 11, and therefore denies the same.

12. President Clinton is without knowledge or information sufficient to form a belief as to the truth of the allegations set forth in paragraph 12, and therefore denies the same.

13. President Clinton is without knowledge or information sufficient to form a belief as to the truth of the allegations set forth in paragraph 13, and therefore denies the same.

14. President Clinton does not recall ever meeting plaintiff, and therefore denies each and every allegation set forth in paragraph 14.

15. While it was the usual practice to have a business suite available for the purpose of making calls and receiving visitors, President Clinton has no recollection of meeting plaintiff, and therefore denies each and every allegation set forth in paragraph 15.

16. President Clinton does not recall ever meeting plaintiff, and therefore denies each and every allegation set forth in paragraph 16.

17. President Clinton denies each and every allegation set forth in paragraph 17, except he admits that on or about May 8, 1991, David Harrington was Director of the Arkansas Industrial Development Commission.

18. President Clinton denies each and every allegation set forth in paragraph 18.

19. President Clinton denies each and every allegation set forth in paragraph 19.

20. President Clinton denies each and every allegation set forth in paragraph 20.

21. President Clinton denies each and every allegation set forth in paragraph 21.

Conditional Denials
Rule 8(b) allows a defendant to either admit, deny, or assert that he "is without knowledge or information sufficient to form a belief as to the truth of an averment." As is typical of answers, this one repeatedly invokes that phrase which, under the rule, "has the effect of a denial."

22. President Clinton denies each and every allegation set forth in paragraph 22.

23. President Clinton denies each and every allegation set forth in paragraph 23.

24. President Clinton denies each and every allegation set forth in paragraph 24.

25. President Clinton denies each and every allegation set forth in paragraph 25.

26. President Clinton denies each and every allegation set forth in paragraph 26.

27. President Clinton is without knowledge or information sufficient to form a belief as to the truth of the allegations set forth in paragraph 27, and therefore denies the same.

28. President Clinton denies that he engaged in any improper conduct with respect to plaintiff. He is without knowledge or information sufficient to form a belief as to the truth of the remaining allegations set forth in paragraph 28, and therefore denies the same.

29. President Clinton is without knowledge or information sufficient to form a belief as to the truth of the allegations set forth in paragraph 29, and therefore denies the same.

30. President Clinton denies that he engaged in any improper conduct with respect to plaintiff. He also denies making the statement attributed to him in paragraph 30. President Clinton is without knowledge or information sufficient to form a belief as to the truth of the remaining allegations set forth in paragraph 30, and therefore denies the same.

31. President Clinton denies that he engaged in any improper conduct with respect to plaintiff. He is without knowledge or information sufficient to form a belief as to the truth of the remaining allegations set forth in paragraph 31, and therefore denies the same.

32. President Clinton denies that he engaged in any improper conduct with respect to plaintiff. He is without knowledge or information sufficient to form a belief as to the truth of the remaining allegations set forth in paragraph 32, and therefore denies the same.

33. President Clinton denies that he engaged in any improper conduct with respect to plaintiff. He is without knowledge or information sufficient to form a belief as to the truth of the remaining allegations set forth in paragraph 33, and therefore denies the same.

34. President Clinton denies that he engaged in any improper conduct with respect to plaintiff. He is without knowledge or information

sufficient to form a belief as to the truth of the remaining allegations set forth in paragraph 34, and therefore denies the same.

35. President Clinton denies that he engaged in any improper conduct with respect to plaintiff. He is without knowledge or information sufficient to form a belief as to the truth of the remaining allegations set forth in paragraph 35, and therefore denies the same.

36. President Clinton is without knowledge or information sufficient to form a belief as to the truth of the allegations set forth in paragraph 36, and therefore denies the same.

37. President Clinton is without knowledge or information sufficient to form a belief as to the truth of the allegations set forth in paragraph 37, and therefore denies the same.

38. President Clinton denies that he engaged in any improper conduct with respect to plaintiff. President Clinton does not recall ever meeting plaintiff, and therefore denies each and every allegation set forth in paragraph 38.

39. President Clinton denies that he engaged in any improper conduct with respect to plaintiff. He is without knowledge or information sufficient to form a belief as to the truth of the remaining allegations set forth in paragraph 39, and therefore denies the same.

40. President Clinton is without knowledge or information sufficient to form a belief as to the truth of the allegations set forth in paragraph 40, and therefore denies the same.

41. President Clinton is without knowledge or information sufficient to form a belief as to the truth of the allegations set forth in paragraph 41, and therefore denies the same.

42. President Clinton denies that he engaged in any improper conduct with respect to plaintiff. To the extent the allegations set forth in paragraph 42 merely refer to or quote from the article in the *American Spectator,* attached as exhibit A to the Complaint, no response is required.

43. President Clinton denies that he engaged in any improper conduct with respect to plaintiff. To the extent the allegations set forth in paragraph 43 merely refer to or quote from the article in the *American Spectator,* attached as exhibit A to the Complaint, no response is required.

44. President Clinton denies each and every allegation set forth in paragraph 44.

45. President Clinton denies that he engaged in any improper conduct with respect to plaintiff. He is without knowledge or information

sufficient to form a belief as to the truth of the remaining allegations set forth in paragraph 45, and therefore denies the same.

Specificity Paragraph 46 is a good example of careful drafting. Under Rule 8(b), "[d]enials shall fairly meet the substance of the averments." General (blanket) denials are strongly disfavored under the Federal Rules.

46. President Clinton denies that he made sexual advances toward plaintiff. He also denies the quote attributed to him in paragraph 46. President Clinton is without knowledge or information sufficient to form a belief as to the truth of the remaining allegations set forth in paragraph 46, and therefore denies the same.

47. President Clinton denies each and every allegation in paragraph 47, except that he admits that a false article was published in the *American Spectator,* that plaintiff spoke publicly on February 11, 1994, and that representatives of plaintiff asked the President to acknowledge certain things which were untrue.

48. Based on information and belief, President Clinton admits that he and those acting on his behalf have denied plaintiff's allegations. Each and every other allegation set forth in paragraph 48 is denied.

49. Based on information and belief, President Clinton admits that his legal counsel made the statements set forth in paragraph 49. Each and every other allegation set forth in paragraph 49 is denied.

50. Based on information and belief, President Clinton admits that White House spokeswoman Dee Dee Meyers made the statement set forth in paragraph 50. Each and every other allegation set forth in paragraph 50 is denied. To the extent paragraph 50 states legal conclusions, no response is required.

51. President Clinton denies each and every allegation set forth in paragraph 51.

52. President Clinton admits that the general public reposes trust and confidence in the integrity of the holder of the office of the Presidency. Each and every other allegation set forth in paragraph 52 is denied.

53. President Clinton denies each and every allegation set forth in paragraph 53, except that he admits he was a member of the Arkansas State Bar on or about May 8, 1991. To the extent paragraph 53 states legal conclusions, no response is required.

54. President Clinton denies each and every allegation set forth in paragraph 54. To the extent paragraph 54 states legal conclusions, no response is required.

55. President Clinton denies each and every allegation set forth in paragraph 55. To the extent paragraph 55 states legal conclusions, no response is required.

56. President Clinton denies each and every allegation set forth

in paragraph 56. To the extent paragraph 56 states legal conclusions, no response is required.

57. President Clinton denies each and every allegation set forth in paragraph 57.

COUNT I: DEPRIVATION OF CONSTITUTIONAL RIGHTS AND PRIVILEGES (42 U.S.C. §1983)

58. President Clinton repeats and realleges his answers to the allegations appearing in paragraphs 1-57 as if fully set forth herein. President Clinton denies that he engaged in any improper conduct or deprived plaintiff of any constitutional right or privilege protected under 42 U.S.C. §1983, and therefore denies each and every allegation set forth in paragraphs 58, 59, 60, 61, 62, 63, 64, and 65. To the extent paragraphs 58-65 state legal conclusions, no response is required.

COUNT II: CONSPIRACY TO DEPRIVE PERSONS OF EQUAL PROTECTION OF THE LAWS (42 U.S.C. §1985 (3))

59. President Clinton repeats and realleges his answers to the allegations appearing in paragraphs 1-65 as if fully set forth herein. President Clinton denies that he engaged in a conspiracy to deprive plaintiff of any constitutionally protected right, and therefore denies the allegations set forth in paragraphs 66, 67, 68, and 69. To the extent paragraphs 66-69 state legal conclusions, no response is required.

COUNT III: INTENTIONAL INFLICTION OF EMOTIONAL DISTRESS

60. President Clinton repeats and realleges his answers to the allegations appearing in paragraphs 1-69 as if fully set forth herein. President Clinton denies that he engaged in any improper conduct with respect to plaintiff or any conduct intended to or which he knew was likely to inflict emotional distress upon plaintiff, and therefore denies the allegations of paragraphs 70, 71, 72, 73, and 74. To the extent paragraphs 70-74 state legal conclusions, no response is required.

COUNT IV: DEFAMATION

61. President Clinton repeats and realleges his answers to the allegations appearing in paragraphs 1-74 as if fully set forth herein. President Clinton denies that he defamed plaintiff in any respect, and therefore denies the allegations appearing in paragraphs 75, 76, 77, 78, and 79. To the extent paragraphs 75-79 state legal conclusions, no response is required.

62. To the extent any allegation set forth in the Complaint is not specifically answered above, it is hereby denied.

AS TO PLAINTIFF'S REQUEST FOR RELIEF

63. President Clinton denies that plaintiff is entitled to any relief whatsoever in connection with the Complaint.

AFFIRMATIVE DEFENSES

President Clinton alleges the following affirmative defenses to the allegations that he engaged in conduct violative of federal or state law.

First Affirmative Defense

Rule 12 Defenses
Here the President as-
serts the Rule 12(b)(6)
defense of failure to state
a claim as a Rule 8(c) affirmative defense. Can it
function as both?

64. The Complaint fails to state a claim upon which relief may be granted.

Second Affirmative Defense

65. Plaintiff's cause of action for intentional infliction of emotional distress is time-barred.

Third Affirmative Defense

66. Plaintiff's defamation claim is barred because, even if the statements could properly be attributed to President Clinton, they are not defamatory.

Fourth Affirmative Defense

67. Plaintiff's defamation claim is barred because, even if the statements could properly be attributed to President Clinton, they are true.

Fifth Affirmative Defense

68. Plaintiff's defamation claim is barred because, even if the statements could properly be attributed to President Clinton, they are privileged or protected by one or more immunities, including, but not limited to, the First and Fourteenth Amendments to the Constitution of the United States and the immunity doctrine established in *Nixon v. Fitzgerald,* 457 U.S. 731 (1982).

Sixth Affirmative Defense

69. Plaintiff's claim that President Clinton is jointly and severally liable for the allegedly defamatory statements attributed to Trooper Danny Ferguson is barred as a matter of law.

Affirmative Defenses
Most affirmative de-
fenses conform to the
typical structure of con-
fession and avoidance;
i.e., even if the allegation
is true, there can be no
recovery. Here, the President raises a variety of affirmative defenses, based
on law (the statute of limitations has expired) and
facts (a third party com-
mitted the harm).

Seventh Affirmative Defense

70. Plaintiff's claims are barred because she did not incur any injury or damages cognizable at law.

Eighth Affirmative Defense

71. Plaintiff's injuries and damages, if any, were caused by the acts of third persons, for which the President is not responsible.

Ninth Affirmative Defense

72. Plaintiff's injuries and damages, if any, were caused by the acts of plaintiff and her representatives, for which the President is not responsible.

Tenth Affirmative Defense

73. Plaintiff is not entitled to punitive damages under the applicable law.

Eleventh Affirmative Defense

74. Plaintiff has failed to plead special damages with particularity as required by Federal Rule of Civil Procedure 9(g).

Wherefore, President Clinton respectfully requests that the Complaint be dismissed and that this Court enter judgment in his favor and grant such other relief as the Court deems just and proper.

Special Damages In certain kinds of cases, including defamation, the pleading rules require that the details of the damages be specified. The reasoning is that one cannot assume that these acts, even if committed, led to harm.

NOTES AND COMMENTS

1. Categories of defenses. Rule 8 provides that a defendant shall "admit or deny the averments" in the complaint; shall "state in short and plain terms" his or her defenses; and "shall set forth affirmatively" each matter that constitutes an affirmative defense. How do denials, defenses, and affirmative defenses differ? Using President Clinton's answer as an example, can you describe the differences among these three concepts?

2. Affirmative defenses. Perhaps the trickiest aspect of drafting an answer is deciding what to plead as an affirmative defense. Rule 8(c) specifies 19 assertions that must be pled as affirmative defenses or waived. Number 20 is "any other matter constituting an avoidance or affirmative defense." There are multiple standards for ascertaining what "other matters" should be classed as affirmative defenses under the FRCP. Some courts focus on whether the assertion fits within the traditional confession and avoidance, or "yes, but" logic; others ask whether it would surprise a plaintiff's lawyer who was reasonably well prepared by its improbability; and yet others focus on whether it turns on information uniquely within the control of the defendant. At the least, a proper affirmative defense inserts new facts into the case, and is not simply a denial of facts alleged in the complaint.

There can be significant consequences from mistaken pleading of affirmative defenses. Although federal procedure is generally lenient regarding amendments, the lawyer who has omitted an affirmative defense might face the frightening prospect of having waived a decisive argument. In practical terms, the judge can exclude evidence at trial that would support an affirmative defense, if it was not pled as such. Why not, then, overlabel defenses as affirmative, which seems to have been the tendency of President Clinton's lawyers? Because the burden of proof usually aligns with the burden of pleading, characterizing something as an affirmative defense might amount to an assumption of the burden of proof on that matter at trial.

Exercise 4—Affirmative Defenses

Consider two possible affirmative defenses: First, President Clinton makes the familiar response that truth is a defense to defamation. (See Paragraph 67 of President Clinton's answer.) Is that correctly labeled as an affirmative defense? Second, Jones's lawyers argued that President Clinton's immunity claim (in Chapter 3) was an affirmative defense, rather than a ground for dismissal. The consequence of their winning on that point would have been that Clinton could not have raised the question before filing his answer.

Neither immunity nor truth as a defense to defamation is in the list of affirmative defenses enumerated in Rule 8(c). Therefore, the question of whether they should be categorized as such turns on whether they would fall within the scope of "any other matter constituting an avoidance or affirmative defense." What are the arguments for and against treating each as an affirmative defense?

3. Brain teaser: The Erie doctrine.   [You should skip this question if you have not yet covered what is known as the *Erie* doctrine in your procedure course.] In Paragraph 66 of the answer, President Clinton invokes the defense that the statements alleged in the complaint (see Paragraphs 48-50), which allegedly implied that Jones was a liar, even if attributable to him, were not defamatory as a matter of law. Because the underlying claim—defamation—arises under state law, it will be state law that determines whether those statements constitute defamation as a matter of law. But what body of law—state or federal—determines whether this is an *affirmative* defense or a simple denial? Under the *Erie* doctrine, federal law governs on issues of procedure, and state law governs on issues of substantive law. Consider which should control on this question.

4. Framing discovery.   To a limited extent, the defendant can use the answer to frame the scope of discovery. If a fact has been admitted, defendant can argue that it should be excluded from discovery on the ground that discovery about an uncontested assertion is unduly burdensome and duplicative. In some situations, a defendant might admit a fairly insignificant fact, even if it could plausibly be denied, in order to try to cut off inquiries into related matters.

5. Don't forget Rule 11.   Recall that Rule 11 applies to answers (and many other documents) as much as to complaints. Are there any portions of President Clinton's answer that might run afoul of his or his attorney's duty to certify that "to the best of [his or her] knowledge, information and belief, formed after an inquiry reasonable under the circumstances . . . the denials of factual contentions are warranted on the evidence or, if specifically so identified, are reasonably based on a lack of information or belief"?

6. The best defense.   Imagine that Clinton wants to sue Jones for malicious prosecution. Could he use this answer as a way of bringing that claim? How?

7. Inconsistent defenses.   In his answer, President Clinton alleges both that plaintiff's injuries were caused by third parties (Paragraph 71) and that they were caused by plaintiff herself (Paragraph 72). Is that permitted under the Rules?

8. Plaintiff's response.   Jones has now been accused of causing the injuries to herself. What can she do to respond to Paragraph 72 of the answer?

9. Drafting technique.   Following is a side-by-side chart of selected paragraphs of the complaint and the corresponding paragraphs of the answer. Compare the carefulness of the language in each. Can you do better? Try redrafting each of the eight paragraphs and write a short memo explaining why you chose to redraft as you did.

Complaint and Answer Comparison

COMPLAINT	ANSWER
10. At approximately 2:30 P.M. on that day, Ferguson reappeared at the registration desk, delivered a piece of paper to Jones with a four-digit number written on it and said: "The Governor would like to meet with you" in this suite number. Plaintiff had never met Defendant Clinton and saw him in person for the first time at the Conference.	10. President Clinton denies the allegations set forth in paragraph 10 to the extent they purport to allege that he requested to meet plaintiff in a suite at the Excelsior Hotel. He is without knowledge or information sufficient to form a belief as to the truth of the remaining allegations set forth in paragraph 10, and therefore denies the same.
14. Jones knocked on the door frame and Clinton answered. Plaintiff entered. Ferguson remained outside.	14. President Clinton does not recall ever meeting plaintiff, and therefore denies each and every allegation set forth in paragraph 14.
30. When Ballantine met Plaintiff at the reception area, she immediately asked Jones what was wrong because Jones was visibly upset and nervous. Plaintiff wanted to talk about something that just happened and wanted to discuss it someplace privately. Ballantine and Jones went to a private area in the office, and later outside. Jones then told Ballantine what had happened with Clinton in the hotel suite. According to Ballantine, Jones told her that Clinton said as she left the room, "I know you're a smart girl and I'm sure you'll keep this to yourself."	30. President Clinton denies that he engaged in any improper conduct with respect to plaintiff. He also denies making the statement attributed to him in paragraph 30. President Clinton is without knowledge or information sufficient to form a belief as to the truth of the remaining allegations set forth in paragraph 30, and therefore denies the same.
47. Because the false statements appearing in the *American Spectator* article that Jones was willing to have sex with Clinton (and the innuendo that she had already done so when she left the hotel suite) threatened her marriage, her friendships, and her family relationships, Plaintiff spoke publicly on February 11, 1994, that she was the "Paula" mentioned in the *American Spectator* article, that she had rebuffed Clinton's sexual advances, and that she had not expressed a willingness to be his girlfriend. Jones and her lawyer asked that Clinton acknowledge the incident, state that Jones had rejected Clinton's advances, and apologize to Jones.	47. President Clinton denies each and every allegation in paragraph 47, except that he admits that a false article was published in the *American Spectator,* that plaintiff spoke publicly on February 11, 1994, and that representatives of plaintiff asked the President to acknowledge certain things which were untrue.

CHAPTER FIVE

Amendments

INTRODUCTION

In the summer of 1997, with the Supreme Court decision behind them and the pleadings completed, both sides turned their attention to moving forward with the litigation process in the trial court. Both sets of lawyers began making discovery requests. This moment in a lawsuit—immediately prior to the onset of the usually expensive discovery stage—often leads to renewed settlement discussions, which is what happened in *Jones v. Clinton*. On August 5, Bennett invited Davis and Cammarata to his office, and the two teams negotiated into the night. They tentatively agreed that the President would pay Jones $700,000 and, in addition, issue a statement that would express regret but not constitute an admission. Recall that $700,000 was the total amount that Jones had sought in her complaint. The lawyers thought they had a deal.

Once again, however, the deal fell through. Jones refused to accept the settlement. Her lawyers were furious. On August 19, they wrote her a 12-page letter urging her to accept the offer, stating in part: "Your focus has changed from proving that you are a good person, to proving Clinton is a bad person. That was never your objective in filing suit." Jones could not be persuaded, however. Accounts of the case report that among those urging her not to settle were her husband and informal advisers who had begun to act as counselors and supporters. Another lawyer working with the "elves"—the lawyers volunteering their time to work on her case—told *Washington Post* reporter Michael Isikoff: "We were terrified that Jones would settle. It was contrary to our purpose of bringing down the President."

Judge Wright announced her ruling on President Clinton's Rule 12(c) motion on August 22, 1997, during a status conference; the opinion was filed on August 25. On the next day, she issued a scheduling order in which the following deadlines were set:

- witness lists were to be exchanged by December 5, 1997;
- discovery was to be concluded by January 30, 1998;
- any further pretrial motions were due by March 13, 1998;

- pretrial information sheets (preparatory to pretrial orders) were due April 24, 1998; and
- trial was to begin on May 27, 1998.

On August 29, Davis and Cammarata wrote Jones again, this time to inform her that they would not continue to represent her. On September 8, they filed a formal motion to withdraw, which Judge Wright granted. The *Washington Post* carried the story of the lawyers' withdrawal. Among the readers who saw it was John Whitehead, the president of an organization called the Rutherford Institute based in Charlottesville, Virginia. Founded in 1982, the Rutherford Institute describes itself as an ACLU for conservative causes, established to support legal actions for civil liberties. (*See www.rutherford.org.*) Ironically, Whitehead, like Judge Wright, had also been a student at the University of Arkansas Law School while President Clinton was a professor there and had interviewed Clinton for the student newspaper.

Whitehead called Susan Carpenter-McMillan, who had become Jones's public relations adviser and general confidante, and told her that Rutherford would pay the legal expenses of Jones's continuing litigation. Rutherford did not have lawyers on staff who would be available to undertake the legal work in-house, but he referred her to a firm where a member of Rutherford's board of directors was a partner. That firm—Rader, Campbell, Fisher and Pyke, of Dallas—took over as Jones's lawyers on October 1.

Jones's new lawyers added an unexpected twist to the lawsuit: They sought leave under Rule 15 to amend the complaint.

PLAINTIFF'S MOTION FOR LEAVE TO FILE FIRST AMENDED COMPLAINT AND BRIEF THEREON

TO THE HONORABLE JUDGE OF SAID COURT:

Plaintiff hereby moves the Court, in accordance with Federal Rule of Civil Procedure 15(a), for leave to file Plaintiffs First Amended Complaint herein and for good cause would show the Court as follows.

1. As this Court is aware, the Court issued its Memorandum Opinion and Order on Defendant Clinton's Motion for Judgment on the Pleadings on or about August 22, 1997, a mere two (2) months ago. This Memorandum Opinion effected several changes to the nature of Plaintiff's pleadings in her original Complaint, the primary changes being to dismiss Plaintiff's defamation claim against Defendant Clinton and to dismiss Plaintiff's claim for deprivation of a protected liberty interest in her reputation.

2. As the Court's record will reflect, Plaintiff's new counsel of record entered their appearance herein on or about October 1, 1997, and they have been studying the Court's Memorandum Opinion since their entry into this case only 26 days ago.

3. As a result of Plaintiff's new counsels' review of the Memorandum

Opinion and their review of the facts surrounding this case as presently known, Plaintiff has determined that it is appropriate to amend her Complaint in certain respects. In this connection, Plaintiff hereby tenders to the Court a full, complete, and true copy of her proposed Plaintiff's First Amended Complaint which is attached hereto as Exhibit A and incorporated herein by reference for all purposes. As the Court will observe, the primary changes to be effected by this amended pleading are: (a) to drop Plaintiff's remaining defamation count against Defendant Ferguson and Plaintiff's remaining loss-of-reputation claims in order to simplify the issues for discovery and trial and to concentrate on the claimed constitutional violations; (b) to clarify Plaintiff's constitutional and civil-rights claims and conform them more fully to the facts previously plead, especially with respect to Plaintiff's equal-protection arguments concerning her disparate treatment as a State employee and her claims about Defendants' interference with her right to petition for redress of her grievances; and (c) to seek a declaratory judgment from the Court concerning substantially the same causes of action previously plead.

4. As the Court's docket sheet will reflect, discovery and other pretrial activities are just now starting in this case, after having been delayed by Defendants for three (3) years while they pursued unsuccessfully their novel immunity claims. Accordingly, there was no reason or opportunity for any party to seek to amend its pleadings before disposition of these purely defensive and dilatory claims.

5. Plaintiff maintains that the omission of her remaining defamation and reputation-loss claims will simplify the issues for discovery and trial and will significantly reduce anticipated discovery battles that this Court would otherwise need to address.

6. Plaintiff would point out that the Court's current August 25, 1997 Scheduling Order anticipates that requests to amend pleadings will be taken up after the parties' Pretrial Conference Information Sheet is filed herein on or about April 24, 1998. Obviously, the instant request for leave to file an amended complaint is presented approximately six (6) months before this April 1998 due date set by the current Scheduling Order.

7. This Motion is supported by the language of Rule 15(a) itself, which states that leave of court to amend shall be freely given when justice so requires. Moreover, the Supreme Court has ruled that: "If the underlying facts or circumstances relied upon by a plaintiff may be a proper subject of relief, . . . the leave [to amend] sought should, as the rules require, be 'freely given.'" *Foman v. Davis,* 371 U.S. 178, 182 (1962). Moreover, when the facts underlying a previously plead claim are substantially similar to those which form the basis of a proposed new claim to be added by amendment, a trial court should grant leave to amend the complaint to add the new count. *Buder v. Merrill, Lynch, Pierce, Fenner & Smith, Inc.,* 644 F.2d 690 (8th Cir. 1981).

WHEREFORE, PREMISES CONSIDERED, Plaintiff prays that the Court grant leave to file Plaintiff's First Amended Complaint as attached hereto as Exhibit A and for such other and further relief, special or general, at law or in equity, to which Plaintiff may be justly entitled.

EXCERPTS OF FIRST AMENDED COMPLAINT

[Italicized text indicates additions to original complaint; strike-out indicates text from the original complaint that was dropped.]

This is the first mention of plaintiff's new claim of a violation of her First Amendment right to petition the government for redress for that violation.

31. Ballantine urged Jones to report the incident *to the police or to her AIDC superiors.* Plaintiff refused, fearing that, if she did so, no one would believe her account, that she would lose her job, and that the incident would endanger her relationship with her then-fiancé (now husband), Stephen Jones. *Plaintiff responded that it was the State Police themselves who had just jointly perpetrated, with Defendant Clinton, this heinous conduct upon her and that Defendant Clinton had sternly admonished her that her boss at the AIDC was Defendant Clinton's very good friend. Thus, Plaintiff realized that the police and the AIDC would stifle any petition of hers for redress, and she correctly feared that, if she did so report, she would lose her job.*

This paragraph introduces the concept of "third-party favoritism" as a form of sexual harassment.

39. Jones continued to work at AIDC even though she was in constant fear that Governor Clinton might take retaliatory action against her because of her rejection of his abhorrent sexual advances *and in order to further chill and squelch her potential reporting of these incidents to appropriate authorities.* Her enjoyment of her work was severely diminished. In fact, she was treated in a hostile and rude manner by certain superiors in AIDC. This rude conduct had not happened prior to her encounter with Clinton. Further, after her maternity leave she was transferred to a position which had no responsible duties for which she could be adequately evaluated to earn advancement. The reason given to her by her superiors for the transfer was that her previous position had been eliminated. This reason was untrue since her former position was not abolished. It was a pretext for the real reason which was that she was being punished for her rejection of the various advances made by Clinton described above. In addition, the job in which she was placed called for a higher grade and pay, yet she was not paid more money than she received in her previous position. Although other employees received merit increases, Jones never received a raise beyond a cost of living increase. *This discriminatory treatment contrasts vividly with Defendants' treatment of other women who succumbed to Defendant Clinton's predatory custom, habit, pattern, and practice of using State payroll, time, vehicles, personnel, and resources to solicit sexual favors and who provided such favors because Defendants systematically granted, directly and indirectly, governmental and employment benefits, appointments, advancements, raises, promotions, positions, and perquisites to such other women.*

43. The *American Spectator* account also asserted that the troopers' "'official' duties included facilitating Clinton's cheating on his wife. This meant that, on the State payroll, and using State time, vehicles, and resources, they were instructed by Clinton on a regular basis to approach women and to solicit their telephone numbers for the Governor, to drive him in State vehicles to rendezvous points and guard him

during sexual encounters; to secure hotel rooms and other meeting places for sex: . . ." and various other things to facilitate Clinton's sex life including "to help Clinton cover-up his activities by keeping tabs on Hillary's whereabouts and lying to Hillary about her husband's whereabouts." Although this pattern of conduct by Clinton may be true, the magazine article concluded, evidently from interviews with troopers from Clinton's Security Detail, including Ferguson, that "all of the women appear to have been willing participants in the affairs and liaisons." *This reported pattern of conduct by Defendant Clinton is accurate and reflects Defendants' unconstitutional actions taken under color and pretense of state law, regulation, custom, usage, habit, pattern, and practice.*

44. Since Jones ("Paula") was one of the women preyed upon by Clinton and his troopers, including by Defendant Ferguson, in the manner described above, those who read this magazine account could conclude falsely that Jones ("Paula") had a sexual relationship and affair with Clinton. ~~Jones's reputation within her community was thus seriously damaged.~~

The dropped sentence reflects plaintiff's decision to drop any defamation claim. Why might a defamation claim cause more trouble than it was likely worth? Consider its ramifications for the scope of discovery.

60. Defendant Clinton, *individually and* as Governor of Arkansas, acting under color *and pretense* of state law, *regulation, custom, usage, habit, pattern, and practice,* discriminated against Plaintiff because of her gender by sexually harassing and assaulting her on May 8, 1991, and thereafter, and this deprived Jones of her right to equal protection of the law. *Defendant Clinton, further so acting, also discriminated against Plaintiff because of her sex by systematically granting, directly and indirectly, governmental and employment benefits, appointments, advancements, raises, promotions, positions, and perquisites to other women who succumbed to Defendant Clinton's predatory custom, usage, habit, pattern, and practice of using State payroll, time, vehicles, personnel, and resources to solicit sexual favors and who provided such favors, while continually denying, directly and indirectly, any such appointments, advancements, raises, promotions, positions, and perquisites to Plaintiff because she would not accede to Defendant Clinton's repeated solicitations of sex from her. This conduct further deprived Plaintiff of her right to equal protection of the law. Additionally and alternatively, Defendant Ferguson was a willful participant in said joint action with Defendant Clinton in committing such discriminatory conduct, and there was a mutual understanding and a meeting of the minds between them in perpetrating such heinous conduct, as evidence by, inter alia, Defendant Ferguson's admission to Plaintiff that "we do this all the time for the Governor."*

Paragraphs 60-65 appear as part of plaintiff's revised statement of Count I. Does the added language constitute a new claim?

61. Further, *Defendant Clinton* ~~he~~ continued personally, and through agents, *directly and indirectly,* to impose a hostile work environment on Plaintiff in which she feared the loss of her employment and the possible adverse employment actions against her, including job discrimination and monitoring of her personal life. As described above she was placed in a category separate from other public employees in that she was actually subjected to *rudeness and* hostility by her superiors, which deprived her of an opportunity for advancement and she suffered an economic deprivation. *In contrast, other women who succumbed to*

> *Defendant Clinton's said predatory pattern and practices and provided him sexual favors were not subjected to such a hostile work environment but were, in fact, frequently granted employment benefits, appointments, advancements, raises, promotions, positions, and perquisites, directly and indirectly, by Defendants and their subordinates in government.*

This paragraph contains the statement of the new First Amendment claim.

> 63. ~~Plaintiff also was entitled to a due process liberty interest in her reputation as an honest public employee. Clinton's actions and statements deprived Jones of these rights.~~ *Plaintiff also was entitled to freedom of speech and the absolute right to petition the Government for redress of her grievances under the First Amendment of the United States Constitution. By virtue of Defendant Clinton's overt and covert warnings, admonitions, intimidations, and threats to Plaintiff's boss, and by virtue of Defendant Ferguson's pointed inquiries and implied threats to Plaintiff regarding "how's Steve," Defendants, acting under color and pretense of state law, regulation, custom, and usage, intentionally infringed and violated Plaintiff's said First Amendment rights, privileges, and immunities and deprived her of same by chilling and squelching Plaintiff's exercise of such rights in reporting Defendants' heinous conduct to government authorities for proper redress.*

Note that Ferguson is added as a co-defendant as to Count I. Similar paragraphs added him as "jointly and severally liable" under Counts III and the new Count IV. In the original complaint, he was included only in Count II (conspiracy).

> 65. The above-described actions of Clinton were undertaken when he was acting under the color of state law, as Governor of Arkansas, *and said actions of Defendant Ferguson were undertaken when he was acting under the color and pretense of state law as an Arkansas State Trooper and Police Officer.* and *S*aid actions deprived Jones of federal equal protection, ~~and~~ due process *and free speech and petition* rights guaranteed by the Fifth and Fourteenth Amendments of the United States Constitution, and *caused Plaintiff actual damage and injury, for which she hereby sues Defendants, jointly and severally. Said conduct is* made actionable by 42 U.S.C. §1983 (The Civil Rights Act).

Additionally, the First Amended Complaint contained a new Count IV. The original Count IV pled defamation, and was dismissed as to President Clinton (but not Ferguson) by the judge's decision on the Rule 12(c) motion. The new Count IV did not assert an additional substantive claim, but sought a declaratory judgment as to elements of the other counts.

OPPOSITION TO PLAINTIFF'S MOTION TO AMEND THE COMPLAINT

After repeated representations to this Court, the Supreme Court and the public at large that the chief aim of her suit was to redeem her reputation, plaintiff now seeks to amend her complaint to drop her only remaining claim for defamation, and to add other, specious claims against the defendants. Plaintiff's motion to amend should be rejected because it is futile, in that it seeks to plead claims which are not actionable; seeks to replead claims that have been dismissed; and seeks redundant and inappropriate declaratory relief. The proposed amendments are also prejudicial and untimely.

We believe, moreover, that the amended complaint is disingenuous and was not submitted in good faith. . . . Plaintiff clearly hopes and intends that the amendment will dramatically shift the focus of the case away from Paula Jones's few alleged contacts with President Clinton, and toward gossip and innuendo concerning the President's alleged conduct with other women—rumor and gossip that plaintiff says she did not even know about at the time, and which could not have impacted her rights. For all these reasons, plaintiff should not be permitted to amend her complaint. . . .

Plaintiff seeks to expand her Section 1983 claim to assert that she was discriminated against because women who purportedly "succumbed" to then-Governor Clinton's alleged sexual overtures allegedly were rewarded with government jobs, promotions, and other benefits while she was denied such benefits because she refused the Governor's alleged advances. These allegations fail to support a claim for either *quid pro quo* or hostile environment sex harassment because such third-party favoritism does not constitute disparate treatment on the basis of sex, and in any event, plaintiff could not have suffered sex discrimination based on conduct of which she was unaware.

There is virtually universal agreement among the circuits that a claim of sex discrimination cannot be founded, without more, on the assertion that the plaintiff was disadvantaged in her working conditions because the defendant favored other employees who willingly engaged in sexual conduct with the defendant. As one court explained, "preferential treatment on the basis of a consensual romantic relationship between a supervisor and an employee is not gender-based discrimination," because all other workers, male or female, are equally disadvantaged by it. [citation omitted] Accordingly, so-called "paramour" or third-party favoritism, standing alone, does not state an actionable claim.

Plaintiff has suggested that her claim is valid nonetheless because she is not simply alleging that other alleged sexual partners of the Governor received preferential treatment, but also that she was denied benefits because of her refusal to "succumb." This distinction fails because plaintiff does not and cannot allege that she knew of the alleged preferential treatment of others at the time, or that it occurred in her work place. Plaintiff also fails to identify any employment benefits or opportunities that she was entitled to but which were given to someone else who consented to sexual relations with the defendant. Without such allegations, her claim is subject to dismissal. . . .

The defendants, moreover, ought not to be penalized because plaintiff and her first counsel had a falling out and plaintiff's new counsel has just "studied" the case and wishes to pursue a new agenda through an amended complaint. Plaintiff had ample opportunity to amend prior to now. There was an eight-month period between the date the original complaint was filed and the date the presidential immunity issue was appealed, and another five months have elapsed since jurisdiction was returned to the District Court. Accordingly, plaintiff has no valid reason for delay.

We respectfully submit, moreover, that the Court's scheduling order, relied on by plaintiff, does not contemplate that plaintiff may amend the complaint to dramatically change the scope and direction of litigation at any time up until two weeks before trial. Rather, that order merely reflects the standard practice that amendments may be made before trial in order to conform the complaint to the evidence adduced during discovery—providing there is no prejudice to the defendants and the amendments are in good faith.

Finally, we submit that plaintiff will not be prejudiced if amendment is disallowed. First, plaintiff has not even initiated discovery on her core claim concerning the defendants' alleged conduct toward her. Most significantly, the original complaint—even minus the defamation claim, which plaintiff is free to dismiss at any time—amply achieves plaintiff's legitimate litigation ends. Accordingly, the amended complaint should be rejected.

Order Granting Motion for Leave to Amend
Nov. 24, 1997

. . . Rule 15(a) of the Federal Rules of Civil Procedure provides that leave to amend complaints shall be freely granted "when justice so requires." The determination of whether the motion to amend is granted is left to the sound discretion of the trial court. There is no absolute or automatic right to amend. Unless a substantial reason exists to deny leave to amend, however, the discretion of the trial court is not broad enough to permit denial. *Foman v. Davis,* 371 U.S. 178, 182 (1962). Factors which the court should consider in determining whether to grant leave to amend include undue delay, bad faith, dilatory motive on the part of the movant, repeated failure to cure deficiencies by amendments previously allowed, undue prejudice to the opposing party, and futility of amendment.

Plaintiff first requests that she be allowed to drop her remaining defamation count against Ferguson and her remaining loss-of-reputation claims in order to simplify this lawsuit and concentrate on the claimed constitutional violations. The Court has considered the matter and will grant plaintiff's request to drop these claims from her lawsuit. Although plaintiff states that the omission of her remaining defamation count and her remaining loss-of-reputation claims from her lawsuit will simplify the issues for discovery and trial and will significantly reduce anticipated discovery battles, the Court, in allowing plaintiff to drop these claims, is not thereby indicating how it will rule on any evidentiary issues that later arise in this lawsuit. Any such issues will be taken up on an issue-by-issue basis as they may arise in the course of discovery and/or the trial.

Plaintiff also requests that she be allowed to amend her complaint in order to clarify her constitutional and civil rights claims and conform them more fully to the facts previously plead, especially with respect to her equal protection arguments concerning her disparate treatment as a State employee and her claims about defendants' interference with her right to petition for redress of her grievances. In response, the President points out that this request is really an attempt to add three new grounds for recovery under 42 U.S.C. §1983: (1) a *quid pro quo* third-party favoritism claim in which plaintiff alleges that the Governor granted governmental and employment benefits to other women who succumbed to his solicitation of sexual favors while plaintiff was denied such benefits because she would not accede to his solicitations of sex from her; (2) a hostile environment third-party favoritism claim in which plaintiff alleges she suffered a hostile environment because other women who succumbed to the Governor's "predatory pattern and practices and provided him sexual favors" were not subjected to a hostile environment but were granted favors and benefits which she was denied; and (3) a First Amendment claim in which plaintiff alleges she was deprived of her Constitutional right to free speech and to petition the government for redress by virtue of the Governor's "overt and covert warnings, admonitions, intimidations, and threats to plaintiff." The President argues that the proposed amended complaint should be disallowed as these new causes of action fail to state claims and would thus not survive a motion to dismiss.

It is true that most courts that have considered the matter have concluded that preferential treatment on the basis of a consensual romantic relationship between a supervisor and an employee is not, standing alone, sex discrimination. *See, e.g., Thomson v. Olson,* 866 F.Supp. 1267, 1272 (D.N.D. 1994), *aff'd,* 56 F.3d 69 (8th Cir. 1995); *Piech v. Arthur Anderson,* 841 F.Supp. 825, 828 (N.D.Ill. 1994). Such alleged favoritism is not discrimination based on gender since all workers, male or female, are disadvantaged by it. *See Taken v. Oklahoma Corp. Comm'n,* 125 F.3d 1366, 1370 (10th Cir. 1997); *Harvey v. Chevron,* 961 F.Supp. 1017, 1029 (S.D.Tx. 1997); *Miller v. Aluminum Co. of Am.,* 679 F.Supp. 495, 501 (W.D.Pa.), *aff'd,* 856 F.2d 184 (3rd Cir. 1988).

> Here, the judge is distinguishing between the relevance of certain facts to plaintiff's existing claims and whether her newly pled facts state a viable different claim. What part of Rule 15 supports her reasoning as to proof at trial?

Similarly, "[a] co-worker's romantic involvement with a supervisor does not by itself create a hostile work environment," *Candelore v. Clark County Sanitation District,* 975 F.2d 588, 590 (9th Cir. 1992), especially where, as in this case, there is no allegation that plaintiff was aware of any such alleged relationship. Cf. *Taken,* 125 F.3d at 1370 (no hostile working environment where plaintiffs did not work with other woman). Accordingly, to the extent plaintiff is seeking to plead as distinct causes of action a *quid pro quo* third-party favoritism claim or a hostile environment third-party favoritism claim, those claims will not be recognized. In so ruling, however, the Court is not thereby indicating how it will rule on any evidentiary issues that later arise in this lawsuit. Any such issues will be taken up on an issue-by-issue basis as they may arise in the course of discovery and/or the trial. Thus, while the Court is not recognizing plaintiff's third-party favoritism allegations as distinct causes of action, the Court will permit their inclusion in the amended complaint for the purpose of clarifying plaintiff's constitutional and civil rights claims as far as proof at trial is concerned.

With respect to plaintiff's First Amendment claim, plaintiff asserts that the Governor's "overt and covert warnings, admonitions, intimidations, and threats to Plaintiff to 'keep this to yourself' (or words to that effect) and that he would speak to Plaintiff's boss, and by virtue of Defendant Ferguson's pointed inquiries and implied threats to Plaintiff regarding 'how's Steve,'" deprived her of her First Amendment rights by "chilling and squelching Plaintiff's exercise of such rights in reporting Defendants' heinous conduct to governmental authorities for proper redress." Again, to the extent plaintiff is attempting to plead as a distinct cause of action a First Amendment claim in which she alleges she was deprived of her Constitutional right to free speech and to petition the government for redress, this claim will not be recognized. The allegations of the complaint establish that plaintiff has spoken on the matters that are the subject of this lawsuit, and, in any case, the comments attributed to the defendants do not, as a matter of law, constitute a threat of specific future harm, a requirement for such a claim. Nevertheless, these same essential allegations were included in the original complaint and may have some bearing on other claims in plaintiff's lawsuit. Accordingly, as was the case with plaintiff's third-party favoritism claims, the Court will permit their inclusion in the amended complaint for the purpose of clarifying plaintiff's Constitutional and civil rights claims as far as proof at trial is concerned.

. . . Likewise, the Court will construe plaintiff's prayer for a declaratory judgment in Count IV of the amended complaint as having no effect as any relief that plaintiff obtains in this lawsuit will, in the absence of settlement, be by way of a jury verdict. Accordingly, while the Court has no objection to the inclusion of these matters in plaintiff's amended complaint, they are of no effect as far as this Court is concerned and will not be recognized for purposes of the issues that remain in this lawsuit. . . .

NOTES AND COMMENTS

1. *Plaintiff's theory of amendment.*   How would you describe what the plaintiff was trying to achieve by this motion for leave to amend? Did the third-party favoritism allegations constitute a new claim? How would you characterize it? What were plaintiff's strongest arguments in support of the motion?

2. *"New" facts.*   What allegations of fact did plaintiff add to her complaint by this amendment? Obviously, none of these facts was truly new; everything that had happened in 1991 had already happened. The amendment illustrates a point that we noted in Chapter 1: different lawyers "discover" and develop the same facts differently, and there are almost always multiple options for how facts describing a particular event are woven together to support legal claims.

Exercise 5—Revising the Theory of the Case
Redraft the plaintiff's theory of the case based on the amended complaint.

3. *Defendant's theory of opposition.*   President Clinton's lawyers argued that what plaintiff described as new claims could not survive a Rule 12(b)(6) motion. How did Clinton's futility theory interact with the function of a motion to dismiss? Did it matter whether the third-party favoritism allegations constituted a new claim? What were the biggest weaknesses in Clinton's argument in opposition?

4. *New parties to old claims.*   Although in general he plays a minimal role in the lawsuit, Defendant Ferguson's presence is a factor in this motion. Were there new claims as to him?

Exercise 6—Analyzing an Opposition to Amendment
The arguments against amendment that you just read were those raised by President Clinton's lawyers. Assume that Defendant Ferguson has objected to

the aspects of the amendment that affect him. As Judge Wright's law clerk, write a memorandum to her analyzing whether those amendments meet the criteria of Rule 15.

5. The judge's ruling.   In what ways did the plaintiff win this motion? In what ways did the defendant win? What will be the most significant impact of this ruling?

CHAPTER SIX

Discovery: Devices and Defenses

INTRODUCTION

Discovery was probably the most significant and most controversial aspect of *Jones v. Clinton*. As *Washington Post* reporter Michael Isikoff noted presciently in the article he wrote at the time the complaint was filed, "Regardless of whether Clinton is victorious, federal court rules may give Jones's lawyers the opportunity to take sworn depositions from witnesses, including former members of Clinton's gubernatorial security detail who have said they solicited women for the governor. This process could keep alive for some time politically damaging questions about the president's private conduct."[1]

President Clinton's strategy of delay contributed to keeping those questions pending. Stuart Taylor, Jr., writing in *The American Lawyer* shortly before the President won reelection in November 1996, summed up the developments to that date:

> Jones's lawyers have visions of putting the president between the rock of damaging admissions and the hard place of possible perjury . . . Bennett has shut them out, so far, by losing on the presidential immunity claim in the district court and appealing, and then losing in the Eighth Circuit and appealing again, first for en banc review, then for Supreme Court review. Meanwhile, there has been no factual answer for Clinton to file. No depositions. No interrogatories. No discovery into whether there is, in fact, a distinguishing mark. No trial.[2]

Once discovery began in the fall of 1997, its intensity amounted to a virtual blitzkrieg. The court's docket of records in the case includes all pleadings, motions, responses, cross-motions, and judicial rulings. Of the 505 documents in the docket, more than 60 percent—323, by far the largest category—relate to issues of discovery. Many of the 323 documents include voluminous exhibits and attachments; the result

---

1. Michael Isikoff, "Clinton Named Defendant in Sexual Harassment Suit," *Washington Post*, May 7, 1994 at A-1.
2. Stuart Taylor, Jr., "Her Case Against Clinton," The American Lawyer, Nov. 1996 at 57.

is thousands of pages pertaining to discovery. In addition, the parties conducted 62 depositions.

Although *Jones v. Clinton* may have been unique in the consequences of its discovery phase, it was not unusual in the proportion of discovery disputes to the overall number of contested issues in a given case. Discovery is often the most protracted and most expensive stage in litigation.[3] And it is also often the most significant phase: "One of the striking things about American discovery is that parties often do reveal damaging information, and the importance of that discovered material in litigation cannot be overstated."[4]

The original drafters of the FRCP intended discovery to replace the tricks and surprises that often occurred during trials with a rational, systematic pretrial exchange of information. The Supreme Court concurred. "[T]he deposition-discovery rules are to be accorded a broad and liberal treatment. No longer can the time-honored cry of 'fishing expedition' serve to preclude a party from inquiring into the facts underlying his opponent's case. Mutual knowledge of all the relevant facts gathered by both parties is essential to proper litigation." *Hickman v. Taylor*, 329 U.S. 495, 507 (1947). Fact revelation was thus removed (in theory) from trial and shifted to a pretrial stage that was to be primarily self-executing, as a mutual responsibility of opposing counsel, involving little of the judge's time. (*See, e.g.*, Rule 29, which allows counsel to alter by stipulation the limitations on discovery set by the remainder of the Rules.) Thus, trial was to become "less a game of blind man's bluff and more a fair contest with the basic issues and facts disclosed to the fullest extent practicable." *United States v. Procter & Gamble*, 356 U.S. 677, 683 (1958).

In the culture of law practice, however, discovery has evolved into what is often a highly contentious phase, producing a substantial amount of litigation ancillary to the merits. Especially in high-stakes cases between well-financed opponents, the gestalt of discovery can become more like a free-fire zone.[5]

Efforts by Clinton's lawyers to secure copies of documents provide a relatively mild example of satellite litigation regarding discovery:

1. Defendant's Request for Production of Documents
2. Plaintiff's Document Production Responses
3. Letter sent by Defendant's Counsel to Plaintiff's Counsel noting missing Documents
4. Motion by Defendant to Compel Plaintiff's Production of Documents
5. Statement by Plaintiff in Opposition to President Clinton's Motion to Compel Production of Documents
6. Motion by Defendant to Hold in Abeyance the Motion to Compel
7. Renewed Motion by Defendant to Compel a Response from Plaintiff to Request for Production of Documents

---

3. Preliminary Draft of Proposed Amendments to the Federal Rules of Civil Procedure 2-3 (August 1998), reprinted in 181 F.R.D. 18, 25-26 (1998).

4. Richard L. Marcus, Discovery Containment Redux, 39 B.C. L. Rev. 747, 750 (1998).

5. High-stakes cases, which tend to be discovery-heavy, account for about one-third of the caseload of federal courts. John S. Beckerman, Confronting Civil Discovery's Fatal Flaws, 84 Minn. L. Rev. 505, 506 (2000). In the majority of cases, discovery works well. *Id.* at 507. Nonetheless, throughout the system, "discovery disputes and 'hardball' litigation tactics are far more common today than they used to be." *Id.* at 509.

8. Response by Plaintiff to Defendant Clinton's Motion to Compel a Response from Plaintiff to Request for Production of Documents
9. Reply by Defendant Clinton to Plaintiff's Response to Motion to Compel a Response from Plaintiff to Request for Production of Documents

Two weeks after the ninth set of papers, Judge Wright ruled on the issues presented.

As one response to the problem of extensive litigation over seemingly basic questions, the Judicial Conference adopted a series of amendments to the discovery rules, including the mandatory initial disclosure requirement, a ban on any other discovery prior to a meeting between counsel, additional mandatory disclosures prior to trial, a maximum number of interrogatories, and a time limit on depositions. Many of these changes were promulgated first as an option for district courts in 1993, and then as a nationwide command in 2000. At the time of the *Jones v. Clinton* litigation, the Eastern District of Arkansas had opted out of the mandatory initial disclosure rule.

Another of the changes to Rule 26 adopted in 2000 altered the scope of discovery. Prior to 2000, Rule 26(b)(1) permitted discovery "regarding any matter, not privileged, which is relevant to the subject matter involved in the pending action." The 2000 amendment narrowed the scope of Rule 26 by creating two subcategories of permissible discovery: matters discoverable without judicial oversight and a broader scope subject to judicial approval. Thus, the current rule permits attorney-managed (without a judge's order) discovery of matters that are "relevant to the claim or defense of any party." It allows discovery under the old standard of "relevant to the subject matter involved in the action" only upon motion, when it is ordered by the judge "for good cause shown." The Advisory Committee notes regarding the changes state:

> The Committee intends that the parties and the court focus on the actual claims and defenses involved in the action. The dividing line between information relevant to the claims and defenses and that relevant only to the subject matter of the action cannot be defined with precision. A variety of types of information not directly pertinent to the incident in suit could be relevant to the claims or defenses raised in a given action. For example, other incidents of the same type . . . could be properly discoverable under the revised standard. . . . [I]nformation that could be used to impeach a likely witness, although not otherwise relevant to the claims or defenses, might be properly discoverable. In each instance, the determination . . . depends on the circumstances of the pending action. . . . In general, it is hoped that reasonable lawyers can cooperate to manage discovery without the need for judicial intervention. When judicial intervention is invoked, the actual scope of discovery should be determined according to the reasonable needs of the action.

Jones v. Clinton was litigated under the previous, broader standard. As you read this and the following chapter, consider whether you think that the current version of Rule 26 would have made a difference in any of the discovery litigation had it been in effect. Also consider how the new rule would affect the drafting of the pleadings.

The purpose of this chapter is to illustrate the mechanics of discovery and to lay the groundwork for the analysis of relevance and privacy issues in the next chapter. The section on devices contains examples of each of the most significant forms of discovery, as used in *Jones v. Clinton:* interrogatories, requests for production of documents, requests for admissions, and depositions. The section on defenses contains excerpts from discovery materials in which issues of privilege, work product, and undue burden were contested.

As you read these documents, refer to Rules 26 to 37. Then, for each document excerpted in this chapter, consider the following:

- Does it meet the standard for relevance to claims or defenses set by the current Rule 26(b)(1)?
- Does it comply with the standards set by the rule governing that form of discovery?
- How does the request advance the goals of the party seeking the information?
- Are there grounds for objecting to the request?

Exercise 7—Formulating a Discovery Plan

Assume that you are an associate assigned to work with Robert Bennett. Draft a discovery plan for President Clinton. What are your most important objectives in this lawsuit? What constraints must you consider? Which documents will you consult in developing such a plan? Almost always, you would begin with the complaint. Return to your analysis from Chapter 1 of the elements of each of plaintiff's claims, and revise it in light of Judge Wright's ruling on the Rule 12(c) motion and the Amended Complaint. Reread the Answer. Which discovery devices will be the best methods to achieve those goals? In what sequence do you expect to use these devices? How will you decide which persons to depose and in what order to do the depositions? Note the potential importance of the information that private fact-gathering efforts may have produced. (See "Case Planning" section of Chapter 1.) Although you can assume that any discovery plan will shift as the case goes forward, you undertake discovery without one at your peril.

DEVICES

Interrogatories

The submission of *interrogatories*—written questions that elicit written answers—is the most basic and usually the least expensive form of discovery. One of its routine functions, that of requiring the other party to furnish names and addresses of prospective witnesses, is now included in the initial mandatory disclosure. R. 26(a)(1)(A). It is still the mechanism by which counsel establish the outlines of the opponent's theory of the facts, by asking for disclosure of how that party will present the story of what happened that led to the dispute. In turn, the party receiving the interrogatories can often discern her opponent's theory by reading closely which questions are being asked.

The first example is taken from the interrogatories that Clinton posed to Jones. In almost all instances, the answers to interrogatories are written by lawyers, not by the party to whom they are directed. (Interrogatories can only be directed to parties, not to nonparty witnesses.)

PLAINTIFF'S RESPONSES AND OBJECTIONS TO THE FIRST
SET OF INTERROGATORIES OF DEFENDANT
WILLIAM JEFFERSON CLINTON

. . . 6) Interrogatory: List each and every action taken with respect to your
employment at AIDC that you contend was, or may have been, taken as a result
of the alleged events on May 8, 1991, including but not limited to, all pay raises
you claim you were entitled to but did not receive.

Objection: Plaintiff objects to this Interrogatory to the extent that it suggests that the adverse employment decisions made with respect to her, and at issue in this case, were a response solely to the incident which occurred on May 8,
1991, rather than in response to that incident and to the other incidents described
in the Complaint and to plaintiff's refusal, throughout the relevant time period, to
see, or to engage in sex with, defendant Mr. Clinton.

Response: Without waiving the foregoing objection, plaintiff states that in
response to the incidents described in the Complaint I was asked by a member of
his security detail for my telephone number, and asked if I would meet with Mr.
Clinton while his wife was out of town. This was clearly a request that I engage in
sex with Mr. Clinton. Private details of my life were investigated, by persons whose
names I do not know, and the information thus gathered was displayed to me in a
manner that was intended to frighten me, and that did frighten me: it suggested
that I was being watched and/or followed, by law enforcement personnel, at then-
Governor Clinton's request, because Mr. Clinton wanted to engage in sex with me
and as a way of inducing me to engage in sex with him, or as a way of punishing
me because I refused to do so. These facts also made clear to me that my refusal
to engage in sex with Mr. Clinton on May 8, 1991, had not been forgotten by him
or his security detail, but was instead remembered and itself the source of continued interest and attention directed by them towards me. This led me to believe, as
I still do, that my refusal to engage in sex with Mr. Clinton was communicated to
others, at my place of employment; that it was understood by the Governor and
his security detail that this refusal was a bad thing; that it justified the stalking I experienced; and that it also justified other kind of work-related punishment such as
denial of pay increases; denials of promotions; denials of the opportunity to apply
for other and better positions; and denial of the opportunity to have actual substantive job responsibilities.

I was physically touched by Mr. Clinton again after May 8, 1991, and at
the time of this second touching Mr. Clinton falsely claimed to certain persons that
he and I were "a couple." All of these incidents occurred while I was either involved with, or engaged or married to, Stephen Jones.

Throughout the period I worked at the AIDC I was never given a raise, although I was eligible for cost of living and merit raises which I cannot now identify
with any greater detail. At various times, in order to advance my career, to earn
more money, or to better myself, I sought to apply for other jobs, but I was effectively discouraged and prevented from doing so for reasons unrelated to my abili-
ties. Apart from these substantive displays of hostility, I was ostracized by the people with whom I worked in purely emotional ways—for example, during my second
year at AIDC I was singled out on Secretaries Day as the only person at my level
not given flowers. Even the accountant got flowers.

> In July, 1992, I went on maternity leave for 6 weeks, to which I was enti-
> tled according to the state employee handbook. Even though the handbook stated
> that anyone who took maternity leave could come back to the same position and
> job title that she had before, when I came back after 6 weeks, I no longer had my
> job. Pam Hood had been given my job. I was put at a desk outside Clydine Pen-
> nington's office, and was given nothing to do. I was just a gopher, running docu-
> ments back and forth to the Capitol [sic] twice daily.
>
> I do not know who was directly responsible for my demotion after my ma-
> ternity leave. I do not know who was directly responsible for my never getting a
> raise or a promotion, or for my being effectively prevented from applying for other
> positions, or for my being ostracized at my workplace. I believe that Mr. Clinton
> was ultimately responsible for these adverse employment experiences, and that he
> communicated the disfavor he felt towards me to someone at the AIDC who was
> in a position to impose these punishments.
>
> I believe that Mr. Clinton and members of his security detail, whom I can-
> not now identify with any greater specificity, were responsible for my being investi-
> gated, watched, or followed. Mr. Clinton and members of his security detail were
> responsible for using private information to frighten me and to attempt to induce
> me to meet with, and to engage in sex with, Mr. Clinton. Mr. Clinton was responsi-
> ble for touching me and for claiming to others that he and I were "a couple."
>
> Plaintiff has prepared this Response before reviewing her employment rec-
> ords with the AIDC. Plaintiff expressly reserves the right to supplement this Re-
> sponse after reviewing those records and other discovery relevant hereto. . . .

NOTES AND COMMENTS

1. Redrafting. Assume that plaintiff's response (as written in the first person) was her answer, in her words, to the interrogatory. As her lawyer, it is now your job to edit it, or not. How would you revise it? What would be the advantages and disadvantages of editing this response?

2. Follow-up. Assume that you represent President Clinton. Based on the interrogatory response that you just read, what would you ask next? Would you file additional interrogatories or use another discovery device?

The second example of interrogatories focuses on the questions, rather than the answers. Following is an excerpt from Jones's Second Set of Interrogatories to Clinton. They serve two functions: (1) identification of persons who, on plaintiff's theory, could help her case but about whom only the defendant knew (Nos. 10, 11, 16, 17, and most of 19) and (2) learning defendant's version of the background facts (No. 19(a)). In the next chapter, we will analyze the relevance and privacy issues raised by these interrogatories.

SECOND SET OF INTERROGATORIES FROM PLAINTIFF
TO DEFENDANT CLINTON

TO: William Jefferson Clinton

Pursuant to Rules 26 and 33 of the Federal Rules of Civil Procedure, Plaintiff Paula Jones hereby propounds the following written interrogatories to you. You are required to serve a written response, in full compliance with the applicable rules of procedure, on or before Monday, November 3, 1997.

Please answer each of the following enumerated interrogatories separately and fully, in writing, and under oath. A request for identification of any particular document or thing includes a request for identification of the original of that document or thing, as well as identification of each and every photocopy or duplicate of that document or thing, and each and every draft of the document or thing.

> This kind of highly specific definition is commonly used in discovery, as a method of eliminating possible bases for nondisclosure.

In answering the following interrogatories, you are to provide not only the information within your direct personal knowledge, but also the information within the knowledge of your attorney(s), any investigator employed by you or by your attorney(s), or any consultant or expert witness employed by you or by your attorney(s).

The following interrogatories are continuing. After serving your initial response to these interrogatories, please supplement your response whenever any information responsive to them is recalled or received by you or your attorney(s).

> Note that Rule 26(e)(2) imposes the same duty of supplementation regardless of whether counsel states it in the document.

If, in response to a particular interrogatory, an objection is interposed, and the objection applies to some but not all of the information requested, please provide in your answer all responsive information which the objection does not apply. Any and all objections should be interposed by the deadline for your initial response, or will be considered waived.

> The specificity requirement in this paragraph derives from Rule 33(b)(2). Case law has held that objections are waived unless stated at the time of responding.

. . . INTERROGATORY NO. 10: Please state the name, address, and telephone number of each and every individual (other than Hillary Rodham Clinton) with whom you had sexual relations when you held any of the following positions:

a. Attorney General of the State of Arkansas;
b. Governor of the State of Arkansas;
c. President of the United States.

INTERROGATORY NO. 11: Please state the name, address, and telephone number of each and every individual (other than Hillary Rodham Clinton) with whom you proposed having sexual relations, or with whom you sought to have sexual relations, when you held any of the following positions:

a. Attorney General of the State of Arkansas;
b. Governor of the State of Arkansas;
c. President of the United States. . . .

> INTERROGATORY NO. 16: Please state the name, address, and telephone number of each and every female (other than Hillary Rodham Clinton) whom you kissed during a private meeting between you and the female at any time when you held any of the following positions:
>
>   a. Attorney General of the State of Arkansas;
>   b. Governor of the State of Arkansas;
>   c. President of the United States.
>
> INTERROGATORY NO. 17: Please state the name, address, and telephone number of each and every person who was asked by you to arrange a private meeting between you and any female (other than Hillary Rodham Clinton), attended by no one else, at any location other than your office, at any time when you held any of the following positions:
>
>   a. Attorney General of the State of Arkansas;
>   b. Governor of the State of Arkansas;
>   c. President of the United States. . . .
>
> INTERROGATORY NO. 19: On May 8, 1991, did you enter a numbered suite or room not a conference room, but a suite or room furnished for overnight lodging at the Excelsior Hotel in Little Rock, Arkansas? If so, please state:
>
>   a. Why you entered the suite or room;
>   b. The name of each and every other person who was present in the suite or room at any time when you were there;
>   c. The name of each and every person who arranged to make the room available to you; and
>   d. Whether the Excelsior Hotel was paid for the suite or room and, if so, the name of the person who paid for it. . . .

President Clinton objected to the first four interrogatories above on relevance and privacy grounds, and refused to answer pending a ruling by Judge Wright. Following is the entirety of his response to Interrogatory 19:

> 19. President Clinton has no recollection of whether a suite or room was available for his use in connection with the May 8, 1991 Governor's Quality Conference.

NOTES AND COMMENTS

1. Duty to respond. Is President Clinton's response to Interrogatory 19 sufficiently complete? Can he simply rely on present recollection or does he have a duty of reasonable inquiry before answering? Rule 33 does not speak directly to this point, but the mandate in 33(b)(1) that interrogatories shall be answered "fully" has been interpreted to require such a duty. *Brunswick Corp. v. Suzuki Motor Co., Ltd.*, 96 F.R.D. 684, 686 (E.D. Wis. 1983) (Japanese corporation required to obtain information from its U.S. subsidiaries, even if they are separate corporations). If a party is unable to obtain answers through reasonable inquiry, he is required to describe the efforts used in the inquiry. 4A, James W. Moore, Moore's Federal Practice ¶¶33.25, 33.26 (2d ed. 1996).

Exercise 8—Drafting Interrogatories

Assume for purposes of this exercise that the judge has ruled that there will be no discovery into the past sexual activities of either party. Further assume that in his mandatory disclosure under Rule 26(a)(1)(A), President Clinton stated that there were no witnesses to the alleged events other than the parties. The current Rules limit the number of interrogatories to 25. Rule 33(a). Draft a set of interrogatories from Jones to Clinton.

2. Other options.   Assume that, after these answers are submitted, President Clinton's own lawyers go through his official files in the Arkansas state records office, which are massive. They locate files organized chronologically (including those covering May 1991), files of his public speeches, files of expenses paid with state funds, correspondence files, and files with the personnel records of state troopers assigned to protect him. Under Rule 33, what may his lawyers do?

Requests for Production of Documents and Things

In a case involving many documents, production requests can impose enormous burdens on parties and, as a result, are frequent triggers for objections. Document management during discovery has occupied many an associate's billable hours. Another example of the premise of attorney self-management in the discovery system is that Rule 34(a) permits the discovery of "any designated documents," and it is the attorneys who designate. Note that Rule 34 defines *documents* as "including writings, drawings, graphs, charts, photographs, phono-records, and other data compilations from which information can be obtained, translated, if necessary, by the respondent through detection devices into reasonably usable form." As you can imagine, the number of items subject to Rule 34 requests can be enormous.

In *Jones v. Clinton,* the facts that gave rise to the claim did not involve documents. Thus, the document requests focused only on possible ancillary documents. Are they "reasonably calculated to lead to the discovery of admissible evidence" under Rule 26(b)(1)? To which aspects of her case would plaintiff argue that they are relevant?

FIRST SET OF REQUESTS FROM PLAINTIFF TO DEFENDANT CLINTON FOR PRODUCTION OF DOCUMENTS AND THINGS

TO: William Jefferson Clinton

Pursuant to Rules 26 and 34 of the Federal Rules of Civil Procedure, Plaintiff Paula Jones hereby requests that you produce, for inspection and copying, all of the documents and tangible things described in the enumerated requests below. You are required to serve a written response, in full compliance with the applicable rules of procedure, on or before Monday, November 3, 1997.

Why such detail? See Rule 34(b).

Paula Jones requests that the production begin at 10:00 a.m. on Tuesday, November 4, 1997, and that the production take place at the offices of your attorney, Robert S. Bennett, Skadden, Arps, Slate, Meagher & Flom LLP, 1440 New York Avenue, N.W., Washington, D.C. 20005-2111.

This and the following two paragraphs expand the definition of *document* beyond that found in the rule. Courts have upheld such expansions, and they have gradually worked their way into the boilerplate of discovery documents.

. . . "Document" means any tangible thing on which appears, or in which is stored or contained, any words, numbers, symbols, or images. . . .

A request for any particular document or thing is a request for the original, for each and every photocopy or duplicate of that document or thing, and for each and every draft of the document or thing. . . .

You are to produce not only the documents and things in your immediate possession, but also those over which you have custody or control, including but not limited to documents and things in the possession, custody, or control of your attorney(s), any investigator employed by you or by your attorney(s), or any consultant or expert witness employed by you or by your attorney(s).

. . . REQUEST FOR PRODUCTION NO. 5: Please produce each and every document, if any, containing notes of any conversation during which was mentioned any one or more of the following individuals:

All but the last of the requests included here concern documents that refer in some way to the plaintiff. On what basis might you object to producing them if you were President Clinton's attorney?

a. Paula Jones; . . .

REQUEST FOR PRODUCTION NO. 9: Please produce each and every document containing a reference to Paula Jones. . . .

REQUEST FOR PRODUCTION NO. 11: Please produce each and every document containing a statement by any person who has had, or who claims to have had, sexual relations with Paula Jones.

REQUEST FOR PRODUCTION NO. 12: Please produce each and every document mentioning the name of any person who has had, or who claims to have had, sexual relations with Paula Jones.

REQUEST FOR PRODUCTION NO. 19: Please produce the entire contents of each and every file having as its title or identification (or as a part of its title or identification) the name Paula Jones.

REQUEST FOR PRODUCTION NO. 20: Please produce each and every written statement by anyone about Paula Jones.

REQUEST FOR PRODUCTION NO. 21: Please produce each and every document containing, or purporting to contain, a statement by Paula Jones about any of the facts alleged by her in this case. . . .

Will insurance documents lead to the discovery of admissible evidence? Older conflicting case law on this question was resolved in favor of disclosure, and Rule 26(a)(1)(D) now includes such documents as part of initial mandatory disclosure.

REQUEST FOR PRODUCTION NO. 60: Please produce each and every insurance agreement under which any person carrying on an insurance business may be liable to satisfy part or all of a judgment which may be entered in this civil action or to indemnify or reimburse for payments made to satisfy a judgment which may be entered in this civil action.

NOTES AND COMMENTS

1. Initial disclosures.   In the 2000 amendments to the Rules, which were not in effect for this case, a new requirement of initial disclosure pertaining to documents was added. R. 26(a)(2). Note that it differs from Rule 34 in two important ways other than timing: First, it requires that certain documents can be identified or listed, in lieu of producing copies. Second, its scope is limited to documents that a party "may use to support its claims or defenses, unless solely for impeachment." By comparison, the scope of documents discoverable under Rule 34 is coextensive with the scope of Rule 26(b)(1) and would cover documents that are potentially harmful to a party's case as well as those that she intends to use.

2. Striking the right balance.   The samples from *Jones v. Clinton* hint at the breadth possible for document requests. Document discovery was not always so wide-ranging. As originally adopted in 1938, Rule 34 required a showing of good cause before any document had to be produced. Since then, "there has been a gradual but sweeping transformation in American jurisprudence as to the right of a party claiming injury to obtain documents from alleged wrongdoers."[6] Of course, defendants have equal rights to obtain documents.

The 2000 amendments capped the number of interrogatories and the number and length of depositions, but did not impose caps on document requests (although local rules may address this issue under Rule 26(b)(2)). In practice, limitations on the number of document requests tend to be imposed on a case-by-case basis, subject only to the general bounds set by Rule 26(b)(1). Should there be an amendment to the Rules that would provide a more generic form of limitation? Can you draft one? One difficulty in proposing a numerical cap is that document requests can be drafted as highly specific descriptions or broad catch-all demands; however, the same is true for interrogatories.

3. The difference a word makes.   One story that illustrates the importance of the fine points of drafting arose when attorneys for Jones served a subpoena duces tecum on Linda Tripp. (A subpoena duces tecum requires that an individual appear and that she bring certain items with her.) Tripp wanted to retain custody and control of the audiotapes she had made of conversations with Monica Lewinsky. The subpoena required her to produce all "writings" at the time of her deposition. Because the subpoena did not specify data sources other than writings (e.g., tapes), her lawyer was able to avoid producing copies of the tapes. (Eventually, these tapes were obtained by the Office of Independent Counsel.)

4. Objections.   What procedure should a party follow to object to document requests? *See* Rule 34(b). President Clinton objected to Requests 5, 9, 11, 12, 19, 20, and 21 on the ground that all such documents were protected by the work product doctrine of Rule 26(b)(3). What steps would opposing counsel take to force production? The issue did not proceed any further in the *Jones* case because President Clinton, after objecting, stated for each of the above requests that he had "no documents responsive to this Request."

---

6. Geoffrey C. Hazard, Jr., From Whom No Secrets Are Hid, 76 Tex. L. Rev. 1665, 1684 (1998).

Requests for Admissions

Requests for admissions under Rule 36 serve a very different function from other discovery devices in that they operate primarily to lock in the other party's version of the case or to obtain concessions, rather than to obtain information. Responses to requests for admissions are binding, unlike responses to interrogatories. Compare Rule 36(b) to Rule 33(c). In this respect, a request for admissions functions like the complaint because it elicits binding responses to specific factual allegations.

Another similarity between requests for admissions and pleadings is that the language of Rule 36(a), in the second paragraph, closely tracks that of Rule 8(b) on "general rules of pleading": Responses "shall fairly meet the substance" of the admission requested, and "when good faith requires that a party qualify an answer or deny a part of the matter of which an admission is requested, the party shall specify so much of it as is true and qualify or deny the remainder." Moreover, responses to a Rule 36 request cannot simply assert "lack of knowledge or information sufficient to form a belief as to the truth of an averment," which is permitted under Rule 8(b). A party responding to a Rule 36 request "cannot give lack of information or belief as a reason for failure to admit or deny unless the party states that the party has made a reasonable inquiry, and that the information known or readily obtainable by the party is insufficient to enable the party to admit or deny." Rule 36(a).

The biggest difference between Rule 36 requests and pleadings is that Rule 36 gives the *defendant* an opportunity to assert factual contentions that the plaintiff must admit or deny. Why does this not occur earlier in the case?

The timing (usually late in discovery) of this device illustrates the philosophy of the FRCP in action. Rather than frontload this function into the pleadings phase, forcing greater precision and finality onto the allegations of the complaint and the defenses of the answer, the Rules allow the parties to frame the key assertions in their theory of the case after they have had the opportunity to engage in discovery.

FIRST SET OF REQUESTS FROM PLAINTIFF TO DEFENDANT CLINTON FOR ADMISSIONS

TO: William Jefferson Clinton

Pursuant to Rules 26 and 36 of the Federal Rules of Civil Procedure, Plaintiff Paula Jones hereby requests that, on or before Monday, November 10, 1997, you serve a written response separately answering each of the requests enumerated below. Any matter admitted by you in response to these requests is conclusively established unless the Court on motion permits withdrawal or amendment of the admission. Any admission made by you in response to these requests is for the purpose of the above-referenced civil action only and is not an admission for any other purpose, nor may it be used against you in any other proceeding. . . .

REQUEST FOR ADMISSION NO. 1: Please admit or deny the following: On May 8, 1991, Defendant Clinton was the Governor of the State of Arkansas.

REQUEST FOR ADMISSION NO. 2: Please admit or deny the following: On May 8, 1991, the Governor of the State of Arkansas was the highest ranking officer of the executive branch of the government of the State of Arkansas.

REQUEST FOR ADMISSION NO. 3: Please admit or deny the following: On May 8, 1991, the Arkansas Industrial Development Commission was an agency of the government of the State of Arkansas.

The first six requested admissions are straightforward and would eliminate the need to produce proof on them at trial.

REQUEST FOR ADMISSION NO. 4: Please admit or deny the following: On May 8, 1991, the Arkansas Industrial Development Commission was part of the executive branch of the government of the State of Arkansas.

REQUEST FOR ADMISSION NO. 5: Please admit or deny the following: On May 8, 1991, David Harrington was the Director of the Arkansas Industrial Development Commission.

REQUEST FOR ADMISSION NO. 6: Please admit or deny the following: Defendant Clinton appointed David Harrington to the position of Director of the Arkansas Industrial Development Commission.

REQUEST FOR ADMISSION NO. 7: Please admit or deny the following: On May 8, 1991, David Harrington was a friend of Defendant Clinton.

REQUEST FOR ADMISSION NO. 8: Please admit or deny the following: On May 8, 1991, Defendant Clinton attended a conference at the Excelsior Hotel in Little Rock, Arkansas. . . .

How would you respond to Requests 7, 8, and 11?

REQUEST FOR ADMISSION NO. 11: Please admit or deny the following: The conference which took place on May 8, 1991, at the Excelsior Hotel in Little Rock, Arkansas, was sponsored by the Arkansas Industrial Development Commission. . . .

REQUEST FOR ADMISSION NO. 35: Please admit or deny the following: On May 8, 1991, at the Excelsior Hotel, Defendant Clinton directed Defendant Ferguson to tell Paula Jones (whose name at that time was Paula Rosalee Corbin) that Defendant Clinton would like to meet her (or words to that effect).

REQUEST FOR ADMISSION NO. 36: Please admit or deny the following: On May 8, 1991, at the Excelsior Hotel, Defendant Clinton directed Defendant Ferguson to tell Paula Jones (whose name at that time was Paula Rosalee Corbin) that Defendant Clinton would like to meet her in a certain numbered room (or words to that effect).

Plaintiff did not expect President Clinton to admit the remaining requests, so what was their function? Note the subtle differences in language among the requests.

REQUEST FOR ADMISSION NO. 37: Please admit or deny the following: On May 8, 1991, at the Excelsior Hotel, Defendant Clinton asked Defendant Ferguson to tell Paula Jones (whose name at that time was Paula Rosalee Corbin) that Defendant Clinton would like to meet her (or words to that effect).

REQUEST FOR ADMISSION NO. 38: Please admit or deny the following: On May 8, 1991, at the Excelsior Hotel, Defendant Clinton asked Defendant Ferguson to tell Paula Jones (whose name at that time was Paula Rosalee Corbin) that Defendant Clinton would like to meet her in a certain numbered room (or words to that effect). . . .

REQUEST FOR ADMISSION NO. 52: Please admit or deny the following: While he was Governor of the State of Arkansas, Defendant Clinton had sexual relations with at least one woman (other than Hillary Rodham Clinton), and at least one member of the Arkansas State Police facilitated at least one meeting between Defendant Clinton and the woman.

The requests beginning with No. 52 are the ones President Clinton challenged, as you will see in the next chapter. Why didn't he simply deny them?

REQUEST FOR ADMISSION NO. 53: Please admit or deny the following: While he was Governor of the State of Arkansas, Defendant Clinton had sexual relations with at least one woman (other than Hillary Rodham Clinton), and at least one member of the Arkansas State Police concealed at least one meeting between Defendant Clinton and the woman.

REQUEST FOR ADMISSION NO. 54: Please admit or deny the following: While he was Governor of the State of Arkansas, Defendant Clinton had sexual relations with at least one woman (other than Hillary Rodham Clinton), and at least one member of the Arkansas State Police assisted Defendant Clinton in concealing at least one meeting between Defendant Clinton and the woman.

REQUEST FOR ADMISSION NO. 55: Please admit or deny the following: While he was Governor of the State of Arkansas, Defendant Clinton had sexual relations with at least one woman (other than Hillary Rodham Clinton) who was, at the time of the sexual relations, an employee of the State of Arkansas (or an agency thereof).

REQUEST FOR ADMISSION NO. 56: Please admit or deny the following: While he was Governor of the State of Arkansas, Defendant Clinton had sexual relations with at least one woman (other than Hillary Rodham Clinton) who later became an employee of the State of Arkansas (or an agency thereof).

REQUEST FOR ADMISSION NO. 57: Please admit or deny the following: While he was Governor of the State of Arkansas, Defendant Clinton had sexual relations with women (other than Hillary Rodham Clinton), and members of the Arkansas State Police arranged meetings between Defendant Clinton and the women.

REQUEST FOR ADMISSION NO. 58: Please admit or deny the following: While he was Governor of the State of Arkansas, Defendant Clinton had sexual relations with women (other than Hillary Rodham Clinton), and members of the Arkansas State Police facilitated meetings between Defendant Clinton and the women.

REQUEST FOR ADMISSION NO. 59: Please admit or deny the following: While he was Governor of the State of Arkansas, Defendant Clinton had sexual relations with women (other than Hillary Rodham Clinton), and members of the Arkansas State Police concealed meetings between Defendant Clinton and the women.

REQUEST FOR ADMISSION NO. 60: Please admit or deny the following: While he was Governor of the State of Arkansas, Defendant Clinton had sexual relations with women (other than Hillary Rodham Clinton), and members of the Arkansas State Police assisted Defendant Clinton in concealing meetings between Defendant Clinton and the women.

REQUEST FOR ADMISSION NO. 61: Please admit or deny the following: While he was Governor of the State of Arkansas, Defendant Clinton had sexual relations with women (other than Hillary Rodham Clinton) who were, at the time of the sexual relations, employees of the State of Arkansas (or an agency thereof).

REQUEST FOR ADMISSION NO. 62: Please admit or deny the following: While he was Governor of the State of Arkansas, Defendant Clinton had sexual relations with women (other than Hillary Rodham Clinton) who later became employees of the State of Arkansas (or an agency thereof).

REQUEST FOR ADMISSION NO. 63: Please admit or deny the following: While he was Governor of the State of Arkansas, Defendant Clinton had sexual relations with a woman whom he, as Governor, appointed to a position as a judge in the State of Arkansas. . . .

NOTES AND COMMENTS

1. Just say no?   What is to stop a party faced with requests for potentially damaging admissions from simply denying everything? Read Rule 37(c)(2). Do other portions of Rule 37 apply also?

2. Fee shifting.   Given the possible sanctions, can you see why Jones's lawyers included requests for admissions as to assertions that they knew Clinton would deny? Can a party use this device to obtain attorneys' fees that would not otherwise be awardable?

Depositions

Within the discovery phase, it is often *depositions*—testimony taken when opposing counsel face each other and question witnesses, out of the presence of the judge—that produce the most hostile encounters. The lawyer conducting the deposition may pose objectionable questions, but, unlike at trial, the lawyer representing the witness often cannot obtain immediate relief from a judge who has heard the exchange and can rule on whether the questions are out of order. Not surprisingly, such exchanges occurred with some frequency in *Jones v. Clinton.*

As stated earlier, the philosophy of the Rules is that discovery is attorney-managed and self-executing. The assumption of the drafters was that opposing counsel, if unable to reach the judge by such means as telephone, would either negotiate the disputes or enter the objection on the record and proceed with the deposition. Rule 30(d)(1) recognizes three exceptions that allow the deposition to be halted: a lawyer "may instruct a deponent not to answer only when necessary [1] to preserve a privilege, [2] to enforce a limitation [as to relevancy, for example] directed by the court [in an order prior to the deposition], or [3] to present a motion" asserting bad faith questioning. The bad faith motion requires "a showing that the examination is being conducted in bad faith or in such manner as unreasonably to annoy, embarrass, or oppress the deponent or party." R. 30(d)(4).

In response to a number of depositions that were halted by counsel and followed by motions for protective orders and/or motions to compel answers, Judge Wright issued the following order, imposing an additional restriction on the invocation of a bad faith objection:

Order of January 9, 1998

The Court hereby instructs all parties to strictly follow Fed. R. Civ. P. 30(d)(1) in the depositions that remain. This means that any objection to evidence during a deposition "shall be stated concisely and in a non-argumentative and non-suggestive manner," and without any coaching of the witness as to what previous discovery may or may not have disclosed. The parties may attempt to contact the Court to resolve a dispute if they so desire, and this Court will be perfectly willing to rule on any such objections. If, however, the Court is for some reason not available, the party objecting to the questioning may do no more than object in a manner provided by Fed. R. Civ. P. 30 and allow the questioning to proceed. If the party objecting feels the questioning is in bad faith, their recourse is to later move for sanctions. The Court will hold in abeyance any request for an extension of the discovery deadline that has or will be made depending on how the discovery process proceeds from here on out.

Shortly after she issued this order, Judge Wright agreed to a request by President Clinton's lawyers that she personally attend his deposition, to be conducted in Washington, on January 17, 1998. Do you understand why they felt it was important that she be present?

Even a contentious deposition, however, can produce valuable information. Compare the following excerpt of the deposition of Paula Jones with the answer to the interrogatory question that you read earlier in this chapter. Both concern the topic of whether there was an adverse impact on her job status as a result of the alleged incident. Recall that adverse job impact was an essential element of plaintiff's sexual harassment claim.

DEPOSITION OF PAULA JONES

By Mr. Bennett: . . .

Q. Now on July 1st, 1991, you received a cost-of-living increase, didn't you?

A. Probably. I don't know what date it was. But I know I received what everybody else got each year.

Q. Now also on July 1st, 1991, you were upgraded from a Grade 9 to a Grade 11, the very grade you mentioned, weren't you?

A. I don't recall.

Q. Well, do you dispute that that's what the records show?

Mr. Campbell: Objection. No foundation. No evidence in the record.

By Mr. Bennett:

Q. Do you dispute—you can answer.

A. No.

Note that an objection does not prevent questions from being reasked and then answered.

Q. So you did get a Grade 11, didn't you?

A. That's what I'm saying. I don't really know how the grades went. I don't know how the grades went. I don't know what I came in as and I don't know what I left as. So I don't know.

Q. Well, you went from, on July 1, 1991, according to the records, you went from a Grade 9 to a Grade 11. Did you ever apply for a Grade 12 or 13 or 14?

Mr. Campbell: Objection. No foundation. No evidence in the record.

By Mr. Bennett:

Q. Did you ever apply for a grade higher than 11?

A. Yes. I believe I did.

Q. When?

A. I don't know. I just—those few times when I would talk to Clydine and she would say that, I would go ahead and fill out an application maybe or something.

Q. All right. And on March 11th, 1992, you received a merit increase?

A. Um-huh.

Q. Didn't you?

A. Probably. That's what everybody else received too.

Q. And on—

A. Cost-of-living raise.

Q. And on July—no. I said merit increase.

A. Oh, I don't know what that is.

Q. You know there's a difference between a merit increase and a cost-of-living increase, you know that?

A. No.

Note that Bennett clarifies the record on the type of pay increase. Otherwise, he would not be able to use this transcript later, as, for example, support of a summary judgment motion.

Q. You don't know that you got both cost-of-living increases and merit increases when you worked at AIDC?

A. I don't know if I did or not. . . .

By Mr. Bennett:

Q. On the incident—the incident which allegedly occurred at the Excelsior Hotel on May 8th, 1991, did anybody at AIDC ever mention [it] to you at any point in time while you worked there?

A. Pam Blackard.

Q. How did Pam Blackard know about it?

A. Because she was there.

Q. She wasn't in the room, was she?

A. No. But she was at the conference and knew what had took place that day.

Q. But you told Pam Blackard, didn't you?

A. What went on in the room?

Q. Yes.

A. Yes.

Q. You didn't tell her everything that went on in the room, though, did you?

A. Yes. Eventually. Yes, I did.

Q. At the time?

A. Oh, no, not at the time.

Q. All right. Now you were here for Pam Blackard's deposition, weren't you?

A. Yes.

Q. And did you hear Pam Blackard testify that she never told anybody at AIDC, that you swore her to secrecy, or words to that effect?

A. Yes.

Q. Do you believe Pam Blackard wouldn't have told anybody?

A. Yes. I believe that.

Q. Other than Pam Blackard, did you tell anybody at AIDC?

A. No, I did not.

Q. All right. Now my question to you is, during the period of time that you worked at AIDC, did any of your supervisors or anyone else mention to you that they were aware of the incident which allegedly occurred in the room at the Excelsior Hotel?

A. No.

Q. Did anybody say to you that you weren't getting a promotion because you wouldn't give sex to Governor Clinton?

A. No.

Q. Did anyone ever say to you that if you gave sex to Governor Clinton that you would get promoted or get a raise or get a better job?

A. No. But I'm sure they would never say that if they did know about it.

Mr. Bristow: Objection. It's not responsive.

By Mr. Bennett:

Q. Do you know of anybody at AIDC who knew about this incident other—let me finish— other than Pam Blackard?

A. Not to my knowledge. Personally, nobody mentioned it to me. That doesn't mean they didn't know.

Q. You don't know of anybody, though, do you?

A. Un-uh. . . .

NOTES AND COMMENTS

1. An end run.   Unlike the three preceding discovery devices, depositions can be used to obtain information from nonparties as well as parties. That distinction would seem to signify a goal of making discovery less intrusive for nonparties. Agreeing to be deposed might be thought to be less burdensome than writing answers to interrogatories or complying with requests for production of documents.

Not surprisingly, however, attorneys have found an effective substitute for the absence of document requests as to nonparties. Read Rule 45. Note that it appears in Section VI of the Rules, titled "Trials." (See sample subpoena in Appendix 3.) Is Rule 45 more or less protective of nonparties who must produce documents than Rule 34 is of parties who must produce documents?

2. Distant witnesses. What if the witness lives at substantial distance from the court where the case is being litigated? Under Rule 45(a)(2), a deposition subpoena must issue from the district court in which the deposition will be taken. Under Rule 45(b)(2), authority to command attendance at a deposition is limited to persons who live in the district where the court is located or within 100 miles of the court's location. Thus, attorneys have to secure a subpoena from the home district of the witness if that person lives beyond district boundaries or more than 100 miles away. In the *Jones* case, that led to a subpoena issuing from the Eastern District of Virginia for Kathleen Willey, a former White House employee who at one time alleged that President Clinton had groped her during a meeting in the oval office. She objected, and plaintiff's motion to compel testimony by Willey was litigated in the Eastern District of Virginia. Her deposition was taken with Judge Robert Merhige of that court in attendance.

DEFENSES: PRIVILEGE, WORK PRODUCT, AND UNDUE BURDEN

The devices identified in the previous section—interrogatories, requests for production of documents, requests for admissions, and depositions—are the primary tools of the discovering party. Now we turn to the question of what defenses the party being discovered can assert against them. We defer the issues of relevance and privacy to the next chapter because they merit more extensive treatment. What follows is an introduction to three often-used defenses in discovery: privilege, work product, and undue burden.

Rule 26(b)(1) allows discovery of materials "not privileged," a standard that governs regardless of which device is used. The privilege most often asserted as a bar to discovery is the attorney-client privilege, which provides protection for confidential (i.e., not waived by the presence of a third party) communications between attorney and client made for the purpose of furnishing or obtaining legal advice or assistance. The Federal Rules of Evidence do not define the exact bounds of this privilege, but instead defer to federal common law interpretation of its scope (or to state law, in a diversity case). Fed. R. Evid. 501.

Under attorney-client privilege, the rationale for excluding otherwise admissible and perhaps quite relevant and material evidence is that effective representation in an adversarial system necessitates carving out a protected zone for full and frank communication between attorney and client. Implicit in this rationale is the assumption that the communication relates to how well the attorney can represent her client in her role as an attorney. The privilege allows the client to receive "the aid of persons having knowledge of the law and skilled in its practice." *United States v. Zolin,* 491 U.S. 554, 562 (1989). A number of courts have held that the privilege applies only to communications made for the purpose of securing legal advice. *See In Re Bieter Co.,* 16 F.3d 929, 936 (8th Cir. 1994); *United States v. El Paso Co.,* 682 F.2d 530, 538 (5th Cir. 1982); *United States v. Kovel,* 296 F.2d 918, 922 (2d Cir. 1961). Should the privilege apply when the attorney and client are discussing public relations aspects of the lawsuit? Especially in today's media environment, has that become simply one component of legal work?

A similar question applies to the work product doctrine. Evolving from *Hickman v. Taylor* into Rule 26(b)(3), the work product doctrine shields from discovery materials that are prepared in anticipation of litigation or for trial, which could reveal an attorney's strategy and assessments of the case. Rule 26(b)(3) specifically extends coverage to nonattorneys. It is now clear that accountants and private investigators, for example, are covered by the work product doctrine. Are the memoranda or notes of a person who does public relations or public speaking about the case, on behalf of the client, also covered? What if that person has been retained or selected by the attorney? What if she regularly consults with the attorney?

The phrase "undue burden" is often used in discovery disputes as a shorthand reference to the general limitations imposed by Rule 26(b)(2), which provides that the trial judge has the discretion to limit burdensome discovery, even if that discovery would otherwise be permissible under the criteria set by Rule 26(b)(1). (Rule 26(b)(2) also provides the authority to expand discovery, by lifting the limits imposed by the Rules on the number of interrogatories and requests for admissions, and on the number and length of depositions. Recall that these limits did not apply to *Jones v. Clinton*.) There are three bases for such limitations: (1) "the discovery is unreasonably cumulative or duplicative, or is obtainable from some other source that is more convenient, less burdensome or less expensive"; (2) the party seeking discovery has already had ample opportunity during discovery to acquire the information; and (3) the discovery sought is disproportional to the value of the information, "taking into account the needs of the case, the amount in controversy, the parties' resources, [and] the importance of the issues at stake," as well as the importance of the information. In the Advisory Committee Notes to the 2000 amendments, the committee stated that "courts have not implemented these limitations with the vigor that was contemplated." Accordingly, the final sentence of Rule 26(b)(1), which cross-references (b)(2), was added "to emphasize the need for active judicial use of subdivision (b)(2) to control excessive discovery."

The following materials raise all of these questions.

In 1997, Paula Jones authorized two public relations agents to begin and run the Paula Jones Legal Fund (PJLF). According to press reports, they guaranteed that from the funds they raised, a minimum of $100,000 would go to Jones; in return, they would be authorized to pay themselves a fee of up to $300,000. Reports also surfaced that none of the proceeds were being used to pay Jones's lawyers or litigation expenses, but that a number of more personal expenses were being paid with the fund-raising proceeds. President Clinton's lawyers sought to discover more information by deposing Cindy Hays, the director of the Fund. Would information about the PJLF meet the Rule 26(b)(1) threshold of relevance for purposes of discovery? Would the change made to that rule in 2000 affect your answer? Even if it did satisfy the criteria for relevance, should it have been shielded from disclosure as a product of the attorney-client relationship?

Hays responded to the subpoena for a deposition with a motion for a protective order. Later, both the Fund and Jones filed similar motions. Following are excerpts from the ensuing litigation:

**PRESIDENT CLINTON'S OPPOSITION TO MOTIONS
FOR PROTECTIVE ORDER REGARDING SUBPOENA
TO CINDY HAYS**

President Clinton is entitled to make inquiries into plaintiff's motives and grounds for making the charges contained in her suit, and in particular, whether she is pursuing the charges in order to profit from the lawsuit and attendant publicity, or in order to embarrass and attack the President politically. We also are entitled to inquire into the payment of plaintiff's legal costs in connection with her demand for legal fees. *See* Compl. ¶¶79 a-d. Information about the Legal Fund would shed light on all these issues.

A party's motives always are relevant to that party's credibility and the credibility of her allegations. The terms, conditions, profitability, and source of support for the Legal Fund all go to plaintiff's motives and credibility. If, for example, discovery disclosed that the Fund paid plaintiff's personal expenses or that she otherwise profited from the Legal Fund, that would be relevant to her motives for filing suit. Deposition testimony obtained to date makes plain that the plaintiff has received money from the Fund for her personal expenses. Similarly, if discovery showed a publicist, publisher, or media outlet was funding this litigation, or that political opponents of the President were funding the litigation, that would go directly to plaintiff's credibility.

Moreover, there is much information related to the Fund which would be highly relevant to plaintiff's prayer for fees, including:

- whether plaintiff already has recovered her legal expenses and is not "out-of-pocket" for them;
- whether plaintiff or her counsel is going to seek double recovery—once from the Fund and once from the defendants;
- whether the Fund includes a mechanism for returning contributions in the event plaintiff recovers fees; and
- whether donors are advised when they contribute that plaintiff also may obtain recovery of fees pursuant to statute.

Furthermore, in the course of serving as plaintiff's agent and issuing press releases, it is reasonable to assume that Ms. Hays spoke to plaintiff about the allegations in the Complaint and plaintiff's purpose in filing suit. Obviously, plaintiff's statements on those subjects are directly relevant here.

Ms. Hays's objection that the request for documents pertaining to plaintiff is burdensome and "overbroad as to time and subject matter" also is unfounded. We understand that Ms. Hays did not know plaintiff prior to undertaking to serve as director of plaintiff's Fund. Hence, any information or documents she may have regarding plaintiff inherently would be limited in time and scope. This is borne out by the date and

Rule 26(b)(5) requires that an attorney who asserts privilege or work product must specify which privilege is being asserted as to each document or inquiry, and describe in general terms the documents being withheld. This has come to be known as the "privilege log."

descriptions of the documents on Ms. Hays's "privilege" log, which are limited in number and which all relate to this matter.

The Legal Fund is a business that solicits money widely from anyone who wants to contribute. Indeed, it has its own "web site" that broadly publicizes the details of this litigation, and which invites donors to "click here to contribute." . . .

. . . In particular, information about who is paying one's legal fees is not privileged. Similarly, an organization's tax returns are not privileged and can be discovered, if relevant. And although the list reflects documents that embody communications from lawyers, they apparently refer to lawyers for plaintiff, not for Ms. Hays or the Legal Fund. Accordingly, these documents too would not be privileged.

REPLY OF CINDY HAYS TO PRESIDENT CLINTON'S OPPOSITION TO MOTIONS FOR PROTECTIVE ORDER REGARDING SUBPOENA TO CINDY HAYS

The "alter ego" doctrine usually arises in corporate law, when a court disregards the corporate structure and treats individual shareholders as responsible for corporate acts. Here, PJLF is asserting that because it is the alter ego of plaintiff (attribution in reverse direction of the normal use of the doctrine), it has the same attorney-client relationship with her attorneys that she does.

. . . Hays is not a mere "third-party witness" but rather is the agent of plaintiff operating under a specific power of attorney which is in the record. Moreover, the Fund is the alter ego of plaintiff. . . .

Attorney Gil Davis could testify that he hired Hays to assist all counsel and Jones herself in various aspects of the litigation. He specifically advised Hays that all communications between herself and Jones or counsel and those communications with third parties of an investigative nature were privileged and confidential and could not be disclosed without the express approval of Jones or her lawyers. Statements Hays made in public were approved or pre-authorized by counsel (e.g., Davis or attorney Cammarata authorized Hays on occasion to respond to Robert Bennett's ubiquitous public statements about plaintiff).

The creation of a "Paula Jones Legal Fund" web page and the use of the name, "Paula Jones Legal Fund" were at the behest of counsel. The communications related to these decisions were privileged. Web page content was intensely scrutinized by Davis and Cammarata prior to publication. These efforts related to a strategy necessitated by the media campaign being waged against Jones in the press by the defendant's attorneys. Davis asked Hays to attempt to organize and manage the efforts to track attorney leaks and comments. Davis and Cammarata attempted to deal with the media assault both ethically and from a litigation perspective and extensive efforts were required in this regard.

A spontaneous, grass roots outpouring of support for Paula Jones resulted from the use of the name "Paula Jones Legal Fund" and the creation of an Internet web page. The plaintiff accepted a blue jeans endorsement ("No Excuses Jeans") that generated desperately needed income, given her rising expenses. Jones and Hays sought donations from private individuals and public interest groups alike in order to help defray the enormous cost of defending defendant's national media blitz, and that of answering the interlocutory appeal to the U.S. Supreme Court. Uniformly, Jones and Hays sought gifts and donations on the specific basis that the identity of the giver would remain anonymous as is spelled out on the web page.

Hays acted as a coordinator of these efforts, always on the advice of Jones's counsel, and always from a litigation perspective. In essence, she acted as the eyes and ears of Davis and Cammarata in all that she did, working directly with and for Jones and the attorneys in the litigation effort. She was specifically authorized to act as Jones's agent related to fundraising, as is shown by the power of attorney already in the record.

From the outset, decisions related to these efforts were on the advice of counsel and were obviously directly related to the litigation effort. Except as to her specific public statements, all of Mrs. Hays's communications, including those related to the creation and management of the fund, were protected attorney-client, work product, investigative, "self-critical analysis," and inter- and intra-party communication.

Defendant urges that information relating to the Fund is discoverable because it is relevant to the prayer for attorneys' fees in the Complaint. He claims that he needs information on out of pocket expenses, whether donors will be repaid if there is a fee award and the mechanism for returning contributions because plaintiff has opened up this area by seeking an award of fees in a request for relief. But such discovery is unnecessary at this time since plaintiff is not yet a prevailing party under 42 U.S.C. §1988. Moreover, even if the matter were relevant, in the discretion of the Court it should be deferred until after trial. A request for attorneys' fees "raises legal issues collateral to the main course of action." *White v. New Hampshire Dept. of Social Security*, 455 U.S. 445, 451 (1982). Any such discovery is unnecessary at this time. This rationale is merely a device to permit a fishing expedition into Fund affairs.

Similarly the contention that if a media outlet or a Republican made a donation to the case that this would "go directly to plaintiff's credibility" is another false rationale which permits the intimidation of fund donors or plaintiff. There is no link between a donor actually being a Republican or a media outlet and whether plaintiff is telling the truth about the underlying incident which constitutes the core of the complaint. What happened in a hotel room that day will lead to the discovery of admissible evidence, not who donated years later to support this case against the most powerful person in the world. Plaintiff's credibility is not affected by who donated to her legal fund.

That a media outlet might have a financial interest in this litigation does not affect plaintiff's credibility either. Intense scrutiny and monetary interest on the part of the media is inescapable and proves nothing with respect to the motives of the plaintiff. . . .

PRESIDENT CLINTON'S OPPOSITION TO MOTIONS OF PAULA JONES AND
PAULA JONES LEGAL FUND FOR PROTECTIVE ORDER

. . . All [the] privilege assertions rest on the contention, unsupported in
fact or by citation to case law, that everyone affiliated with the Fund is an agent of
plaintiff or her counsel, and that they and the Fund are engaged almost exclusively
in activities that are privileged because all of their conduct relates to the litigation.
These contentions stretch reality beyond recognition. The documents we have
seen show that the Fund exists primarily for two purposes—to do public relations
and to raise money for plaintiff's legal and personal expenses. None of these activities is privileged.

First, we return to the well-established rule—uncontested by the Fund,
Ms. Hays, or plaintiff—that the act of paying another's legal bills is not privileged
conduct, and does not place the payor in an attorney-client relationship with the client or make the payor an agent of the attorney. That being the case, it is difficult
to see how persons engaged in raising funds to pay legal fees would be subject to
any privilege—even if they were a lawyer's agents for that purpose.

Second, while we do not dispute that lawyers can rely on nonlawyers for
assistance and in appropriate circumstances remain within the bounds of privilege,
the activities of press agents—even if undertaken in support of litigation—do not
come within those bounds, because they are not providing legal advice or preparing for trial. The documents show that Ms. Hays functioned only as a press spokes-
person for Ms. Jones, and billed the Fund for her services as a "consultant"—not a
paralegal, as is now contended. Ms. McMillan, for her part, goes on the air almost
daily on behalf of Ms. Jones. Therefore, even if the Fund, Ms. McMillan, or Ms.
Hays operate under counsel's direction, and even if the Fund's activities could be
said in some way to "advance interests related to the lawsuit," their activities and
communications are not subject to the attorney-client privilege. . . .

Order of November 25, 1997

. . . Plaintiff . . . states that any communications between herself and Ms.
Hays that were "made for the purposes of facilitating the rendition of professional
legal services by Ms. Jones's lawyers to Ms. Jones" are privileged. Thus, the privilege assertions of the PJLF, Ms. Hays, and the plaintiff, as noted by the President,
essentially rest on the contention that everyone affiliated with the fund is an agent
of plaintiff or her counsel, and that all of the activities of themselves and the fund
are privileged because all such activities relate to the litigation.

The prerequisites for a claim of privilege are found in proposed Federal Rule
of Evidence 503, which is also known as Supreme Court Standard 503. . . . The
rule provides:

A client has a privilege to refuse to disclose and to prevent any other person from disclosing confidential communications made for the purpose of facilitating the rendition of professional legal services to the client, (1) between himself or his representative and his lawyer or his lawyer's representative, or (2) between his lawyer and his
lawyer's representative, or (3) by him or his lawyer to a lawyer representing another

in a matter of common interest, or (4) between representatives of the client or between the client and a representative of the client, or (5) between lawyers representing the client.

The Court has considered the matter and has no doubt that the President is entitled to at least some of the communications he seeks. . . .

. . . [T]he Court does not, at least as a general matter, consider communications regarding media events and the like to be sufficiently related to the core litigation such that any privilege could be asserted. If, however, the parties are unable to resolve the matter on their own, the Court will review the communications *in camera* and make a privilege determination on a document-by-document basis. . . .

Order of December 4, 1997

. . . [T]he parties have submitted for *in camera* review those documents to which the parties cannot agree are or are not privileged. The Court has reviewed these documents under the standards governing the attorney-client privilege, the work product doctrine, and other privileges asserted by the parties. Essentially, the court considers to be privileged those documents which can fairly be said to involve trial strategy and settlement negotiations between plaintiff, her attorneys, and her representatives. Conversely, the court does not consider those documents involving fund raising, public relations strategy, and tax returns to be subject to any privilege in this litigation (although some of these documents may or may not be privileged in other contexts). Accordingly, the Court directs that the following documents . . . be disclosed to the President. [The order contains a list of documents as identified by stamped number.]

NOTES AND COMMENTS

1. Why so little mention of work product?   Since the documents at issue here apparently were the product of nonattorneys, why did Jones's lawyers so heavily stress attorney-client privilege rather than work product? Presumably, at least one reason was that attorney-client privilege is absolute. Discovery is permitted only of matters "not privileged" as Rule 26(b)(1) states at the outset; thus, privileged materials are immune from discovery (unless the privilege is waived). The work product provisions of the rule, however, allow for balancing the risk of harm against the probative value of the documents being sought. Rule 26(b)(3) permits disclosure of work product documents if one can demonstrate substantial need of the materials and the inability without undue hardship to obtain their substantial equivalent by other means.

2. On not making law.   Judge Wright's orders settle the questions raised in this case on a document-by-document basis; she does not "make law." Since she identifies only certain documents for release, one can infer that she did find other documents to be privileged, although she does not specify whether she is relying on the attorney-client privilege or the work product doctrine. (Work product is not properly referred to as a privilege, although many attorneys, including Judge Wright, use the term.) In a situation involving frequent contact between Jones's supporters in the fund and her attorneys, consider the difficulty of segregating what is from and what is not work product. Judge Wright opted for a hands-on approach of reviewing the documents as the most efficient way to decide the dispute.

Exercise 9—Analysis of Work Product Doctrine

Rule 26(b)(3) includes "consultant" in the list of a party's representatives whose materials may be covered by the work product doctrine. Should Hays be considered a consultant? Consider the policy concerns behind the work product doctrine: As with attorney-client privilege, the goal is to facilitate the most effective representation by counsel. If it were limited to attorneys (and their direct employees), any reliance on nonattorney experts such as accountants or investigators would be unprotected. Under the Rule 26(b)(3) model, the nonattorneys, even if independent of the law firm, are acting as agents for the attorney in their work on a particular case. Write an analysis of whether the Paula Jones Legal Fund would fit into that model, in light of the purposes of the work product doctrine.

3. Overbreadth as undue burden.   Hays and the PJLF assert undue burden, but then do not place much reliance on it. Their contention as to burden was that the list of documents sought by subpoena duces tecum was "overbroad as to time and subject matter." President Clinton responded that the limited time in which the Fund had existed and in which Ms. Hays knew Ms. Jones served to place reasonable bounds on the request. Apparently, Hays and PJLF did not pursue the point further. Imagine that the volume of documents was much greater or that all PJLF documents had been shipped to a storage facility in Oregon. What factors would the court consider in assessing burden? *See* Rules 45(c)(3)(A)(iv) and 26(b)(2).

4. Less burdensome alternative.   Another common variation on the Rule 26(b)(2) undue burden objection is that the information is readily obtainable by alternative means. President Clinton objected on those grounds to an interrogatory that asked him to state "the name, address, and telephone number of each and every person who worked in the Governor's Mansion" while he was Governor. Judge Wright granted his motion for a protective order and "require[d] that plaintiff obtain this information elsewhere, e.g., through employment records." Order of December 11, 1997.

CHAPTER SEVEN

Discovery: Relevance and Privacy

INTRODUCTION

When Jones's new lawyers entered the case on October 1, 1997, the first document they served on Clinton's lawyers was the set of interrogatories excerpted in the last chapter.[1] Within a few weeks, they also served the requests for production of documents and the requests for admissions. These discovery efforts became the focus of litigation over the extent to which information concerning Clinton's past sexual encounters were relevant to Jones's allegations. It was this dispute, and Judge Wright's ruling, that established the basis for a subpoena to Monica Lewinsky and for the questions concerning Lewinsky at the President's deposition that ultimately became the basis for articles of impeachment and his trial in the Senate.

On October 30, concerned by the "publicity concerning discovery in this matter," Judge Wright secured the consent of all parties to a confidentiality order to govern discovery. The order forbade the parties and their attorneys and agents from disclosing the identity of persons being deposed or the questions being asked at the depositions, and also prohibited the disclosure or release of any discovery documents. (The full text of the order is in Chapter 9 on Joinder and Intervention, which describes efforts to intervene by media organizations seeking access to discovery materials.) It soon became evident from press reports that the order was being violated, and a number of individuals found that their private lives had become topics for public discussion.

Jones's lawyers served notices of deposition on women about whom they had information suggesting a past sexual relationship with the President. Seven women contested the notices, and they became Jane Does 1 through 7 in the court's records. For each, Judge Wright allowed their motions to quash the subpoena for their depositions to be filed under the pseudonym of Jane Doe. Although most of these docu-

---

1. The Plaintiff's First Set of Interrogatories had been filed by Jones's previous lawyers. The first set consisted of six questions, all concerning the alleged events of May 8, 1991; none inquired into Clinton's relationships with other women.

ments have now been unsealed, the women remain named solely as Jane Does, with both their names and potentially identifying text redacted. Judge Wright permitted almost all of the depositions.

In addition to the privacy rights of President Clinton and the Jane Does, another set of constitutional rights formed the basis of a discovery dispute in *Jones v. Clinton*. In this third example, it arose from the efforts by President Clinton to discover information concerning the Paula Jones Legal Fund. In the last chapter we considered the defenses based on privilege and work product raised by the Fund's director. In this chapter we will explore whether the Fund had a right under the First Amendment to prevent disclosure of the names and other information concerning the individuals who donated money to it.

Each of these discovery disputes pitted the broad concept of relevance in Rule 26 against a competing claim of constitutional rights.

RELEVANCE AND PRIVACY ISSUES AS TO PARTIES

PRESIDENT CLINTON'S MOTION FOR PROTECTIVE ORDER

President Clinton, through counsel, pursuant to Rule 26(c) of the Federal Rules of Civil Procedure, hereby moves for a protective order to properly limit the scope of discovery in this case. Plaintiff has served discovery request on the President . . . seeking any rumor, innuendo, gossip, or allegation of purported sexual conduct by President Clinton with anyone, at almost any time, regardless of whether the purported conduct would constitute harassment.

Plaintiff's claims in this case, however, are that the President, while governor, acted under color of state law to subject her to *quid pro quo* and hostile environment sexual harassment while she worked at the Arkansas Industrial Development Commission (AIDC) in 1991, thereby depriving her of her civil rights and inflicting emotional distress.

Accordingly, as fully discussed in the accompanying memorandum of law, much of the discovery sought by plaintiff is irrelevant to her claims. Specifically, the following is irrelevant to plaintiff's claims:

(i)   alleged incidents that occurred before or after the defendant was Governor are irrelevant, since they could not constitute actions taken under color of state law . . .

(ii)   alleged incidents that occurred outside of AIDC are irrelevant since they could not constitute evidence of *quid pro quo* sexual harassment in that work place;

(iii)   alleged incidents of which plaintiff had no knowledge are irrelevant because they could not have contributed to plaintiff's perception that her work environment was hostile;

(iv)   alleged incidents of consensual behavior are irrelevant because they would not be harassment or discrimination; and

(v) alleged incidents that are remote in time—whether before or after the allegations in the Complaint—are irrelevant and discovery into them would be unduly burdensome.

Therefore, President Clinton respectfully requests that the Court enter a protective order limiting the scope of discovery to purported incidents, if any, of nonconsensual conduct by him occurring close in time, and in the same work place—the AIDC—as the events alleged in the Complaint. . . .

MEMORANDUM IN SUPPORT OF PRESIDENT CLINTON'S MOTION FOR A PROTECTIVE ORDER

. . . Plaintiff has directed interrogatories to the President asking him to identify every woman other than his wife with whom he has had sexual relations, every woman he has kissed in private, every woman to whom he has made sexual advances, and every woman who has ever asserted that she had sexual relations with him. All these requests pertain to the period when he was Attorney General of Arkansas, Governor of Arkansas, or the President of the United States—virtually his entire adult working life.[2]

These overbroad yet intrusive interrogatories are supplemented by fourteen similarly obnoxious, repetitive Requests for Admissions which plaintiff submitted to the President.[3] . . .

B. Plaintiff Seeks Information That Is Irrelevant to Her Claims.

There is no general rule regarding the discoverability of a defendant's sexual misconduct with persons other than the plaintiff in sexual harassment cases. Whether alleged other acts of sexual misconduct by the defendant are discoverable turns on the specific nature of the claims in the law suit. . . .

While the scope of discovery permitted under Rule 26(b) is broad, it should not be construed to allow "fishing expeditions." "Some threshold showing of relevance must be made before parties are required to open wide the doors of discovery and to produce a variety of information which does not reasonably bear upon the issues in the case." [citation omitted] The Court, moreover, is empowered to preclude unduly burdensome, harassing, or embarrassing discovery, even where it arguably is relevant. Fed. R. Civ. P. 26(c).

In this regard, even someone who is a President or Governor has a sphere of privacy which courts should respect. This is especially so here, where the Supreme Court instructed this Court to consider

> Note that the argument shifts from relevance to privacy and back to relevance. The two points are related but distinct. How do you think the argument should be phrased?

---

2. [Text of Interrogatories, 10, 11, 16, and 17 from Plaintiff's Second Set of Interrogatories; see Chapter 6, *supra.*]

3. [Text of Requests for Admission, Nos. 52-64; see Chapter 6, *supra.*]

"[t]he high respect that is owed to the office of the Chief Executive" in determining the scope of discovery in this case.

In sexual harassment cases in particular, even those that do not involve a high-ranking official, courts have declined to permit unwarranted invasions of a party's privacy. Such limitations "are consistent with both the letter and the spirit of Rule 26 and necessary to prevent unnecessary embarrassment and invasions of [a party's] private life." *Longmire v. Alabama State Univ.*, 151 F.R.D. 414, 418 (M.D. Ala. 1992).

Longmire is directly on point here. In *Longmire,* plaintiff brought *quid pro quo* and hostile environment sexual harassment claims based on Title VII, Section 1983 and the state tort of outrage against her supervisor and her employer, Alabama State University. She sought discovery into other sexual activities by her supervisor both while he was employed at another university and during a previous period of employment at Alabama State.

The court limited discovery to incidents that were alleged to have occurred in the same work place, during the time plaintiff was employed there. The court deemed the defendant's conduct at other times and in other places of employment to be irrelevant. *See also Garvey v. Dickinson College,* 763 F. Supp. 799, 801-02 (M.D. Pa. 1991) (excluding evidence of sexual harassment outside the academic department where plaintiff worked); . . . .

Incidents of which the plaintiff was unaware also are irrelevant to a hostile environment claim. *Longmire* at 417. This is yet another reason why incidents remote in time or place from plaintiff's work at AIDC would be irrelevant.

Alleged consensual conduct between the defendant and another woman also is not relevant here. Sexual harassment is, by definition, unwelcome, nonconsensual sexual conduct. Nonetheless, plaintiff is expected to argue that evidence of consensual conduct would be relevant to a claim of disparate treatment, which she seeks to include in her proposed Amended Complaint. However, courts . . . recognize that a disparate treatment/sex discrimination claim cannot be based on allegations that a co-worker received preferential treatment because she consented to sexual relations with a supervisor. *See e.g., Becerra v. Dalton,* 94 F.3d 145, 149-50 (4th Cir. 1996); *Ellert v. Univ. of Texas,* 52 F.3d 543, 546 (5th Cir. 1995); *Thomson v. Olson,* 866 F. Supp. 1267, 1271-72 (D.N.D. 1994), *aff'd,* 56 F.3d 69 (8th Cir. 1995). Accordingly, incidents of consensual conduct would not be relevant to plaintiff's claims, even if she were permitted to amend her Complaint.

Finally, it is a fundamental rule of discovery in all types of cases—not just sexual harassment cases—that events that occurred remote in time from those alleged in a complaint are generally not relevant or probative. Discovery into such events therefore would be unduly burdensome. . . .

Compare the arguments made here, about what evidence could be relevant to a proper claim of harassment, with the arguments that Clinton's lawyers made in the Rule 12(c) motion. Is there a consistent theory of the case? Is this a second bite at the apple?

PLAINTIFF'S MEMORANDUM IN OPPOSITION TO THE MOTION OF DEFENDANT CLINTON TO LIMIT DISCOVERY

When this case began Mr. Clinton approached this Court, on a completely barren record, and contended in the most vigorous possible terms—and invoking every ounce of the dignity and importance of his high public office—that his status as President of the United States prevented plaintiff from litigating her case as effectively as she would have been able to do if she were suing anyone else in the world. Because he was trying to cut plaintiff off before she got anywhere at all, his motion to stay this case was based on no actual facts, and no actual evidence regarding the issues, such as interference with his duties, that he claimed was presented. Indeed, his goal was to prevent plaintiff from gathering any facts, so he himself had none to offer. This Court, of course, rejected the bulk of his argument; the Court of Appeals rejected it in its entirety; and the Supreme Court did as well, in a 9-0 vote that left no room for uncertainty: this plaintiff, the Supreme Court has commanded, must be treated like any other unless a showing is made that national security, or similar weighty interests, require otherwise. . . .

Now Mr. Clinton comes again to this Court, on an entirely barren record. Because his goal is precisely to prevent plaintiff from gathering any facts, he has none himself to support the arguments he makes. This deficiency exists even though his arguments—about relevance, about probity, about potential prejudice—are themselves entirely about evidence and are completely fact-bound. Arguments about these issues cannot be assessed in a theoretical vacuum, any more than this Court could assess his claim of interference with presidential duties in the absence of any facts showing such interference. There will certainly come a time to address the evidentiary issues raised by this case, when motions *in limine* are made, when evidence is proffered—*after* a discovery record has been made. That time is not now.

It is thus important to remember what Mr. Clinton would apparently rather forget: that this is not a motion *in limine,* but a discovery motion. This motion does *not* turn on whether the discovery sought will in fact be admissible, but upon whether there is *any* possibility that the discovery *might,* directly or indirectly, lead to admissible evidence. For by its express terms, "Rule 26(b)(1) of the Federal Rules provides that discovery need not be confined to that which is admissible as evidence, but that which is reasonably calculated to lead to the discovery of admissible evidence." . . .

Indeed, as Rule 26(b)(1) itself says, "[i]t is not ground for objection that the information sought will be inadmissible at trial if the information sought appears reasonably calculated to lead to the discovery of admissible evidence." Fed. R. Civ. P. 26(b)(1). The courts must "interpret 'relevant' broadly to mean matter that is relevant to anything that is or may become an issue in the litigation." . . .

First, the discovery sought by Mrs. Jones is reasonably calculated to lead to the discovery of admissible evidence under Fed. R.

Once again, plaintiff's strategy is to stress the procedural posture of the case and the law of procedure, rather than the law governing the claim of sexual harassment.

Evid. 404(b). That provision mandates the admission into evidence of "other crimes, wrongs, or acts . . . [to prove] motive, opportunity, intent, preparation, plan, knowledge, identity, or absence of mistake or accident." Numerous courts in sexual-harassment cases have recognized that Rule 404(b) justifies broad discovery into a defendant's sexual conduct toward persons other than the plaintiff. As one such court recently explained:

> The principle is well established that [other] acts and statements should be admitted where necessary to show state of mind. This is the policy reflected in Fed. R. of Evid. 404(b), under which evidence of prior bad acts which would otherwise be inadmissible may be introduced to show intent, motive, knowledge, and the like.

Logan v. Colonial Williamsburg Hofer Properties, Inc., 1997 U.S. Dist. LEXIS 1335, at *3. . . .

> Judge Wright indicated that she would permit evidence on the new allegations pled in the amended complaint even though they did not stand on their own as independent claims. (See Chapter 5.) Here you see the impact on discovery.

. . . [T]he discovery Mrs. Jones seeks is not only relevant merely to Mr. Clinton's intent and state of mind; it is relevant to *the very fact of discrimination* against her. Mrs. Jones has now sought, based upon new information available, to amend her complaint to allege that her equal protection rights were also violated by the fact that women who accepted Mr. Clinton's sexual advances received employment benefits, raises, and promotions from governmental authority, while those (like Mrs. Jones) who refused Mr. Clinton's advances were denied such benefits. That makes Mr. Clinton's treatment of other women *directly* relevant to the proof of an additional equal-protection violation and of the central element of one kind of *quid pro quo* sexual harassment claim. Mr. Clinton's assertion to the contrary is premised upon the shameless miscitation of a line of cases that stand merely for the proposition that, standing alone, preferences given to a single paramour do not amount to gender discrimination. Those cases, however, make clear that where there is more—such as the denial of preferences to those who spurn sexual advances, as alleged here—a sexual harassment claim will plainly lie. . . .

. . . [E]ven putting aside all the reasons, discussed above, why consensual incidents are discoverable, plaintiff submits that consent cannot be made the dividing line for *discovery* for two reasons: first, it is extremely difficult for anyone to define; and second, its presence or absence in any given case must be investigated even if consent is ultimately to determine the line between admissible and inadmissible evidence.

To see why this is so, one need only attempt to answer the following question: if discovery is to be limited to nonconsensual incidents, who is to determine which ones may be discovered? Mr. Clinton? Clearly not—and not only because, as an interested party, he might intentionally miscategorize an incident, but also because he may have convinced himself that a woman consented when in fact she did not.

Indeed, the entire question of consent to the "requests" or demands of a high-ranking public official, who travels (and who is alleged to procure women) with armed guards, is itself a difficult subject. Must there be physical resistance to establish a lack of consent? Is there consent if a woman's presence alone with him is procured, as it was here, by the fraudulent implication that "the Governor" wished to "meet" with a state employee, presumably for something having to do with state business—such as the plaintiff's employment? Is there "consent" if a female state employee engages in sex because she believes she must do so to preserve her employment status? Because she wishes to better it? Because she believes she can only better it, in competition against women who do engage in sex with Mr. Clinton, if she does so as well?

Like his rejected demand for immunity, Mr. Clinton's plea for protection from this sort of discovery simply cannot be granted—it cannot even be intelligently assessed—on a totally empty record. The Court must have facts before it to decide which incidents are relevant and which are not. That is why, even in [cited cases], the determination was made not at the discovery stage but in a motion *in limine* immediately before trial. These motions, moreover, were briefed with an accurate and complete picture of the facts that were to be admitted or excluded. The relevance of the facts, their probity, their potential for causing prejudice, could all be assessed by the court. . . .

Yet another independent ground for denial of Mr. Clinton's motion is the plain relevance of the requested discovery to the issue of punitive damages. The Complaint here seeks punitive damages, and the Eighth Circuit Model Civil Jury Instructions §4.53 contains the punitive damages instruction that will, in all likelihood, be submitted to the jury in this case. The comments to those instructions note that one factor that may be considered by the jury in assessing punitive damages is "the likelihood that the Defendant would repeat the conduct if a punitive award is not made." This comports with the well-settled rule that one of the central purposes of punitive awards is to deter the wrongdoer and others from engaging in similar conduct.

> Note the importance of having sought punitive damages as relief.

It follows that, just as the commentary to the Eighth Circuit Model Civil Jury Instructions makes clear, evidence of similar wrongful acts by a defendant is relevant to the assessment of punitive damages, even and especially if the similar conduct involved persons other than the plaintiff. The cases admitting such evidence are legion. . . .

Jones's lawyers filed a Motion to Compel Responses to the contested interrogatories, as well as their Opposition, *supra,* to the President's Motion for a Protective Order. Clinton's lawyers then filed the following response to Jones's Motion to Compel.

PRESIDENT CLINTON'S OPPOSITION TO PLAINTIFF'S MOTION TO COMPEL RESPONSES TO PLAINTIFF'S SECOND SET OF INTERROGATORIES

. . . The Court has stated that it does not want to treat discovery in this case any differently than it would in a sexual harassment case involving a corporate executive defendant. We know of no case where a court has compelled discovery into the *consensual* sexual conduct of an individual sexual harassment defendant outside the plaintiff's immediate work place, much less into consensual *or* even sexually harassing conduct for a period spanning 20 years. . . .

Plaintiff has suggested that a free-ranging inquest into the President's alleged sexual conduct with other women is warranted because his alleged use of his security detail to escort him to purported rendezvous with other women makes his alleged conduct with those women—regardless of whether it was consensual or nonconsensual—relevant to show a pattern and practice of misuse of government resources. . . .

. . . [A] President or Governor does not forfeit his right to privacy in personal conduct simply because he lives in government-provided housing, is transported to personal activities in government vehicles, or is accompanied by a government-funded security detail wherever he goes. If a Governor or President takes a government car or security detail to go to church, to visit his parents, or to attend private functions at the homes of his friends—even if they are friends of the opposite sex—this is not an abuse of office, and does not render any consensual activities that take place on these private outings any less private, or unlawful or improper.

Even if there was evidence that a state trooper was "involved" in "facilitating" private consensual activities of the Governor, that evidence, we respectfully submit, is *not* relevant to show that the Governor abused State resources to "procure" women or to act as a "sexual predator." Any ruling of this Court that permits discovery into personal matters based solely on the fact that the President or Governor was accompanied by a security detail threatens serious damage to the privacy of all high-ranking government officials who must, unfortunately in this day and age, depend on security details to ensure their safety 24 hours a day.

Discovery of this broad and intrusive nature, moreover, is counter to the Supreme Court's pronouncement concerning the appropriate scope of discovery in this case—which, we respectfully submit, directed the trial Court to consider not only the President's *time* with respect to discovery, but the *dignity of his office* as well. The Court stated not only that the "potential burdens on the President . . . are appropriate matters for [the district court] to evaluate in its management of the case," but also that "*[t]he high respect that is owed to the office* of Chief Executive . . . is a matter that should inform the conduct of the entire proceeding, including the timing and *scope* of discovery." *Clinton v. Jones,* 117 S. Ct. 1636, 1650-51 (1997) (emphasis added). . . .

The court has the power to restrict or prohibit discovery that invades a party's privacy interests, or for any other good cause under Rule 26(c). *See Seattle Times v. Rinehart,* 467 U.S. 20, 35 n.21 (1984). . . . In this case in particular, there is a very real danger that the compulsory processes of the Court will be abused. . . .

> In seeking to compel the President to answer interrogatories about conduct that occurred since he became Chief Executive, plaintiff is disavowing the most significant representation she has made to all the courts that have reviewed this case. From the outset, plaintiff forcefully asserted that her suit should be allowed to proceed because she is seeking to hold the President accountable for alleged conduct he undertook *before* he became President, and that this litigation therefore would not interfere with that office. Now that these arguments have carried the day with the Supreme Court, plaintiff has posed a series of interrogatories aimed directly at the defendant's conduct as President. For this reason alone, her motion to compel answers to interrogatories . . . should be denied insofar as they include conduct that occurred since President Clinton became Chief Executive.
>
> . . . [T]his Court, the Circuit Court of Appeals, and the Supreme Court implicitly relied on plaintiff's repeated representations that such broad-ranging discovery would not occur in this case, because it involved only a few alleged contacts between Ms. Jones and the President. In view of these representations, plaintiff should be estopped from seeking broader discovery now. . . .

Order of December 11, 1997

. . . Interrogatories No. 10 and 11 ask the President to state the name, address, and telephone number of each and every individual (other than Hillary Rodham Clinton) with whom he has had sexual relations or with whom he proposed or sought to have sexual relations when he held any of the following positions: (1) Attorney General of the State of Arkansas; (2) Governor of the State of Arkansas; and (3) President of the United States. Interrogatory No. 17, in turn, asks the President to state the name, address, and telephone number of each and every person who was asked by him to arrange a private meeting between himself and any female (other than Hillary Rodham Clinton), attended by no one else, at any location other than his office, at any time when he held any of the positions listed in interrogatories No. 10 and 11. The President objects to these interrogatories on grounds that (i) they are irrelevant and unlikely to lead to the discovery of admissible evidence; (ii) they are over broad and unduly burdensome, especially because they span a period of 20 years; (iii) in light of plaintiff's deposition testimony [that she was unaware of any relationships involving the defendant while she was employed at AIDC], this discovery is wholly unnecessary; and (iv) plaintiff should be estopped from pursuing this discovery based on prior representations to the Court.

The Court has considered these interrogatories and will limit their scope to some extent. First, because the Court considers any relationship, proposed relationships, or arranged meetings that occurred 20 years ago to be too remote in time to the allegations of plaintiff's amended complaint, the Court will establish a time frame that spans 5 years prior to May 8, 1991 (the date of the alleged incident that is the primary subject of this lawsuit), up to the present. Second, the Court will limit the class of individuals within this time frame to two categories, those who were state or federal employees, and those whose liaisons with Governor

Clinton were procured, protected, concealed, and/or facilitated by State Troopers assigned to the Governor.

The Court finds, therefore, that the plaintiff is entitled to information regarding any individuals with whom the President had sexual relations or proposed or sought to have sexual relations and who were during the relevant time frame state or federal employees. Plaintiff is also entitled to information regarding every person whom the President asked, during the relevant time frame, to arrange a private meeting between himself and any female state or federal employee which was attended by no one else and was held at any location other than his office.[4] The Court cannot say that such information is not reasonably calculated to lead to the discovery of admissible evidence.

The Court further finds that plaintiff is entitled to information regarding any individuals, whether or not state or federal employees, whose liaisons with Governor Clinton were procured, protected, concealed, and/or facilitated by State Troopers assigned to the Governor.[5] Such information may bear on plaintiff's efforts at establishing a pattern or practice of conduct. Again, the Court cannot say that such information is not reasonably calculated to lead to the discovery of admissible evidence.

In limiting the interrogatories at issue in this Order to a time frame that does not exceed 5 years prior to May 8, 1991, the Court is not thereby stating that it intends to limit the deposition testimony of President Clinton to that time frame. As the Court has stated earlier, the Court anticipates that it will have opportunity to rule later on the scope of President Clinton's deposition. It is possible that the Court would permit plaintiff to question the President with regard to matters that fall outside that time frame if she has an independent basis for inquiring into such matters. The Courts simply will not require the President to formulate time-consuming and burdensome responses to written interrogatories requesting information beyond that time frame. . . .

> The scope of what is relevant is linked here to the particular discovery device. For the defendant's deposition, Judge Wright may permit a broader inquiry.

NOTES AND COMMENTS

1. *Missing citations.*   One notable characteristic of Judge Wright's ruling is that she cites no case law in support of her reasoning. In fact, there was little case law on this point at the time, and there remains relatively little. Moreover, most of the precedent that does exist is from district courts rather than appellate courts. Why might this be the state of the law? One reason is because this is a discovery question,

4. Of course, any alleged relationships and/or arranged meetings with a federal employee that occurred when the President was not in a position to directly affect that individual's employment, *i.e.*, when he was still Governor and was not President-elect, would fall outside of the guidelines the Court today establishes. Likewise, any alleged relationships and/or arranged meetings with a state employee that occurred when the President was no longer in a position to directly affect that individual's state employment would also fall outside of the Court's guidelines. [Footnote 2 in the original document.]

5. Any alleged relationships or proposed relationships that did not involve state or federal employees and were not procured, protected, concealed, and/or facilitated by State Troopers assigned to the Governor go well beyond the issues in this case. [Footnote 3 in the original document.]

not an interpretation of the underlying substantive law, although the two are obviously related. In discovery matters, the Rules give the judge broad discretion to shape the contours of permissible discovery, through the wide scope of relevance under Rule 26(b)(1) and the pragmatic balancing of relevance versus privacy intrusions sketched out in Rule 26(b)(2). Thus, in discovery, the trial judge has authority that is reviewable in theory, but often not in practice. As one noted civil procedure scholar stated:

> [T]he trial judge, when acting on a discovery dispute, is in most cases virtually immune to appellate supervision . . . Appellate review of trial court discovery rulings is rare; when review does occur, the appellant must demonstrate that the trial court "abused its discretion," a standard guaranteeing substantial insulation from appellate supervision.

Stephen C. Yeazell, The Misunderstood Consequences of Modern Civil Process, 1994 Wis. L. Rev. 631, 651-652.

Is this good process policy? *Compare Stalnaker v. K-Mart Corp.*, 1996 WL 39777563 (D. Kan.), in which a district court permitted discovery in a sexual harassment suit of defendant's consensual sexual relationships with other K-Mart employees and relied on a confidentiality order to protect the defendant and nonparties against invasions of privacy. Judge Wright also utilized a confidentiality order (see Introduction to this Chapter). In his Opposition to Plaintiff's Motion to Compel, excerpted *supra*, President Clinton argued as follows:

> Due to the unusually high-profile nature of the litigation, the unique status of the defendant, and intense public interest in the titillating nature of plaintiff's allegations, it is highly unlikely that any confidentiality order, however carefully crafted, will prevent unauthorized disclosure if the President is compelled to answer these intrusive and embarrassing interrogatories. In such a situation, the Court clearly has the authority to restrict the scope of discovery, or to disallow it altogether.

Despite many leaks of supposedly confidential information to the press, no one on either side of the litigation in *Jones v. Clinton* was ever penalized for violating the confidentiality order. Was Judge Wright wrong to rely on such an order? Was her reliance correct, but her enforcement too weak? How can attorneys respond if such an order, increasingly common in litigation, is being violated?

2. No appeal.   Another reason that there is so little appellate law on discovery is that discovery orders are usually not appealable until the end of the case (under the final judgment rule). (See Chapter 12.) In retrospect, it seems remarkable that this ruling, which became so consequential, was not appealed. When we get to Chapter 12, we will consider whether this decision should have been classified as falling within one of the exceptions to the final judgment rule.

3. Equal treatment.   Judge Wright approached the minefield of discovery issues that she had to decide in this case with the goal of treating the President as she would treat any other defendant in such a case. Certainly she had discretion under Rule 26, however, to adjust her rulings based on his status as President. Should she have taken his unique status into account? Why or why not?

4. The nature of the claim.   Discovery may be even more important in some types of cases than in others. In a variety of civil rights claims, including employment discrimination, the plaintiff has the burden to demonstrate some aspect of defendant's motivation or intent; in such cases, extensive discovery may be necessary.[6] Additional considerations apply to sexual harassment cases:

> Sexual harassment cases generally involve no witnesses, and the only way the plaintiff can prove that this happened was to show that there was a pattern. Moreover, the only way he or she, usually she, can prove that there is a pattern is to try to get other instances before the trier of fact. So, if you say that you cannot ever inquire into activities that the defendant says were consensual, you may insulate defendants from accurate charges.

Cass Sunstein, Lessons from a Debacle: From Impeachment to Reform, 51 Fla. L. Rev. 599, 613 (1999). Sunstein's argument illustrates the potential impact of the law of procedure, and specifically the law of discovery, on substantive law—in this case, that of employment discrimination. In *Jones v. Clinton,* the plaintiff used the kind of "pattern" argument to which Sunstein alludes.

Exercise 10—Balancing Privacy and the Scope of Discovery

Now that you have read the decision that set in motion the chain of events that led to President Clinton's impeachment, try your hand at doing a better job. Assume that the Order of December 11 was Judge Wright's first draft. She has asked you, as her clerk, to write a more fully reasoned decision. She is sufficiently torn about the question that she also tells you that you are free to propose a different outcome in your rewrite. How would you decide this question? Judge Wright wants you to supply a more general analysis of the goals of discovery, the balancing of interests, and the parameters of her authority and discretion under Rule 26, and then apply that analysis to the particular items of discovery at issue here.

PRIVACY INTERESTS OF NONPARTY WITNESSES

Should it make a difference in weighing the right to discovery against privacy rights whether the affected individual is a nonparty? Should persons who have not initiated nor been named a party in litigation have stronger claims to privacy than a party? Several courts have held that a person's nonparty status should be considered a significant factor when a court weighs whether proposed discovery is unduly burdensome. *Katz v. Batavia Marine,* 984 F.2d 422, 424 (Fed. Cir. 1993) (and cases cited therein); *Allen v. Howmedica Leibinger,* 190 F.R.D. 518, 521 (W.D. Tenn. 1999).

In *Jones v. Clinton,* plaintiff's lawyers sought to depose a number of women whom they suspected of having been sexually involved with the President. As you

---

6. Richard L. Marcus, Discovery Containment Redux, 39 B.C. L. Rev. 747, 751 (1998) ("the very structure of employment discrimination law seems to have been founded partly on the availability of broad discovery").

read in the Order of December 11, Judge Wright set three boundaries of relevance for the scope of discovery into that issue: (1) five years before and after May 1991, (2) only where the woman worked in a state or federal government agency, and (3) where Clinton allegedly used a state trooper to facilitate a liaison.

How to apply and enforce that order became a problem, however. Women who received notices of deposition challenged them on grounds of their right of personal privacy. In addition, they submitted affidavits in an attempt to foreclose the basis for a deposition, using the guidelines from Judge Wright's earlier ruling. Following is the most (in)famous of the Jane Doe affidavits, that of Jane Doe No. 6:

AFFIDAVIT OF JANE DOE #6

1. My name is Jane Doe #6. I am 24 years old and I currently reside at 700 New Hampshire Avenue, N.W., Washington, D.C. 20037.

2. On December 19, 1997, I was served with a subpoena from the plaintiff to give a deposition and to produce documents in the lawsuit filed by Paula Corbin Jones against President William Jefferson Clinton and Danny Ferguson.

3. I can not fathom any reason that the plaintiff would seek information from me for her case.

4. I have never met Ms. Jones, nor do I have any information regarding the events she alleges occurred at the Excelsior Hotel on May 8, 1991 or any other information concerning any of the allegations in her case.

5. I worked at the White House in the summer of 1995 as a White House Intern. Beginning in December 1995, I worked in the Office of Legislative Affairs as a staff assistant for correspondence. In April 1996, I accepted a job as assistant to the Assistant Secretary for Public Affairs at the U.S. Department of Defense. I maintained that job until December 26, 1997. I am currently unemployed but seeking a new job.

6. In the course of my employment at the White House I met President Clinton several times. I also saw the President at a number of social functions held at the White House. When I worked as an intern, he appeared at occasional functions attended by me and several other interns. The correspondence I drafted while I worked at the Office of Legislative Affairs was seen and edited by supervisors who either had the President's signature affixed by mechanism or, I believe, had the President sign the correspondence itself.

7. I have the utmost respect for the President who has always behaved appropriately in my presence.

8. I have never had a sexual relationship with the President, he did not propose that we have a sexual relationship, he did not offer me employment or other benefits in exchange for a sexual relationship, he did not deny me employment or other benefits for rejecting a sexual relationship. I do not know of any other person who had a sexual relationship with the President, was offered employment or other benefits in exchange for a sexual relationship, or was denied employment or other benefits for rejecting a sexual relationship. The occasions that I saw

the President after I left my employment at the White House in April 1996, were official receptions, formal functions or events related to the U.S. Department of Defense, where I was working at the time. There were other people present on those
occasions.

9. Since I do not possess any information that could possibly be relevant
to the allegations made by Paula Jones or lead to admissible evidence in this
case, I asked my attorney to provide this affidavit to plaintiff's counsel. Requiring
my deposition in this matter would cause disruption to my life, especially since I
am looking for employment, unwarranted attorney's fees and costs, and constitute
an invasion of my right to privacy.

I declare under the penalty of perjury that the foregoing is true and correct.

Monica S. Lewinsky

Monica S. Lewinsky

Judge Wright denied all requests by the Jane Does who sought to avoid deposition. When the depositions proceeded, the three sets of attorneys (for the plaintiff,
for the defendant, and for the witness) frequently battled over which questions could
be asked. Thus, Judge Wright was forced to revisit the question of the scope of discovery into the President's personal relationships, in the context of the rights of particular witnesses.

*[In the following excerpt, "X" marks a place where the court redacted the text
to remove a name. "XXX" marks a place where a long passage is redacted, presumably to remove text that would identify the deponent or describe facts or allegations of a personal nature.]*

Order of January 9, 1998

During the course of several telephone conferences concerning motions for
protective orders and to quash notices of depositions filed by Jane Doe [X], Jane
Doe [X], and Jane Doe [X], this Court, in essentially denying these motions, ruled
that a factual predicate must be established with each deponent prior to inquiring
into any alleged sexual activity between the deponent and President Clinton. . . .

In ruling that a factual predicate must be established with each
deponent prior to inquiring into any alleged sexual activity, it was the
intent of this Court that the plaintiff not be allowed to *immediately*
question the deponents about any sexual behavior between themselves and the President. The Court was attempting to provide some,
admittedly minimal, protection to these and any future deponents by
requiring that the plaintiff refrain from asking embarrassing, personal questions
about sexual activities unless the plaintiff first established that the answers might
be relevant to plaintiff's case against the President. In this regard, the plaintiff
should first establish that the deponent personally knew then-Governor Clinton
and had some contact with him. If the deponent was a state employee before, dur-

This clarification of her
prior ruling ensures that
all of the depositions will
go forward, regardless of
any assertions in affida-
vits.

ing, or after her contact with the Governor, and if the plaintiff otherwise has a good faith basis for the inquiry (such as sworn testimony of other witnesses), then plaintiff may proceed to ask the personal, embarrassing questions about sexual activities between the Governor and the deponent. If the deponent was not ever a state employee, she may be asked whether she ever applied for a state job and/or whether she ever discussed state employment with Governor Clinton or whether she had any reason to believe that he otherwise knew of her interest in such employment or even mentioned the possibility of employment to her.

As to deponents who were not state employees, such questions as whether they have ever been in an airplane with Governor Clinton, whether the Governor has phoned them at home or at work, whether they have spoken on the telephone with the Governor, whether they have corresponded with the Governor, whether they have been alone with the Governor, whether they have had social contact with the Governor, whether they have had a meeting with the Governor, what the purpose of any such meetings were, etc., are all proper questions in this Court's view and are not dependent upon some nexus between state employment or facilitation of state troopers having been established. Indeed, it is the *answers* to these questions that may well establish such a nexus. What if, for example, the answers to some of these questions revealed that the subject matter of alleged phone calls between the Governor and a deponent were about obtaining state employment and what would be required of the deponent before such employment could be obtained? Or, what if the answers to other such questions that, yes, the deponent indeed had a meeting with the Governor and, further, that such meeting was facilitated by a state trooper? These are matters that go to the heart of plaintiff's lawsuit and the Court thus cannot say that such questions are not reasonably calculated to lead to the discovery of admissible evidence. The Court will therefore permit such questions and will permit plaintiff to go beyond the deponents' statements to establish a nexus as long as there is a good faith basis for doing so. [XXX]

More problematic is the question whether establishment of a nexus to state troopers is a sufficient foundation to trigger embarrassing questions addressed to Jane Doe [X] and Jane Doe [X] in the absence of any evidence that these individuals were state employees at any time. The defendants contend that any evidence of sexual liaisons with these women is irrelevant to the issues of the case and is being sought only to embarrass the President. Plaintiff has argued that evidence of such meetings with females who are not employees is nevertheless relevant to show that the Governor, as a state actor, engaged in a pattern or practice of using state troopers to procure sex in violation of females' constitutional rights. Even · though facially this argument has appeal, the Court considers it now only in the context of Jane Doe [X] and Jane Doe [X] and finds that the evidence thus far does not support plaintiff's argument that the "trooper nexus" establishes such a pattern or practice with respect to these two deponents. [XXX] Similarly, Jane Doe [X] testified that she was not and has not been a state or federal employee. However, the Court will permit counsel for the plaintiff to inquire of both Jane Doe [X] and Jane Doe [X] concerning whether they have ever discussed with Governor or President Clinton the possibility of employment with either state or federal government or whether they have ever applied for such employment or whether he ever offered such employment. If the answer to any of these questions is in the affirma-

> As Judge Wright notes two paragraphs later, this is an unusual degree of detail for a trial judge to specify as to the proper line of questioning in a deposition. Remember, though, that virtually every deposition generated motions by both sides.

tive, then counsel may continue the deposition by asking the personal and potentially embarrassing questions concerning their alleged sexual relationship with President Clinton. . . .

The Court would not bother to go through the machinations of limiting deposition testimony in the manner set forth in this Order were it not for the high degree of public interest in this litigation and the potential for embarrassing the deponents and the President with damaging and irrelevant information. In the typical case, the Court would not bother to restrict deposition testimony and would merely disallow, following a motion *in limine,* the evidence at trial if the prejudicial value substantially outweighs the probative value of such evidence or if the evidence is irrelevant to the issues in this case.

Although the Court has not made any final rulings with regard to what evidence will be admitted or excluded at any trial (and nothing in this Order should be construed as indicating how this Court will so rule), it is very likely that a good deal of the matters obtained in discovery will not be deemed admissible into evidence or, if it is, that it will be restricted in some fashion. In addition, should this case survive summary judgment and go to trial, the Court, as previously indicated, anticipates limiting the amount of time and number of witnesses that will be spent on issues of alleged sexual activity of both the President and the plaintiff (should such matters otherwise be deemed admissible). But the issue here is one of discovery, not admissibility of evidence at trial. Discovery, as all counsel know, by its very nature takes unforeseen twists and turns and goes down numerous paths, and whether those paths lead to the discovery of admissible evidence often simply cannot be predetermined. The President denies the plaintiff's allegations and try as it might, the Court simply cannot determine at this juncture what discovery will reveal nor can it at this time make any credibility determinations.

As it has previously indicated, the Court takes no pleasure in having to rule on matters involving alleged sexual activity of the President and the deponents and it is acutely aware of the high respect that is owed to the Office of the Presidency. Indeed, it is because of the importance of this case and this Court's high respect for the institution of the Presidency that the Court has spent many hours in evening telephone conferences allowing counsel for all parties to state their views in a full and frank manner and to talk through the issues with the Court. But it is difficult for the Court to make evidentiary rulings without knowing what the evidence is. In the meantime, the Court will preside over this case by striving to adhere to its duty to follow the laws and Constitution of the United States in a fair and impartial manner. . . .

NOTES AND COMMENTS

1. Distinction but no difference.   Judge Wright gives no apparent weight to the deponents' status as nonparties in her rulings as to the scope of personal questions that could be asked during the depositions. She did, however, go to some lengths to try to preserve their anonymity vis-à-vis the media. Do you think that her approach was a fair balancing of the interest of the plaintiff in seeking information that could lead to the discovery of admissible evidence against the privacy rights of the witnesses? Could she have developed additional or different categories of witnesses who would have been subject to more probing questions? Although it is impossible to know how truthful the other affidavits were, the Lewinsky affidavit certainly illustrates the shortcomings of accepting such statements at face value. On the other hand, there was a line-drawing question as to all of these depositions: whether the relevancy value of possible testimony about intimate relationships justified the degree of intrusion. How would you resolve that question under the proportionality principle of Rule 26(b)(2)(iii)?

2. Collateral consequences.   Judges in other cases have denied discovery requests that delve into similarly sensitive information about nonparties. Consider two oft-cited examples:

(A) In *Rasmussen v. South Florida Blood Service, Inc.,* 500 So. 2d 533 (Fla. 1987), the Florida Supreme Court refused to allow discovery of the names of blood donors. Plaintiff alleged that he had contracted HIV/AIDS through a blood transfusion, and sought the names of donors to a particular facility (although it was not a defendant in the case). The trial court denied the motion by the blood bank to quash the subpoena; the supreme court reversed. "The threat posed by the disclosure of the donors' identities goes far beyond the immediate discomfort occasioned by third-party probing into sensitive areas of the donors' lives. Disclosure of donor identities in any context involving AIDS could be extremely disruptive and even devastating to the individual donor." *Id.* at 537.

(B) In *Williams v. Thomas Jefferson University,* 343 F. Supp. 1131 (E.D. Pa. 1972), the district court refused to allow plaintiff in a medical malpractice action based on abortion to discover the names of women who had previously had abortions performed at the same facility. Plaintiff sought to gather information that could be used to impeach the expected testimony of a defendant doctor. In denying the request, the court wrote that "[t]he consequences of allowing revelation and examination when considered in terms of family relationships and individual friendships could be disastrous." *Id.* at 1132.

On what bases might you distinguish the information that Jones sought from the facts of these cases? Were her relevance arguments stronger or weaker?

Exercise 11—The Role of Public Policy Concerns

One unsettled aspect of discovery law is the extent to which *public policy interests* (interests other than those of the individuals immediately affected) should be taken into consideration in fashioning discovery orders. Using *Jones, Rasmussen,* and *Williams* as examples, write a memorandum to Judge Wright advising her on that question. Note that the latter two cases do not discuss public policy interests; is it a better reading of law to consider them implicit to those outcomes or as unnecessary? How should such interests be addressed, if at all, in future cases that trench on sensitive private information?

DISCOVERY VERSUS THE FIRST AMENDMENT

As you saw in the last chapter, President Clinton sought discovery from the director of the Paula Jones Legal Fund (PJLF), in an effort to show that Jones received personal financial benefit from the fund and, he argued, should therefore be entitled to less credibility. (Had President Clinton filed a Rule 11(b)(1) motion to assert that the lawsuit was brought for improper purposes, the discovery related to the PJLF might have been relevant to that also.) In addition to the attorney-client and work product defenses asserted against the President's discovery efforts, the PJLF also argued that certain information sought by the President was protected by the First Amendment rights of the persons who donated to the fund.

PRESIDENT CLINTON'S OPPOSITION TO MOTIONS FOR PROTECTIVE ORDER REGARDING SUBPOENA TO CINDY HAYS

. . . On October 1, 1997, Ms. Hays was served with a subpoena for a deposition, and to produce documents relating to plaintiff. Ms. Hays is the former director of the Paula Jones Legal Fund ("Legal Fund" or "Fund"), and by her own admission has documents relating to the creation, operation, and finances of that Fund, the amounts and sources of donations to the Fund, statements by plaintiff, and communications between herself and plaintiff and between herself and plaintiff's counsel. Both Ms. Hays and plaintiff filed motions for a protective order.

Ms. Hays asserts that she does not have to submit to a deposition because she fears reprisal for herself and others if the discovery is had, and that having to respond to the subpoena will violate the freedom of speech or association of contributors to the Legal Fund. . . .

Expressive association claims must be predicated on a showing that "first, that a group of people have come together, and, second, that they have come together for the purpose of engaging in some activity protected by the First Amendment." [citation omitted] Providing financial support for an individual's private lawsuit does not rise to the level of "expressive activity" that merits the protection of the First Amendment. To the contrary, where the litigation is simply "a technique of resolving private differences," and is not undertaken to further broader societal policies, supporting the litigation is not "expressive association." *See NAACP v. Button,* 371 U.S. 415, 429 (1963).

In contrast to members of groups like the NAACP, contributors to the Paula Jones Legal Fund are not "members" of any organized association and do not "take positions on public questions" or engage as a group in any activities protected by the First Amendment, such as speech, assembly, petition for redress of grievances, or the exercise of religion. Nor are they engaged in "intimate human relationships" with each other that would fall within the purview of the First Amendment. Moreover, the Fund is not selective and is not exclusionary; anyone who wants to give money may do so; and an unlimited number of people can support the Fund. In short, donors simply are financial supporters to what essentially is a checking account for a private plaintiff's counsel.

The seminal case relied on by plaintiff regarding expressive activity elucidates this distinction. In *NAACP v. Button,* the Supreme Court found that the NAACP "devotes much of its fund and energies to an extensive program" of litigation dedicated to the purpose of "secur[ing] the elimination of all racial barriers." *NAACP v. Button,* 371 at 419-420. Therefore, "[i]n the context of NAACP objectives, litigation *is not a technique of resolving private differences;* it is a means for achieving the lawful objectives of equality of treatment by all government . . . for the members of the Negro community in this country." *NAACP v. Button,* 371 U.S. at 429 (emphasis added).

In the present case, plaintiff cannot have it both ways. Plaintiff has asserted repeatedly that this litigation is intended simply to vindicate her personal rights. That being the case, financial support for this litigation does not rise to the level of expressive activity protected by the First Amendment. However, plaintiff and Ms. Hays now suggest that the Fund exists to support a political cause. If that is true, plaintiff concedes that the lawsuit is politically motivated. Even so, we respectfully submit, support for the Fund does not rise to the level of expressive activity as that term is understood in the cases discussed above: it still is not part of an overarching litigation effort, being fought on multiple fronts, to push a public policy agenda through the courts, as was the case with the NAACP litigation in *Button.*

Even if Ms. Hays could establish that donors to the Fund were engaged in expressive activity, she also would have to show a "reasonable probability that the compelled disclosure . . . will subject them to threats, harassment, or reprisals from either Government officials or private parties." *Buckley v. Valeo,* 424 U.S. 1, 74 (1976). Purely "speculative fears" such as those asserted here do not substantiate a claim of reprisal.

The declaration submitted by Ms. Hays does not establish any link between the instant litigation and her alleged harassment, let alone a reasonable one. Likewise, the declaration submitted by plaintiff avers only that she, like thousands of individuals annually, has been subjected to an IRS audit this year. Plaintiff does not assert that the President was responsible for that, and would have no basis to do so.

Plaintiff also asserts, without foundation, that First Amendment rights are placed at risk by providing the names of contributors to the defendant, simply by virtue of the fact that he "is the most powerful man in the world." This claim is based on the unreasonable and unjustified assumption that anyone who is President would abuse the office—an assumption this Court should not entertain. Thus, even if plaintiff had standing to assert the constitutional rights of others—which she does not—she has provided no evidence to show that her fear of reprisal is reasonable and not speculative.

Finally, any concern over reprisals against individual and corporate contributors can easily be solved by limiting the dissemination of their identities until such time, if ever, they are needed at trial. . . .

REPLY OF CINDY HAYS TO PRESIDENT CLINTON'S OPPOSITION TO MOTIONS FOR PROTECTIVE ORDER REGARDING SUBPOENA TO CINDY HAYS

Defendant President Clinton's Opposition . . . argues that Hays has not established that the Fund engages in any expressive activity protected by the First Amendment because financial support for litigation is not protected by the First Amendment. He argues that First Amendment protection belongs only to members of organizations like the NAACP which take positions on public questions or engage in activity such as filing petitions for the redress of grievances. . . .

Gender harassment is a human rights violation. *See Harris v. Forklift Systems, Inc.,* 510 U.S. _____, 126 L. Ed. 2d 295, 301 (1993) (Title VII is to be broadly construed to permit an action for gender harassment to accord with Congressional intent to strike at the entire spectrum of disparate treatment). When it is alleged that a Governor of a State or a sitting President of the United States is the perpetrator of gender harassment or *quid pro quo* sexual discrimination, the question of whether the laws of the United States will be equally enforced, so as to apply to that Governor or President, is also a matter of paramount concern. So it is both natural and reasonable for citizens and organizations interested in equal enforcement of the law, the Rule of Law, or even the elimination of gender harassment, to band together to support a court case raising such issues. Such activity is fully protected under the First Amendment.

"[S]upport of litigation is a form of expression and association protected by the First Amendment." *Eilers v. Palmer,* 575 F. Supp. 1259, 1261 (D. Minn. 1984). In *Eilers* the court denied discovery of the names of "all individuals and entities who are funding" a lawsuit involving religious programming by an alleged cult. Under the leading Supreme Court authority that court held that

> compelled disclosure of the names of those individuals or groups supporting the plaintiff's lawsuit would create a genuine risk of interference with protected interests in two ways. First, such disclosure might make the plaintiff, or future plaintiffs, reluctant to accept the support of unpopular groups, fearing that evidence of such support would be used at trial to the plaintiff's disadvantage. Second, the supporters themselves, for various reasons, may have a desire for anonymity that might cause them to withhold support knowing that their names would be disclosed.

Id. at 1261. "The right to join together for the advancement of beliefs and ideas is diluted if it does not include *the right to pool money through contributions,* for funds are often essential if advocacy is to be truly or optimally effective." [citation omitted] The acceptance of defendant Clinton's argument that no associational interests are involved herein would prevent the raising of money to support litigation seeking to advance the Rule of Law or the elimination of gender harassment. This "dilution" of the First Amendment should not be countenanced. . . .

. . . This lawsuit is a petition for the redress of grievances. The case takes positions on public questions such as the application of the Rule of Law to the President of the United States and the paramount enforcement of laws against gender harassment. This is First Amendment protected activity. To argue that only groups like the NAACP are protected from the mandatory disclosure of members or donors is incorrect as a matter of law. *Eilers, supra; see NAACP v. Alabama,* 357 U.S. 449, 460 (1958) ("it is immaterial whether the beliefs sought to be advanced by association pertain to political, economic, religious, or cultural matters . . ."). There is nothing in the case law cited by defendant Clinton supporting the proposition that only groups like the NAACP are protected. To read the case law this narrowly is to set the bar too high for those who band together for common objectives which affect the areas of public policy and the Rule of Law. . . .

. . . In *Seattle Times Co. v. Rhinehart,* 467 U.S. 20 (1984) there was a requested disclosure of the identity of contributors to a Foundation which related to core claims in the action. Since the trial court found that this information was necessary to the lawsuit, the disclosure was allowed. However, even after finding that the information went to the "heart of the lawsuit," the trial court still took measures to protect the identity of the individual donors. This was because there had been recent attacks by anonymous individuals and groups on the Foundation's headquarters. The court believed that there might be serious reprisals to the individual contributors as a result of the disclosure of their names. In upholding this decision, the Supreme Court underscored the importance of protecting individuals from such disclosure. . . .

Order of November 25, 1997

. . . While it may be true, as the President argues, that the "primary purpose of the Fund is [not to support activities directly related to advocacy, it may also be the case that] compelled disclosure of the names of individual donors would chill expressive activity not only in this case, but in future cases as well. In this regard, the Court is unable to conclude from this record that the individual donors made their contributions knowing that the contributions would be used, not to support this litigation in order to achieve political and/or policy goals, but rather, as the President argues, to merely pay plaintiff's personal expenses. Accordingly, the Court concludes that the identities of the individual contributors or donors to the PJLF should remain confidential.

The Court does, however, conclude that President Clinton is entitled to discovery from the PJLF, Ms. Hays, and plaintiff with regard to the number of contributions, the amount of money raised so far, communications with donors (with names of individual donors redacted), and information relating to the creation, operation, and finances of the PJLF. . . . The Court cannot say that this information is not reasonably calculated to lead to the discovery of admissible evidence. . . .

NOTES AND COMMENTS

1. Discovery and dissemination.   Many courts have distinguished between the right to discover information and the much more limited "right" to disseminate it. Although a party who obtains information during discovery is free to disseminate it however she wishes absent a court order to the contrary, courts will frequently limit that option as part of a trade-off in which the opposing party is ordered to produce sensitive information. That appears to have been a key principle behind Judge Wright's discovery decision regarding PJLF in *Jones v. Clinton*. That approach is considerably complicated, however, when a government official is the party seeking discovery of the information, and the request involves the identities of his political opponents. The issue confronting Judge Wright here was whether, and how far, to extend that principle to discovery sought by a government official in the course of litigation. If the defendant had been a corporate CEO, how do you think this question should have been decided?

2. Waiver by initiation of litigation?   Should it make a difference that in *Jones* the names are being sought by the defendant, who did not initiate the lawsuit and so who is conducting discovery only because he has been brought into court? In some jurisdictions, certain privileges may be waived if the person files a lawsuit; for example, if a patient files suit against a physician for malpractice, the patient will be considered to have waived the privilege that attached to prior communications with that physician. Is it fair to allow a party to both file a lawsuit and to foreclose discovery of associational activities that relate to the litigation? This is a situation in which it may be significant that the bulk of the First Amendment rights being asserted are held not by either party, but by nonparties. Even if that were not the case, courts are likely to tread very cautiously in this area:

> [W]hile the filing of a lawsuit may implicitly bring about a partial waiver of one's constitutional right of associational privacy, the scope of such 'waiver' must be narrowly rather than expansively construed, so that plaintiffs will not be unduly deterred from instituting lawsuits by the fear of exposure of their private associational affiliations and activities. When such associational activities are *directly relevant* to the plaintiff's claim, and disclosure of the plaintiff's affiliations is essential to the fair resolution of the lawsuit, a trial court may properly compel such disclosure.

Britt v. Superior Court of San Diego County, 574 P.2d 766, 775 (Cal. 1978) (emphasis in the original) (denying attempt by defendant airport authority to discover information concerning plaintiffs' involvement in local political groups organized to oppose airport policies regarding noise and air pollution).

CHAPTER EIGHT

Discovery: Sanctions

INTRODUCTION

Most discovery sanctions are imposed while the case is ongoing, often while discovery is still ongoing. In *Jones v. Clinton,* sanctions were imposed after the case had ended. They were based on an extraordinary set of events that began during the same period that the lawyers were arguing the relevance and privacy issues that you just read in Chapter 7.

On approximately November 18, 1997, Jones's lawyers first learned of the existence of Monica Lewinsky. Several days before, Linda Tripp, who had been taping telephone conversations with Monica Lewinsky, called her book agent, Lucianne Goldberg. Tripp had surmised that she could arrange to be subpoenaed to give a deposition in the *Jones* case, which would provide an opportunity to disclose the Clinton-Lewinsky affair and lay the foundation for a book detailing her impressions of the Clinton White House. Goldberg sought advice about whether Tripp's being deposed would be a smart move from Alfred Regnery, a publisher who specialized in books by conservatives. Regnery in turn called Peter Smith, a financial supporter (see Chapter 1), who referred Goldberg to Richard Porter, one of the lawyers who had become secret helpers for Jones's litigation team ("the elves"). Porter immediately e-mailed George Conway, who had become the chief "elf." Conway faxed the e-mail to Don Campbell, one of Jones's lawyers in Dallas. Three days later, another of Jones's lawyers called Tripp.

On December 5, 1997, Jones's lawyers faxed their proposed witness list to Bennett, including Lewinsky's name, the first mention of her in any documents in the case. On December 19, Lewinsky received a subpoena to testify at a deposition. It was a subpoena duces tecum, instructing her to bring to the deposition "each and every gift" that she had received from Clinton. She responded with the affidavit that you read in the previous chapter, which was filed on January 7, 1998.

The link that led to the President's impeachment occurred when Richard Marcus, the other "elf" most involved in the litigation of the *Jones* case, had dinner with yet another law school classmate, Paul Rozensweig, and told him of the Lewinsky allegations and the existence of Tripp's tapes. Rozensweig was a staff attorney with the Office of Independent Counsel (OIC) Kenneth Starr. Rozensweig conveyed this information to his superiors the next day. On January 12, 1998, OIC lawyers and FBI agents interviewed Tripp. Five days later, Jones's lawyers deposed President Clinton, asking him a series of pointed questions about Lewinsky.

This deposition and its aftermath led to the President's impeachment. Three of the four articles of impeachment presented to the House of Representatives by the Judiciary Committee concerned *Jones v. Clinton.* Both of the articles that the House adopted grew out of the lawsuit. (See Appendix 1: Articles of Impeachment.) The first article charged the President with perjury before the grand jury convened by the Independent Counsel, in that during his grand jury appearance in August 1998, he lied about aspects of his *Jones v. Clinton* deposition testimony, as well as about the details of his affair with Lewinsky.[1] The second article adopted by the House charged him with obstruction of justice in *Jones v. Clinton* for his alleged efforts to influence witnesses just before and just after the deposition.[2] The House rejected two articles: one charged President Clinton with having committed perjury during his January 17, 1998 deposition and in his answers to the interrogatories that you read in Chapter 6;[3] and another alleged perjury in his answers to questions (similar to interrogatories) posed to him by the Judiciary Committee during the impeachment inquiry.[4]

In the Senate, where a two-thirds vote is required for conviction,[5] President Clinton was found not guilty of both of the articles adopted by the House. On the first article, alleging perjury, the vote was 45 guilty, 55 not guilty.[6] On the obstruction of justice article, the vote was 50 to 50.[7]

Although the effort to remove the President from office failed, Judge Wright found him in civil contempt of court and imposed monetary sanctions for providing false testimony during his deposition. In addition, she referred the matter to the State Bar of Arkansas for possible action. On January 19, 2001, the day before he left office, he reached a settlement with the Arkansas state bar disciplinary committee in which he admitted giving false and misleading testimony; his license to practice law in that state was suspended for five years. On the basis of that agreement, Independent Counsel Robert Ray (who had replaced Kenneth Starr) agreed not to file criminal charges arising from any of the matters that had led to the OIC investigation.

Read Rule 37 carefully before you read the following documents. Does it authorize Judge Wright to hold in contempt a party who lies during a deposition? Does it matter that the parties had settled the case before the judge took up the question of contempt, so that no case was pending at the time of her order? What other sources of law could the judge have relied on to sanction a party who had lied?

---

1. The vote was 228 to impeach, 206 against. 144 Cong. Rec. D1217-03, D1217 (1998).
2. The vote was 221 to impeach, 212 against. *Id.* at D1217-03, D1218 (1998).
3. The vote was 205 to impeach, 229 against. *Id.*
4. The vote was 148 to impeach, 285 against. *Id.* at D1217-03, D1219 (1998).
5. U.S. Const. art. I, §3, cl. 6.
6. 145 Cong. Rec. S1457-02, S1458 (1999).
7. *Id.* at S1457-02, S1459.

EXCERPTS OF DEPOSITION TESTIMONY
OF PRESIDENT CLINTON

At the beginning of the President's deposition on January 17, 1998, Jones's lawyers presented a definition of the term "sexual relations" that they had largely copied from a federal statute that President Clinton had signed into law, the Violence Against Women Act. They stated their intent to question the President about his past sexual conduct, as permitted by Judge Wright's discovery order that you read in Chapter 7. Clinton's lawyers objected that certain portions of the proposed definition were unclear. Since she was there, Judge Wright herself revised the definition after hearing the lawyers' arguments. This was the definition of "sexual relations" that she adopted and that was then agreed to by the parties: "A person engages in 'sexual relations' when the person knowingly engages or causes . . . contact with the genitalia, anus, groin, breast, innner thigh or buttocks of any person with an intent to arouse or gratify the sexual desire of any person. . . . 'Contact' means intentional touching, either directly or through clothing."

Q. Do you know a woman named Monica Lewinsky?
A. I do.

Q. How do you know her?
A. She worked in the White House for a while, first as an intern, and then in, as the, in the Legislative Affairs Office. . . .

Q. Is it true that when she worked at the White House she met with you several times?
A. I don't know about several times. There was a period when the, when the Republican Congress shut the Government down that the whole White House was being run by interns, and she was assigned to work back in the chief of staff's office, and we were all working there and so I saw her on two or three occasions then, and then when she worked at the White House, I think there was one or two other times when she brought some documents to me.

Q. Well, you also saw her at a number of social functions at the White House, didn't you?
A. Could you be specific? I'm not sure. I mean when we had, when we had like big staff things for, if I had a, like in the summertime, if I had a birthday party and the whole White House staff came, then she must have been there.
   If we had a Christmas party and the whole White House staff was invited, she must have been there. I don't remember any specific social occasions at the White House, but people who work there when they're invited to these things normally come. It's a—they work long hours—it's hard work, and it's one of the nice things about being able to work there, so I assume she was there, but I don't have any specific recollection of any social event. . . . [Participants took a short break.]

Q. Mr. President, before the break, we were talking about Monica Lewinsky. At any time, were you and Monica Lewinsky together alone in the Oval Office?
A. I don't recall, but as I said, when she worked at the Legislative Affairs Office, they always had somebody there on the weekends. I typically worked some on the weekends. Sometimes they'd bring me things on the weekends.
   She, it seems to me, she brought things to me once or twice on the weekends. In that case, whatever time she would be in there, drop if off, exchange a few words and go, she was there.

I don't have any specific recollections of what the issues were, what was going on, but when the Congress is there, we're working all the time, and typically I would do some work on one of the days of the weekends in the afternoon.

Q. So I understand, your testimony is that it was possible, then, that you were alone with her, but you have no specific recollection of that ever happening?

A. Yes. That's correct. It's possible that she, in, while she was working there, brought something to me and that at the time she brought it to me, she was the only person there. That's possible. . . .

Q. At any time have you and Monica Lewinsky ever been alone together in any room in the White House?

A. I think I testified to that earlier. I think that there is a, it is—I have no specific recollection, but it seems to me that she was on duty on a couple of occasions working for the Legislative Affairs Office and brought me some things to sign, something on the weekend. That's—I have a general memory of that.

Q. Do you remember anything that was said in any of those meetings?

A. No. You know, we just had a conversation, I don't remember. . . .

Q. Have you ever met with Monica Lewinsky in the White House between the hours of midnight and 6 a.m.?

A. I certainly don't think so.

Q. Have you ever met—

A. Now, let me just say, when she was working there, during, there may have been a time when we were all—we were up working late. There are lots of, on any given night, when the Congress is in session, there are always several people around late in the night, but I don't have any memory of that. I just can't say that there could have been a time when that occurred, I just—but I don't remember it.

Q. Certainly if it happened, nothing remarkable would have occurred?

A. No, nothing remarkable. I don't remember it. . . .

Q. When was the last time you spoke with Monica Lewinsky?

A. I'm trying to remember. Probably sometime before Christmas. She came by to see Betty sometime before Christmas. And she was there talking to her, and I stuck my head out, said hello to her.

Q. Stuck your head out of the Oval Office?

A. Uh-huh, Betty said she was coming by and talked to her, and I said hello to her. . . .

Q. I believe I was starting to ask you a question a moment ago and we got sidetracked. Have you ever talked to Monica Lewinsky about the possibility that she might be asked to testify in this lawsuit?

A. I'm not sure, and let me tell you why I'm not sure. It seems to me the, the the—I want to be as accurate as I can here. Seems to me the last time she was there to see Betty before Christmas, we were joking about how you all, with the help of the Rutherford Institute, were going to call every woman I'd ever talked to, and I said, you know—

MR. BENNETT: We can't hear you, Mr. President.

MR. CLINTON: And I said that you all might call every woman I ever talked to and ask them that, and so I said you would qualify, or something like that. I don't, I don't think we ever had more of a conversation than that about it, but I might have mentioned something to her about it, because when I saw how long the witness list was, or I heard about it, before I saw, but actually by the time I saw it her name was on it, but I think that was after all this had happened. I might have said something like that, so I don't want to say for sure I didn't, because I might have said something like that. . . .

Q. Well, have you ever given any gifts to Monica Lewinsky?

A. I don't recall. Do you know what they were?

Q. A hat pin?

A. I don't, I don't remember. But I certainly, I could have.

Q. A book about Walt Whitman?

A. I give—let me just say, I give people a lot of gifts, and when people are around I give a lot of things I have at the White House away, so I could have given her a gift, but I don't remember a specific gift.

Q. Do you remember giving her a gold brooch?

A. No.

Q. Do you remember giving her an item that had been purchased from The Black Dog store at Martha's Vineyard?

A. I do remember that, because when I went on vacation, Betty said that, asked me if I was going to bring some stuff back from The Black Dog, and she said Monica loved, liked that stuff and would like to have a piece of it, and I did a lot of Christmas shopping from The Black Dog, and I bought a lot of things for a lot of people, and I gave Betty a couple of the pieces, and she gave I think something to Monica and something to some of the other girls who worked in the office. I remember that because Betty mentioned it to me.

Q. What in particular was given to Monica?

A. I don't remember. I got a whole bag full of things that I bought at The Black Dog. I went there, they gave me some things, and I went and purchased a lot at the store, and when I came back I gave a, a big block of it to Betty, and I don't know what she did with it all or who got what.

Q. But while you were in the store you did pick out something for Monica, correct?

A. While I was in the store—first of all, The Black Dog sent me a selection of things. Then I went to the store and I bought some other things, T-shirts, sweat shirts, shirts. Then when I got back home, I took out a thing or two that I wanted to keep, and I took out a thing or two I wanted to give to some other people, and I gave the rest of it to Betty and she distributed it. That's what I remember doing.

Q. Has Monica Lewinsky ever given you any gifts?

A. Once or twice. I think she's given me a book or two.

Q. Did she give you a silver cigar box?

A. No.

Q. Did she give you a tie?

A. Yes, she has given me a tie before. I believe that's right. Now, as I said, let me remind you, normally when I get these ties, I get ties, you know, together, and then they're given to me later, but I believe that she has given me a tie. . . .

Q. Did you have an extramarital sexual affair with Monica Lewinsky?

A. No.

Q. If she told someone that she had a sexual affair with you beginning in November of 1995, would that be a lie?

A. It's certainly not the truth. It would not be the truth.

Q. I think I used the term "sexual affair." And so the record is completely clear, have you ever had sexual relations with Monica Lewinsky, as that term is defined in Deposition Exhibit 1, as modified by the court?. . . .

A. I have never had sexual relations with Monica Lewinsky. I've never had an affair with her. . . .

ORDERS IMPOSING SANCTIONS

Jones v. Clinton
36 F. Supp. 2d 1118 (E.D. Ark. 1999)

. . . At his deposition, the President was questioned extensively about his relationship with Ms. Lewinsky, this Court having previously ruled on December 11, 1997, that plaintiff was "entitled to information regarding any individuals with whom the President had sexual relations or proposed or sought to have sexual relations and who were during the relevant time frame [of May 8, 1986, up to the present] state or federal employees." [See Chapter 7.] Based on that ruling, this Court overruled objections during the deposition from the President's attorney, Robert S. Bennett, that questions concerning Ms. Lewinsky were inappropriate areas of inquiry and required that such questions be answered by the President. Having been so ordered, the President testified in response to questioning from plaintiff's counsel and his own attorney that he had no recollection of having ever been alone with Ms. Lewinsky and he denied that he had engaged in an "extramarital sexual affair," in "sexual relations," or in a "sexual relationship" with Ms. Lewinsky. . . .

. . . [F]ederal courts possess the authority to impose sanctions for civil contempt pursuant to the Federal Rules of Civil Procedure and their inherent authority, *see* Fed. R. Civ. P. 37(b)(2) (providing that a court may enter an order treating as a contempt of court the failure of a party to obey the court's orders); *Chambers v. NASCO, Inc.,* 501 U.S. 32, 44 (1991) (noting that the power to punish for contempt is inherent in all courts). . . .

. . . Pursuant to Rule 37(b)(2), a court may hold a party in contempt of court for failing to obey an order to provide discovery and may impose several specific, nonexclusive sanctions to address such misconduct, "the parameters of the available measures being 'such orders in regard to the failure as are just.'" [citation omitted] However, when rules alone do not provide courts with sufficient authority to protect their integrity and prevent abuses of the judicial process, the inherent power fills the gap. In this regard, a court has the "inherent power to protect [its] integrity and prevent abuses of the judicial process" by holding a party in contempt and imposing sanctions for violations of the court's orders. When the source of the civil contempt is a failure to comply with a discovery order, the analysis and available remedies under Fed. R. Civ. P. 37 and the court's inherent power are essentially the same. Two requirements must be met before a party may be held in civil contempt: the court must have fashioned an Order that is clear and reasonably specific, and the party must have violated that Order. Generally, these two requirements must be shown by clear and convincing evidence. Although these requirements apply whether the court is proceeding under the Fed. R. Civ. P. 37 or its inherent power, a court ordinarily should turn to its inherent powers only as a secondary measure when a discovery order has been violated. Accordingly, this Court addresses the President's contumacious conduct under Fed. R. Civ. P. 37(b)(2), finding that rule sufficient in its scope to redress the abuse of the judicial process that occurred in this case.

Fed. R. Civ. P. 37(b)(2) sets forth a broad range of sanctions that a district

How does "inherent power" differ from Rule 37?

court may impose upon parties for their failure to comply with the court's discovery orders. The Rule provides that if a party fails to obey an order to provide or permit discovery, the court "may make such orders in regard to the failure as are just" and, among others, impose the following sanctions: (1) the court may order that the matters regarding which the order was made or any other designated facts be taken as established for the purposes of the action in accordance with the claim of the party obtaining the order; (2) the court may refuse to allow the disobedient party to support or oppose designated claims or defenses, or prohibit that party from introducing designated matters in evidence; (3) the court may strike any pleadings or parts thereof, stay further proceedings until the order is obeyed, dismiss the action or proceeding or any part thereof, or render a judgment of default against the disobedient party; and (4) the court may, in lieu of any of the foregoing sanctions or in addition thereto, enter an order treating as a contempt of court the failure of the party to obey the court's orders. Fed. R. Civ. P. 37(b)(2). In addition to those sanctions, the Rule provides:

> In lieu of any of the foregoing orders or in addition thereto, the court shall require the party failing to obey the order . . . to pay the reasonable expenses, including attorney's fees, caused by the failure, unless the court finds that the failure was substantially justified or that other circumstances make an award of expenses unjust.

On two separate occasions, this Court ruled in clear and reasonably specific terms that plaintiff was entitled to information regarding any individuals with whom the President had sexual relations or proposed or sought to have sexual relations and who were during the relevant time frame state or federal employees. Notwithstanding these Orders, the record demonstrates by clear and convincing evidence that the President responded to plaintiff's questions by giving false, misleading, and evasive answers that were designed to obstruct the judicial process. The President acknowledged as much in his public admission that he "misled people" because, among other things, the questions posed to him "were being asked in a politically inspired lawsuit, which has since been dismissed." . . .

[Excerpts from the President's deposition and grand jury testimony follow.]

Certainly the President's aggravation with what he considered a "politically inspired lawsuit" may well have been justified, although the Court makes no findings in that regard. Even assuming that to be so, however, his recourse for the filing of an improper claim against him was to move for the imposition of sanctions against plaintiff. The President could, for example, have moved for sanctions pursuant to Fed. R. Civ. P. 11 if, as he intimated in his address to the Nation, he was convinced that plaintiff's lawsuit was presented for an improper purpose and included claims "based on 'allegations and other factual contentions [lacking] evidentiary support' or unlikely to prove well-grounded after reasonable investigation." The President never challenged the legitimacy of plaintiff's lawsuit by filing a motion pursuant to Rule 11, however, and it simply is not acceptable to employ deceptions and falsehoods in an attempt to obstruct the judicial process, understandable as his aggravation with plaintiff's lawsuit may have been. . . .

In sum, the record leaves no doubt that the President violated this Court's discovery Orders regarding disclosure of information deemed by this Court to be relevant to plaintiff's lawsuit. The Court therefore adjudges the President to be in civil contempt of court pursuant to Fed. R. Civ. P. 37(b)(2).

The Court now turns to the issue of appropriate sanctions. Several of the sanctions contemplated by Fed. R. Civ. P. 37(b)(2) are unavailable to this Court as the underlying lawsuit has been terminated. The Court cannot, for example, order that the matters upon which the President gave false statements be taken as established, nor can the Court render a default judgment against the President, both of which the Court would have considered had this Court's grant of summary judgment to defendants been reversed and remanded. Moreover, as the Court earlier noted, the determination of appropriate sanctions must take into account that this case was dismissed on summary judgment as lacking in merit—a decision that would not have changed even had the President been truthful with respect to his relationship with Ms. Lewinsky—and that plaintiff was made whole, having settled this case for an amount in excess of that prayed for in her complaint. Nevertheless, the President's contumacious conduct in this case, coming as it did from a member of the bar and the chief law enforcement officer of this Nation, was without justification and undermined the integrity of the judicial system. . . . Sanctions must be imposed, not only to redress the misconduct of the President in this case, but to deter others who, having observed the President's televised address to the Nation in which his defiance of this Court's discovery Orders was revealed, might themselves consider emulating the President of the United States by willfully violating discovery orders of this and other courts, thereby engaging in conduct that undermines the integrity of the judicial system. Accordingly, the Court imposes the following sanctions:

First, the President shall pay plaintiff any reasonable expenses, including attorney's fees, caused by his willful failure to obey this Court's discovery Orders. Plaintiff's former counsel are directed to submit to this Court a detailed statement of any expenses and attorney's fees incurred in connection with this matter. . . .

Second, the President shall reimburse this Court its expenses in traveling to Washington, D.C. at his request to preside over his tainted deposition. The Court therefore will direct that the President deposit into the registry of this Court the sum of $1,202.00, the total expenses incurred by this Court in traveling to Washington, D.C.

In addition, the Court will refer this matter to the Arkansas Supreme Court's Committee on Professional Conduct for review and any disciplinary action it deems appropriate for the President's possible violation of the Model Rules of Professional Conduct. Relevant to this case, Rule 8.4 of the Model Rules provides that it is professional misconduct for a lawyer to, among other things, "engage in conduct involving dishonesty, fraud, deceit or misrepresentation," or to "engage in conduct that is prejudicial to the administration of justice." . . .

Jones v. Clinton
57 F. Supp. 2d 719 (E.D. Ark. 1999)

. . . The Court now turns to the central issue at hand: determining whether the fees and expenses included in the statements of RCFP [Rader, Campbell, et al., the firm representing the plaintiff] and TRI [The Rutherford Institute, co-counsel] are within the scope of this Court's April 12th Order. There are two kinds of civil contempt sanctions a court can impose: coercive and compensatory. A coercive sanction, such as a fine, is designed to force the offending party to comply with a court's order, whereas a compensatory sanction is designed to compensate the nonoffending party for the damage they incur as a result of the offending party's contempt. The matter of the President's contempt involves compensatory rather than coercive sanctions as the Court is not seeking to coerce the President into compliance with any pending court order—the underlying action having been dismissed—and sanctions are being imposed, not only to deter others who might consider emulating the President's misconduct, but to compensate the plaintiff by requiring that the President pay her any reasonable fees and expenses caused by his willful failure to obey this Court's discovery Orders. Accordingly, this Court must determine the sum total of reasonable fees and expenses that plaintiff incurred as a result of the President's willful failure to obey this Court's discovery Orders.

. . . Notwithstanding the narrow and specific nature of the misconduct referenced in the April 12th Order, RCFP and TRI include in their respective statements claims for fees and expenses which clearly cannot be said to have been caused by the misconduct upon which this Court's April 12th Order is based. . . .

Both RCFP and TRI appear to justify the breadth of the fees and expenses included in their statements by arguing, at least in part, that sanctions may be imposed to punish the President's misconduct. RCFP argues, for example, that the President's willful failure to follow this Court's discovery Orders "made a mockery" of both his deposition and all of the proceedings and orders leading up to the deposition, and that he should therefore be made to pay for all of the work done and expenses incurred in the course of events leading up to his deposition and, in particular, all efforts to discover facts concerning Monica Lewinsky. Similarly, TRI asserts that the contemptuous conduct of the President was a "substantial factor" in each of the events for which costs and/or attorney's fees are being sought, and, as previously noted, cautions this Court against imposing *de minimis* consequences on conduct that undermined the integrity of the judicial system.

The Court rejects RCFP's and TRI's apparent understanding of the basis upon which compensatory sanctions may be imposed. Regardless of whether the President's failure to follow this Court's discovery Orders "made a mockery" of the proceedings or even was a "substantial factor" in the events for which fees and expenses are being sought, sanctions for compensatory contempt are not imposed to punish the contemnor, but must be based upon evidence of actual loss. Avoiding imposition of compensatory sanctions that may be characterized as *"de minimis"* simply is not a consideration in determining whether actual loss has been shown.

How does Rule 37(b)(2) treat the issue of imposing sanctions for the purpose of punishment?

The Court also rejects RCFP's argument that because this Court properly could have imposed the sanction of entering judgment against the President on the basis of his contempt of court, plaintiff's counsel would have been justified in seeking compensation for all of their labor and reimbursement for all of the expenses incurred following the President's false answer to Interrogatory No. 10, submitted on December 23, 1997. Specifically, RCFP argues that upon the service of the President's false response to plaintiff's interrogatories, he had a continuing obligation as an officer of the Court and a party subject to the Court's discovery orders to disclose the falsity of his response, and that judgment could have been entered against the President

What authority provides for the possibility of imposing judgment as a discovery sanction?

upon such disclosure. Such a judgment, argues RCFP, could have been entered against the President upon his disclosure of the falsity of his response and would have obviated the need for any further legal services to be rendered or expenses incurred by plaintiff's counsel. RCFP's argument, however, overlooks the probability that any damages awarded to plaintiff as a result of a judgment entered against the President for his civil contempt would not have been based on any fees and expenses incurred by her counsel as a result of the conduct described in this Court's April 12th Order, but would have been damages that plaintiff herself could prove at a subsequent hearing, *i.e.*, damages for alleged deprivation of her constitutional rights and privileges, damages for alleged conspiracy to deprive her of her equal protection and privileges of the laws, and damages for alleged intentional infliction of emotional distress (Counts I-III of plaintiff's amended complaint). Even in the unlikely event that the Court would forego such a hearing on damages, the amount of the judgment would be no greater than the specific amount stated in plaintiff's amended complaint, which is $525,000. Because the parties have already settled this case for $850,000, it is appropriate to limit fees and expenses to those incurred as a result of the misconduct upon which the Court's April 12th Order is based and not engage in speculation concerning what the Court might have ordered had its grant of summary judgment to defendants been reversed on appeal and the case remanded. . . .

[The court allowed fees and expenses to plaintiff's lawyers for the portion of the President's deposition that concerned Lewinsky (approximately 20 percent), for preparation for a deposition of Lewinsky (which ultimately did not occur—see Chapter 12), for a portion of the work on opposing summary judgment and appealing the case to the Eighth Circuit, for researching the law of contempt, and for preparing the fees request itself. The court denied fees for any work done prior to the date of the President's answers to interrogatories, for work related to a conference with the court just prior to the President's deposition, and for work undertaken to persuade the court to reconsider its decision to exclude the Lewinsky testimony.]

The Court takes no pleasure in imposing contempt sanctions against this Nation's President and, no doubt like many others, grows weary of this matter. Nevertheless, the Court has determined that the President deliberately violated this Court's discovery Orders, thereby undermining the integrity of the judicial system, and that sanctions must be imposed to redress the President's misconduct and to deter others who might consider emulating the President's misconduct. . . .

SUSPENSION OF LAW LICENSE

Agreed Order of Discipline
Circuit Court of Pulaski County, Arkansas—January 19, 2001

. . . In this agreed order, Mr. Clinton admits and acknowledges, and the court, therefore, finds:

A. That he knowingly gave evasive and misleading answers, in violation of

Judge Wright's discovery orders, concerning his relationship with Ms. Lewinsky, in an attempt to conceal from plaintiff Jones's lawyers the true facts about his improper relationship with Ms. Lewinsky, which had ended almost a year earlier.

B. That by knowingly giving evasive and misleading answers, in violation of Judge Wright's discovery orders, he engaged in conduct that is prejudicial to the administration of justice in that his discovery responses interfered with the conduct of the Jones case by causing the court and counsel for the parties to expend unnecessary time, effort, and resources, setting a poor example for other litigants, and causing the court to issue a 32-page order civilly sanctioning Mr. Clinton. Upon consideration of the proposed agreed order, the entire record before the court, the advice of counsel, and the Arkansas Model Rules of Professional Conduct, the court finds:

1. That Mr. Clinton's conduct, heretofore set forth, in the Jones case violated Model Rule 8.4(d), when he gave knowingly evasive and misleading discovery responses concerning his relationship with Ms. Lewinsky, in violation of Judge Wright's discovery orders.

Model Rule 8.4(d) states that it is professional misconduct for a lawyer to "engage in conduct that is prejudicial to the administration of justice."

WHEREFORE, it is the decision and order of this court that William Jefferson Clinton be, and hereby is, suspended for five years for his conduct in this matter, and the payment of fine in the amount of $25,000. The suspension shall become effective as of the date of Jan. 19, 2001.

NOTES AND COMMENTS

1. The bounds of Rule 37.   Writing in the *New York Times*, a noted trial lawyer argued that Judge Wright exceeded her authority under Rule 37 because sanctions were imposed after the case had been settled. Nathan Lewin, Not a Civil Action, N.Y. Times, April 4, 1999, at A-25. Lewin quoted Rule 37(b)(2), the provision relied on by Judge Wright: "If a party . . . fails to obey a discovery order . . . *the court in which the action is pending* may make such orders in regard to the failure as are just." (Emphasis added.) The case law as to when a judge's jurisdiction over discovery sanctions expires is not entirely clear. Some case law supports Lewin's argument: *Lowery v. Armstrong World Industries, Inc.,* 1991 WL 126022 (D.D.C. 1991); *Blake Associates v. Omni Spectra,* 118 F.R.D. 283 (D. Mass. 1988). Other cases have granted broader latitude to judges before whom cases had recently ended. *See, e.g., Perkins v. General Motors Corp.,* 965 F.2d 597 (8th Cir. 1992); *Carlucci v. Piper Aircraft Corp.,* 775 F.2d 1440 (5th Cir. 1985); *Jaen v. Coca-Cola Co.,* 157 F.R.D. 146 (D.P.R. 1994). How would you decide that issue? Consider the process policy interests behind either a narrow or expansive interpretation of a district court's authority.

2. Perjury versus lying.   Judge Wright sanctioned President Clinton for having lied during his deposition and in his answer to an interrogatory. The House of Representatives rejected the perjury claim brought against him based solely on those statements. Inconsistent? Not necessarily. *Perjury* is defined under federal law as false material statements made knowingly and under oath either in court or in an ancillary proceeding (such as a deposition).[8]

In his book on the impeachment, Judge Richard Posner treats the law of perjury as implicitly generating "an informal 'privilege' to lie under oath about immaterial matters in order to protect one's personal privacy."[9] Much of the legal debate during President Clinton's impeachment centered on the question of whether his denials of an affair with Lewinsky were material (i.e., directly related to the merits) in the *Jones* case. In Judge Posner's view, Clinton's "lies were material to Paula Jones's case, though only just."[10] Other commentators argued the opposite.[11]

However one comes out on this question, materiality is not required as a prerequisite for contempt sanctions. Thus, Judge Wright did not need to address the issue in her ruling.

Exercise 12—Rule 37 Sanctions

Test your understanding of the operations of Rule 37 with these questions:

(A) To lead to sanctions under Rule 37(b)(2), the conduct must violate an order issued pursuant to one of which three parts of the discovery rules? Which was at issue in *Jones v. Clinton*?

(B) Be sure that you can state the reason why Judge Wright did not rely on Rule 37(c) concerning "failure to disclose; false or misleading disclosure; failure to admit."

(C) Could a judge in the District of Columbia, where the President's deposition was taken, have imposed sanctions under Rule 37(b)(1)? Why not?

(D) In retrospect, and ignoring the real-world political consequences, would the President have been better off had he not appeared at all for his deposition? *See* Rule 37(d).

3. Varieties of contempt. Judge Wright framed the sanction as one for contempt, imposed pursuant to Rule 37(b)(2)(D). This raises the question of which of the two categories of contempt apply: civil or criminal. Under the latter, the defendant is entitled to the procedural protections of a prosecution, including a jury trial and a presumption of innocence unless guilt is proven beyond a reasonable doubt.

---

8. Two federal statutes are relevant to the question of whether President Clinton committed perjury. The first covers out-of-court statements under oath, including in a deposition or in a written statement under penalty of perjury: the individual who "willfully and contrary to such oath states or subscribes any material matter which he does not believe to be true . . . is guilty of perjury and shall, except as otherwise expressly provided by law, be fined under this title or imprisoned not more than five years, or both." 18 U.S.C. §1621. The second statute covers statements made in litigation "proceedings": "Whoever under oath . . . in any proceeding before or ancillary to any court or grand jury of the United States knowingly makes any false material declaration . . . shall be fined under this title or imprisoned not more than five years, or both." 18 U.S.C. §1623.

9. Richard A. Posner, An Affair of State: The Investigation, Impeachment and Trial of President Clinton 45 (1999).

10. *Id.* at 49.

11. *See, e.g.,* Ronald Dworkin, Philosophy and Monica Lewinsky, New York Review of Books, March 9, 2000; Charles W. Collier and Christopher Slobogin, Terms of Endearment and Articles of Impeachment, 51 Fla. L. Rev. 615 (1999); Alan Heinrich, Note: Clinton's Little White Lies: The Materiality Requirement for Perjury in Civil Discovery, 32 Loy. L.A. L. Rev. 1303 (1999).

One of the arguments in Lewin's op-ed was that, because Rule 37 was inapplicable, Judge Wright's only option was to refer the case for prosecution as criminal contempt, an unlikely event in view of the widely held belief that a sitting President is not subject to criminal prosecution.

What Judge Wright describes as *coercive sanctions*—that is, the power to penalize or imprison a person during the course of a case to coerce them into testifying or into compliance with some other court order—falls clearly within civil contempt. By definition, it involves an ongoing lawsuit. Punishment in the form of imprisonment or a fine (payable to the court), imposed for past contumacious acts, is clearly criminal in nature, and could not be imposed without the heightened protections attendant to criminal cases. Judge Wright imposes neither of those forms of contempt, but instead imposed what she described as a second form of civil contempt, which is compensatory rather than coercive. Her order stresses that the monies that the President is ordered to pay are not fines, but compensation for the expenses of the other party and of the court. "[S]anctions for compensatory contempt are not imposed to punish the contemnor, but must be based upon evidence of actual loss." Case law supports Judge Wright's description of compensatory remedies as primarily civil. *See Hicks v. Feiock,* 485 U.S. 624, 631-634 (1988). *But see Gompers v. Buck's Stove and Range Co.,* 221 U.S. 418, 451-452 (1911) (settlement of case terminated right to pursue compensatory contempt).

Exercise 13—Comparing Rule 37 Sanctions with Rule 11 Sanctions

Analyze the possible sanctions in these situations that occurred or could have occurred during *Jones v. Clinton:*

(A) President Clinton made false statements in his deposition testimony. Had the same misrepresentations been contained in an affidavit that he submitted in support of a motion (e.g., for summary judgment), what would the potential sanctions have been?

(B) Assume that Judge Wright had agreed with President Clinton that Jones should be estopped from obtaining discovery into his private life because of the representations made by Jones's lawyers when she opposed his first motion to delay the case; that is, the representations that the litigation of this case would impose minimal intrusions upon the office of the President. (See President Clinton's Opposition to Plaintiff's Motion to Compel in Chapter 7.) Could the President then have obtained sanctions against Jones for having sought the discovery for improper purposes? *Compare* Rule 26(g) to Rule 11(b)(1).

(C) As stated in the Introduction to this chapter, the other charge for which President Clinton was tried in the Senate was obstruction of justice.[12] This article of impeachment accused the President of, among other things, seeking to induce false testimony by two potential witnesses in the *Jones* case: Lewinsky

---

12. Two federal statutes apply: 18 U.S.C. §1512 penalizes anyone who "corruptly persuades another person, or attempts to do so, or engages in misleading conduct toward another person, with intent to influence, delay, or prevent the testimony of any person in an official proceeding." 18 U.S.C. §1503 covers anyone who "corruptly . . . endeavors to influence, obstruct, or impede, the due administration of justice."

and Betty Currie, the President's secretary.[13] Judge Wright did not address these accusations of misconduct in her sanctions order. Could she have? Under what authority could a party be punished if such accusations were true?

4. Inherent powers.   Judge Wright alludes briefly in her opinion to the concept of "inherent powers" as providing an alternative basis for the sanctions that she imposes, but she elects to rely solely on Rule 37. *Inherent powers* is a common law doctrine that predates the FRCP; it accords broad authority to judges to impose sanctions for misconduct by counsel or litigants. *Chambers v. NASCO, Inc.*, 501 U.S. 32 (1991). Courts have invoked their "inherent powers" when misconduct became apparent only after the case had ended. *Id.* at 56; *Carlucci v. Piper Aircraft Corp.*, 775 F.2d 1440, 1447 (11th Cir. 1985).

5. When counsel learns that a client lied.   At the close of President Clinton's testimony in the *Jones* deposition, Robert Bennett, his attorney, had the opportunity to ask him additional questions for the record. The following exchange occurred:

Q. Mr. President, . . . you recall earlier today that Mr. Fisher asked you several questions about Miss Lewinsky?

A. Yes, sir, I do.

Q. And do you recall there was a discussion about an affidavit of Miss Lewinsky generally?

A. Yes, sir, I remember that.

Q. I'm going to read you certain portions of Miss Lewinsky's affidavit, and ask you about them. . . . In paragraph eight of her affidavit, she says this, "I have never had a sexual relationship with the President, he did not propose that we have a sexual relationship, he did not offer me employment or other benefits in exchange for a sexual relationship, he did not deny me employment or other benefits for rejecting a sexual relationship." Is this a true and accurate statement as far as you know it?

A. That is absolutely true. . . .

On September 30, 1998, nearly nine months after the deposition, Bennett sent Judge Wright the following letter:

> As you are aware, [the Lewinsky] affidavit was made part of the record of President Clinton's deposition on January 17, 1998. It has recently been made public in the Starr Report that Ms. Lewinsky testified before a federal grand jury in August 1998 that portions of her affidavit were misleading and not true. Therefore, pursuant to our professional responsibility, we wanted to advise you that the Court should not rely on Ms. Lewinsky's affidavit or remarks of counsel characterizing that affidavit.

Would Bennett have been open to sanctions had he not written the letter? Under what authority?

---

13. For an argument that President Clinton was guilty of obstruction of justice, *see* Posner, *supra* note 9 at 36-58. For an argument that he was not, *see* Jeffrey Rosen, Material Girl, The New Republic, Feb. 8, 1999, at 20ff.

CHAPTER NINE

Joinder and Intervention

INTRODUCTION

Joinder of additional parties can occur at various times during the litigation of a case. In *Jones v. Clinton*, there was one joinder at the outset: Plaintiff's decision to sue two defendants, President Clinton and Arkansas State Trooper Ferguson. From that point forward, the case proceeded with essentially no change in parties—but that was not for lack of effort. A variety of individuals sought to intervene during the course of the lawsuit. A person asserting that he should be heard because he was "one of tens of millions of Americans who voted for President Clinton," the Office of Independent Counsel Kenneth Starr, individuals who received notices of deposition, and a coalition of network broadcast companies and other large news organizations all sought to intervene.

In this chapter, we will first cover the fundamentals of joinder by examining Ferguson's status as co-defendant, as well as hypothetical joinder issues that could have arisen in *Jones v. Clinton*. We will use the first section as a detailed Exercise 14: Variations on Joinder. Moving past the fundamentals, we will then consider an issue that did arise in the case when the news media coalition sought intervention to challenge the judge's order barring public access to all discovery documents. Analysis of whether they should have been permitted to intervene will constitute the second section, Limited Purpose Intervention—A Case Study.

JOINDER

Issues related to the joinder of parties range from the simple to the complex, as the following exercise demonstrates. The interrelationship with subject matter jurisdiction can be decisive.

Exercise 14—Variations on Joinder

Consider each of the following possible joinder issues, based on *Jones v. Clinton* and hypothetical variations on those facts. *If you have already studied subject matter jurisdiction, assume that in this case it is based on diversity of citizenship.* The Complaint includes the same sex discrimination claims as in the real suit, but they are grounded in state, rather than federal, antidiscrimination and constitutional law.

Rule 20 Joinder

(A) Identify the allegations in the Complaint that provide a basis for the joinder of Ferguson under Rule 20. What other concerns about joinder would arise? Would his joinder nonetheless be proper?

(B) Imagine that another woman, Sally Smith, who worked with Jones and continues as an Arkansas state employee, also has alleged that then-Governor Clinton propositioned her. She asserts that the incident occurred approximately one year after the Jones incident, in the Governor's office. She describes the proposition as direct but not offensive. She believes that she did not receive a promotion later that year because she had refused his advances. She received the promotion shortly after Clinton became President. She estimates that she lost approximately $10,000 in pay and benefits from not having received it earlier.

As Jones's lawyer, you are considering whether to add Smith as a second plaintiff when you draft the complaint. Can you join her?

(C) In addition to Smith, imagine that another woman comes forward when you are in the midst of the 1997 discovery: Monica Lee. Lee worked as a White House intern in 1996, and tells you that President Clinton promised her a well-paying job as assistant ambassador to Afghanistan if she would have sex with him. When she refused, she was fired. She has been unable to work since then and has had expensive therapy to cope with the incident; she says that her financial loss exceeds $75,000. She lives in Washington.

As Jones's lawyer, you are considering whether to file a motion to amend the complaint to add Lee as a plaintiff. What should you do? If you seek to join Lee, will the court permit it?

Rule 19 (Necessary Parties) and Rule 14 (Impleader)

For this section of the exercise, assume that you are President Clinton's lawyer and that he is the sole defendant. You are in the middle of the 1997 discovery.

(A) Can President Clinton join State Trooper Ferguson as a necessary party?

(B) You want to sue the *American Spectator* magazine, which published the article that triggered the lawsuit (see Introduction to Chapter 1), for the defamation of your client. You also believe that the magazine defamed Paula Jones. The *American Spectator* is incorporated in California, where it has its sole offices. What mechanisms will you consider to bring the magazine into the lawsuit? Will they succeed?

Rule 24 (Intervention)

(A) Jones's lawyer decided not to join Sally Smith as a plaintiff. Can Smith intervene?

(B) Jones's lawyer decided not to attempt to add Monica Lee as a plaintiff. Can Lee intervene?

Rule 23 (Class Actions)

Sally Smith and Monica Lee tell you that there are dozens of women with whom Clinton has had affairs. Some unknown number of them are or were government employees. Can you litigate *Jones v. Clinton* as a class action?

INTERVENTION

As you can see from working through the preceding examples, one fundamental precept behind the FRCP and joinder is that plaintiffs are given the greatest power to sculpt the contours of a lawsuit. Defendants have less power, and nonparties have the most difficulty in changing the cast of characters selected by the plaintiff.

All Rule 24 motions to intervene require a trade-off between the rights of the parties to control the structure and dynamics of the lawsuit and the rights of others to have a say when they have important rights or interests riding on the outcome of the case. Without intervention, the affected nonparties cannot attempt to influence a decision that could carry major consequences for them. Rule 24 provides for either intervention as of right or permissive intervention depending on the weight of the interest being threatened and the weakness with which existing parties can be expected to protect it.

Limited Purpose Intervention—A Case Study

Motions to intervene "for a limited purpose" take the tension over control of the lawsuit that is intrinsic to the concept of intervention to a new level. "Intervention for a limited purpose" has developed in situations in which a nonparty seeks to join a lawsuit because of the acute impact of a particular ruling or aspect of the case, often related to discovery, but not because the intervenor is seeking relief on the same claim or even would be affected by an outcome based on the merits of claims or defenses. An increasingly common example—and the one from *Jones v. Clinton* on which we will focus—arises when media organizations seek to challenge a judicial ruling that restricts access to what would otherwise be publicly accessible litigation documents.[1]

Thus, the motion we will examine was not on behalf of persons seeking to join *Jones v. Clinton* as full additional plaintiffs or defendants for the duration of the case, as Rule 24 appears to envision intervenors would do. Rather, the proposed intervenors asked to be recognized as a party for a limited purpose only—to challenge particular rulings on motions, or procedures adopted by Judge Wright for conducting

---

1. Another example of a high-stakes civil case in which media organizations sought limited purpose intervention was *Anderson v. Cryovac,* the case that formed the basis for Jonathan Harr's bestseller, A Civil Action (1995). *See Anderson v. Cryovac,* 805 F.2d (1st Cir. 1986).

discovery, or a stringent (in theory, if not in fact) confidentiality order. Both sides in *Jones v. Clinton* at least represented that they wanted the confidentiality order enforced; the media organizations sought to argue, on behalf of themselves and the public, a right to open, above-the-board access to the materials in question, without having to rely on leaks or the spin generated by opposing partisan camps.

The body of law underlying a motion for limited intervention arises from the First Amendment guarantees of freedom of speech and press. In *Richmond Newspapers, Inc. v. Commonwealth of Virginia*, 448 U.S. 555 (1980), the Supreme Court held that absent extraordinary circumstances, a criminal trial had to be open to the press. Following *Richmond Newspapers*, it became common for courts to allow "limited purpose intervention" by media organizations seeking access to proceedings or documents in criminal cases. The Federal Rules of Civil Procedure, and Rule 24 specifically, became implicated when media organizations sought to intervene in highly publicized civil lawsuits such as *Jones v. Clinton*.

Neither Rule 24 nor its Advisory Committee Notes say anything about limited purpose intervention. Arguably that silence is preclusive. However, Rule 24(b) also commits decisions on permissive intervention to the trial judge's discretion. How broadly does that discretion extend? As you read the following materials, consider the process policy concerns that underlie Rule 24 and whether they should be extended to accommodate this new form of intervention. Or should courts simply acknowledge that limited purpose intervention is a new, judge-made procedural doctrine? Would that undermine the FRCP?

A leading case is *Pansy v. Borough of Stroudsburg*, 23 F.3d 772, 778-779 (3d Cir. 1994), in which local newspapers had sought intervention in a suit brought against the borough by its former police chief, who claimed that his civil rights had been violated when he was fired for allegedly mishandling parking meter money. The newspapers sought to intervene solely to challenge a confidentiality order that had sealed the terms of the settlement reached between the parties. The Third Circuit ruled as follows:

> The district court . . . found that the Newspapers did not demonstrate that their interest in the case had anything in common with a question of law or fact in the main action and therefore did not meet the requirements of Fed. R. Civ. P. 24(b)(2).
>
> The district court applied incorrect legal standards in denying the Newspapers' Motion for Intervention. As to the district court's finding that the Newspapers have not shown that their claim has anything in common with a question of law or fact in the case, the district court ruled contrary to a forming consensus in the federal courts. We agree with other courts that have held that the procedural device of permissive intervention is appropriately used to enable a litigant who was not an original party to an action to challenge protective or confidentiality orders entered in that action. [citation omitted] In *Beckman Indus., Inc. v. International Ins. Co.*, 966 F.2d 470 (9th Cir.), *cert. denied*, 506 U.S. 868 (1992), the Ninth Circuit stated:
>
> "[S]pecificity, e.g., that the [intervenors'] claim involves . . . the same legal theory [that was raised in the main action], is not required when intervenors are not becoming parties to the litigation. There is no reason to require such a strong nexus of fact or law when a party seeks to intervene only for the purpose of modifying a protective order." 966 F.2d at 474.
>
> The reasoning in *Beckman* is persuasive, and we adopt it. We therefore reject

the district court's conclusion that the Newspapers have not shown their claim has anything in common with a question of law or fact in the case, and therefore cannot intervene. By virtue of the fact that the Newspapers challenge the validity of the Order of Confidentiality entered in the main action, they meet the requirement of Fed. R. Civ. P. 24(b)(2) that their claim must have "a question of law or fact in common" with the main action.

In *Jones v. Clinton,* a coalition of media groups sought to invoke what the Third Circuit had called the "forming consensus in the federal courts" to intervene. The primary target of their proposed intervention was the Confidentiality Order issued by Judge Wright on October 27, 1997, as the discovery phase was beginning. Discovery documents are not automatically filed with the court,[2] but absent a court order to the contrary, there is no barrier to their dissemination by the parties or others.[3] Judge Wright's Confidentiality Order stated:

Confidentiality Order on Consent of All Parties

Whereas, the Court has determined and counsel for all of the parties agree that this action is a matter in which there has been and will continue to be intense media interest and coverage due to the identity of the parties and the subject matter of this action; and

Whereas, the Court has determined and counsel for all parties agree that the interests of all parties and the judicial system in obtaining a fair and impartial jury and a fair trial for all parties will be prejudiced if the existing pre-trial publicity concerning discovery in this matter were permitted to continue; and

Whereas, the Court has determined and counsel for all parties agree that the interest in an impartial jury and a fair trial greatly outweigh any public interest in access to pre-trial information and proceedings in this matter; and

Whereas, the Court has determined and counsel for all parties agree that no reasonable alternative exists to protect the above-referenced interests;

IT IS HEREBY ORDERED, AND COUNSEL FOR ALL PARTIES CONSENT to the entry of the following confidentiality order to apply to the parties, counsel for the parties, and agents (including spokespersons) for the parties, prohibiting disclosure directly or indirectly of:

1. The time, place, or date on which any deposition is to be taken or the identity of any witness to be deposed; and

2. The content of any deposition, including but not limited to the questions asked, the answers given, whether any objections were made, the substance of any objections, the length of the deposition, whether the deposition went well or poorly, and whether new information was disclosed or old information confirmed; and

3. The content of any written discovery (interrogatories, document requests

---

2. Fed. R. Civ. P. 5(d).

3. For extensive analysis of barring access by nonparties as an issue of discovery law, *see* Arthur R. Miller, Confidentiality, Protective Orders, and Public Access to the Courts, 105 Harv. L. Rev. 427 (1991), and Richard L. Marcus, The Discovery Confidentiality Controversy, 1991 U. Ill. L. Rev. 457.

and requests for admission) sought from any party or third party, the identity of persons or entities from which information is sought, and the content of any responses thereto, including but not limited to the information sought, the responses given, documents produced, whether any objections were made, the substance of any objections, whether the information was helpful or not, and whether any new information was disclosed or old information confirmed.

IT IS HEREBY ORDERED, AND COUNSEL FOR ALL PARTIES CONSENT that all materials, including motions and briefs, filed with the Court concerning discovery matters shall be filed under seal and the parties, counsel for the parties, and agents (including spokespersons) for the parties will not disclose the fact that any such filing has been made or any information concerning the content of such filings, responses thereto or resolution thereof;

IT IS HEREBY FURTHER ORDERED, AND COUNSEL FOR ALL PARTIES CONSENT that counsel for the parties will advise all third parties subject to subpoena, or who otherwise provide information in this case (including documents), of this Confidentiality Order.

The sensational byproduct of this case—the allegation that President Clinton had been sexually involved with Monica Lewinsky during his presidency—surfaced in the mass media in late January 1998. Shortly afterward, a group of media organizations sought limited purpose intervention. The group included the *New York Times*, the Associated Press, *USA Today*, Time, Inc., the Cable News Network, ABC, and NBC. The group filed the following motion:

MOTION FOR LEAVE TO INTERVENE, MOTION TO MODIFY AND/OR RESCIND CONFIDENTIALITY ORDER, AND MOTION FOR ACCESS TO COURT RECORDS AND DISCOVERY

[The above-named media groups] move for leave to intervene in this proceeding for the sole and limited purpose of challenging this Court's Confidentiality Order dated October 27, 1997 ("Confidentiality Order"). Movants further request that this Court rescind or modify the Confidentiality Order and that it lift the restrictions which impede Movants' rights to obtain information concerning the discovery in this cause.

In support of this Motion, Movants state:

1. [Paragraph 1 contains a short description of each of the media organizations.]

2. As members of the news media, each Movant has a direct and substantial interest in promoting and preserving its rights and the rights of the public to be informed about and report on the proceedings in this civil case. Such rights have not been and will not be adequately represented by existing parties to this cause. . . .

4. On October 27, 1997, this Court entered its blanket Confidentiality Order which: (i) seals discovery matters and pleadings filed with the Court, (ii) restricts the dissemination of unfiled discovery, and (iii) prohibits the parties and their counsel from commenting regarding such matters.

---

5. As written, the Confidentiality Order restrains discussion of and restricts access to ALL discovery in this case. It effects a wholesale, blanket restriction on the litigants and their counsel and prohibits them from disclosing not only the substance of discovery, but even the most basic information about discovery, such as who is to be deposed, when, and why. The Order fails to include any specific findings, but is premised solely upon generally articulated concerns that pretrial publicity concerning discovery would prejudice the parties' fair trial rights and that such potential prejudice outweighs the public interest in access to pre-trial discovery proceedings. The Order was entered by this Court without any notice or opportunity to be heard by Movants or other interested members of the media or public.

6. Because the Confidentiality Order requires the sealing of discovery matters filed with the Court, the Order contravenes both the common law and constitutional presumption that court records and proceedings are public property. Closure of judicial records is appropriate only where a compelling governmental interest exists, only where it is likely to be effective in preserving against the perceived harm, and only after considering less restrictive alternatives.

7. Because the Confidentiality Order prohibits the parties from disseminating any discovery materials, the Order is unfounded given that "good cause" does not exist for any protective order restricting disclosure of discovery materials. There has been no specific demonstration that disclosure will cause a clearly defined and serious injury to the fair trial rights of the parties.

8. Because the Confidentiality Order restricts the litigants from speaking about discovery in this case, the Order operates as a gag on speech and interferes with the public's right to obtain information. Such restraints can only be justified in cases of serious and imminent harm to the administration of justice. Further, such restraints cannot be imposed if they will not be effective in preserving the compelling interest at stake.

9. Regardless of the grounds and justification for the Confidentiality Order at the time it was entered, the public interest in discovery proceedings has been enhanced significantly by recent allegations of possible perjury, subornation of perjury, and obstruction of justice at the highest levels of the Executive Branch of the federal government. The public has a legitimate right and compelling interest in being informed about such serious matters. This right substantially outweighs any cause which previously existed for the secrecy of pre-trial discovery matters. Indeed, this interest is all the more compelling in light of the vast array of speculation about discovery materials—speculation which entirely undercuts the very purpose of the Confidentiality Order.

10. The Confidentiality Order has not been effective in protecting against pre-trial publicity. Because of the nature of the claims and the parties, and more significantly because of recent revelations independent of this litigation, pre-trial publicity continues. Accordingly, the Confidentiality Order is not presently likely to advance the interests initially articulated by the Court as grounds for its entry. To the contrary, instead of reducing the possibility of prejudice, the Order is potentially promoting prejudice because by limiting access to the actual facts concerning pre-trial proceedings herein, the Order, without any intention to do so, promotes misinformation, speculation, innuendo, and rumor. . . .

> WHEREFORE, Movants respectfully pray that this Court (a) grant them leave to intervene in this proceeding for the sole and limited purpose of challenging the Confidentiality Order; (b) rescind the Confidentiality Order; and (c) alternatively, release all restrictions on the disclosure and discussion of the discovery materials previously sealed under the Order or determine those materials, which, in light of the peculiar sensitivity overcome the presumption of openness—a presumption particularly apt in a case of such keen public interest.

President Clinton's Opposition focused on the law of public access to discovery documents in civil cases, rather than the criteria for intervention. His primary argument rested on *Seattle Times Co. v. Rhinehart*, 467 U.S. 20 (1984), in which the Supreme Court held that there is no public right of access to discovery documents and that a confidentiality order entered pursuant to Rule 26(c), as Judge Wright's order was, could properly bar disclosure if it was based on "good cause."

Judge Wright agreed with the President and denied the media organizations' motion to intervene or alter the confidentiality order. Judge Wright ruled that good cause existed for the order in two respects: first, that unrestricted access would impair the ability to select a fair and impartial jury should the case go to trial, and second, that the parties had individual interests in personal privacy that merited protection:

Order of March 9, 1998

Rule 26(c) . . . protects privacy interests and specifically includes among its express purposes the protection of a party or person from embarrassment. If ever there was a case necessitating such protection, the case of *Jones v. Clinton* is it. Much of the discovery in this case of alleged sexual harassment has delved deeply into the personal lives of individuals and elicited information that, regardless of its truth or falsity, could prove damaging to reputation and privacy. Many of the media have shown no restraint in their willingness to place such personal information in the public domain despite the pain it may cause. Driven by profit and intense competition, gossip, speculation, and innuendo have replaced legitimate sources and attribution as the tools of the trade for many of these media representatives.

Postscript: The media organizations appealed Judge Wright's decision. During the time when the appeal was pending, Judge Wright granted President Clinton's Motion for Summary Judgment, and dismissed the case. (See Chapter 10.) However, the original confidentiality order remained in effect. The Court of Appeals for the Eighth Circuit remanded this part of the case, directing Judge Wright to reconsider whether the order continued to be justified after the summary judgment decision. *Jones v. Clinton*, 138 F.3d 758 (8th Cir. 1998).

After extensive rebriefing and argument, Judge Wright ruled that she would oversee the gradual unsealing both of documents in the record and of discovery documents acquired by the parties. She indicated that documents that identified the various Jane Does would either remain under seal or be redacted to preserve their anonymity. Lastly, she granted the limited purpose intervention motions filed by several Jane Does, in order that they could have notice and an opportunity to be heard regarding the release of specific documents. (The Jane Does' motions to intervene, as well as the underlying documents, remain under seal.)

NOTES AND COMMENTS

1. Is limited purpose intervention a contradiction in terms?   Reread the text of Rule 24, especially 24(b)(2). In a motion for limited purpose intervention, is there a "claim" that shares a question of law or fact in common with the main action? Read Rules 7(a), 8(a), and 12(b). Together, do they furnish a definition of "claim"? What would it be? Is that too narrow a reading of the meaning of "claim" in Rule 24? Should the nature of the lawsuit or of the public's interest in it be considered a factor? What are the process policy concerns behind either a narrow or a broad definition of "claim"?

2. Slippery slope or reform?   Rule 24(a), with its historical origins in cases involving property rights, provides guidelines for determination of intervention as of right. Rule 24(b)(2) provides a residual catch-all for situations in which there is a question of law or fact in common. Traditionally, courts have been concerned with the question of at what point an intervenor's infringement on plaintiff's right to control the litigation becomes too great. Note that in this extremely sensitive case, both plaintiff and defendant stated that they wanted the confidentiality order; non-parties were seeking to rescind it.

An alternative perspective would be that modern litigation has extended so far beyond the traditional bounds of "parties" and "claims" that we should rethink some of those fundamental concepts. Perhaps a substantial amount of litigation today is not as crisply bipolar as it was when the FRCP were originally written. What is your perspective?

3. Alternative options.   Are the media organizations left without any mechanism for making their views known and seeking access to the documents? The only role available other than that of party would be to participate as an amicus curiae, or friend of the court. What would be the differences between filing an amicus brief and participation as an intervenor, particularly if the organization did not desire or intend to seek monetary or equitable relief? In general, only parties may file motions, such as the motion seeking reconsideration of the confidentiality order. Also, an amicus lacks the right to appeal a ruling. *See* 7C Wright, Miller, and Kane, Federal Practice and Procedure: Civil, 2d. §1923. The denial of a motion to intervene, however, does provide an opportunity to appeal, as occurred in *Jones v. Clinton.* Thus, especially for media organizations likely to seek access to litigation documents repeatedly in high-visibility cases, there is little incentive to forego the motion to intervene.

CHAPTER TEN

Summary Judgment

INTRODUCTION

On February 17, 1998, after the end of discovery, President Clinton filed a motion for summary judgment. This chapter includes an introductory portion of his memorandum of law in support of that motion and then a substantial excerpt from the part addressing the quid pro quo sexual harassment claim. It is followed by the corresponding portion of the plaintiff's memorandum in opposition to summary judgment. Those documents are followed by Judge Wright's decision as to all claims.

As you read the briefs and then the decision, consider how the testing of the quid pro quo claim has proceeded since the beginning of the case. Specifically, compare the arguments by counsel and the judge's resolution of the Rule 12(c) motion with the arguments and ruling on summary judgment. How do they differ? Can you summarize why the judge refused to dismiss the same claim earlier that she dismisses now?

MEMORANDUM IN SUPPORT OF PRESIDENT CLINTON'S MOTION FOR SUMMARY JUDGMENT

President Clinton, through undersigned counsel, hereby moves the Court to enter summary judgment in his favor on all three counts of plaintiff's First Amended Complaint. Summary judgment is properly granted when there is no issue as to material fact and the moving party is entitled to judgment as a matter of law. Fed. R. Civ. P. 56(c); *Celotex Corp. v. Catrett,* 477 U.S. 317, 322-323 (1986). In particular, summary judgment is appropriate when, as here, plaintiff has failed to adduce evidence showing the existence of essential elements of her claims. . . .

President Clinton vehemently denies that the alleged incident at the Excelsior Hotel occurred, or that he acted in any way improperly to-

Even if there are genuine factual disputes about all but one of the elements in a plaintiff's claim, defendant can still win summary judgment.

ward plaintiff. Plaintiff no doubt will contend that this factual dispute precludes summary judgment. However, this factual dispute does not preclude summary judgment because, even as recounted by plaintiff, there has been a failure of proof as to essential elements of plaintiff's claims.

Plaintiff's purported "other acts" evidence concerning other women also is irrelevant to resolution of this Motion, because plaintiff cannot establish that she herself suffered a cognizable injury pursuant to a claim for sexual harassment or outrage. "[A] complete failure of proof concerning an essential element of the nonmoving party's case necessarily renders all other facts immaterial." *Celotex,* 477 U.S. at 323. Plaintiff spent nearly all of her discovery efforts attempting to substantiate rumors that President Clinton made sexual advances to other women—but failed to establish that she personally has a cause of action. Thus, even if plaintiff had evidence with respect to other women that could be said to establish a "pattern and practice" of sexual harassment—which we vigorously contend she does not—such evidence is not material to this summary judgment motion, which turns on plaintiff's failure to prove that she experienced quid pro quo or hostile environment harassment, or that she suffered severe emotional distress. . . .

A.   THE UNDISPUTED FACTS SHOW THAT PLAINTIFF WAS NOT SUBJECTED TO QUID PRO QUO HARASSMENT

As you read, compare the information secured during discovery with the discovery plan that you drafted for the exercise in Chapter 6.

To establish a prima facie case of quid pro quo sexual harassment, plaintiff must put forth evidence to prove, inter alia, that she suffered a tangible detriment as a result of refusing her employer's advances. . . . [T]his requires "a causal link" between the refusal and a resulting tangible job detriment. In particular, a plaintiff's allegation that the defendant made an implied threat of job retaliation does not support a claim for quid pro quo harassment, without evidence that an actual job detriment resulted. Thus, plaintiff must establish (1) that she suffered a tangible job detriment and (2) that the detriment was the result of her refusal to submit to Governor Clinton's alleged unwelcome advances.

Plaintiff's own testimony, the testimony of her three supervisors at the Arkansas Industrial Development Commission ("AIDC") and her state employment records all establish beyond dispute that plaintiff did not experience any tangible job detriment during her employment at AIDC. The undisputed evidence further establishes that those in a position to make decisions about plaintiff's working conditions were unaware of the alleged incident at the Excelsior Hotel, and that neither Governor Clinton nor anyone on his behalf ever asked them to take any job action whatsoever with respect to plaintiff, adverse or otherwise. Accordingly, there was no "tangible job detriment" that "resulted" from plaintiff's purported rejection of Governor Clinton's alleged sexual advances. Hence, there was no quid pro quo harassment.

1.   The Evidence

a.   Plaintiff's Employment Records

Notwithstanding that the plaintiff brought a claim against the President of the United States based on allegations of employment discrimination, Ms. Jones admitted she did not review her own employment records at AIDC prior to filing suit in 1994, and still had not done so at the time of her deposition on November 12, 1997. (Jones Tr. at 33, 76). These records negate any claim of a tangible job detriment, for they show that:

> Beginning here, note the meticulous references to deposition transcripts, affidavits, interrogatories, and other documents— that is, the record that has been compiled in the course of discovery.

- Two months after the alleged incident at the Excelsior Hotel, Ms. Jones's job was reclassified to a higher grade and pay, which increased her annual salary. (Affidavit of Clydine Pennington, Ex. B, ¶6; Arkansas Human Resource Management System Payroll Data Form for P.R. Jones, Ex. B-7).
- On August 28, 1991, nearly four months after the alleged incident, plaintiff's supervisor Clydine Pennington gave her a satisfactory job review. (Ex. B-4).
- In March 1992, on plaintiff's one-year anniversary with AIDC, she received another satisfactory evaluation from Ms. Pennington and Cherry Duckett, Deputy Director of AIDC. (Ex. B-5). This entitled plaintiff to a merit raise, as reflected in Ms. Jones's Payroll Data Form. (Ex. B-7).
- More than one year after the alleged incident, Ms. Jones took maternity leave. Upon her return in September 1992, there was no diminution in Ms. Jones's salary, no change of her job classification, and no change in her job assignment. (See Payroll Data Form, Ex. B-7).
- In an evaluation covering the period of March 1992 until Ms. Jones's voluntary departure from AIDC nearly a year later, Ms. Pennington and another supervisor again gave Ms. Jones a satisfactory job review. (Ex. B-6). Ms. Jones reviewed and signed this evaluation on February 16, 1993. (Id. at 2). Had she remained at the agency one month longer, this satisfactory review would have entitled her to another merit increase. (Pennington Aff. ¶8).
- The records reflect that Ms. Jones was never formally disciplined or reprimanded, and that she separated from AIDC voluntarily in February 1993, 21 months after the alleged incident. (Exs. B-1 to B-13).

b.   Ms. Pennington's Testimony

Clydine Pennington, who was responsible for personnel matters at AIDC, hired Paula Corbin Jones and was the individual primarily responsible for reviewing her work. Her affidavit and testimony establish beyond dispute that Ms. Jones suffered no adverse job actions at AIDC, and certainly none caused by Governor Clinton.

- During Ms. Jones's nearly two-year tenure at AIDC, she received every merit and cost-of-living increase for which she was eligible. (Pennington Aff. ¶6; Deposition of Clydine Pennington ("Pennington Tr."), Ex. C, at 20-26).

- Ms. Pennington was responsible for upgrading Ms. Jones's job from Document Examiner (Grade 9) to Secretary I (Grade 11) on July 1, 1991—two months after the alleged incident. (Pennington Aff. ¶6; Pennington Tr. at 22-23).
- When Ms. Jones returned from maternity leave on September 9, 1992, she was reinstated in an equivalent position with the same rate of pay and benefits that she had before she left. (Pennington Aff. ¶16).
- Only one aspect of Ms. Jones's duties was modified slightly upon her return from maternity leave; rather than being responsible for data entry of AIDC purchase orders and driving records, she was assigned data entry responsibilities for employment applications. (Pennington Aff. ¶17).
- Ms. Jones departed AIDC voluntarily; she was not terminated. In late 1992 or early 1993, Ms. Jones informed Ms. Pennington that she intended to leave AIDC because she was moving to California due to her husband's transfer to another position with Northwest Airlines. (Pennington Aff. ¶18; Pennington Tr. at 60-61).
- At no time prior to Ms. Jones's public statements in 1994 did Ms. Pennington learn of plaintiff's allegations regarding Governor Clinton. Indeed, Ms. Jones informed Ms. Pennington that she had met the Governor at the AIDC conference on May 8, 1991, was excited about having done so, and expressed a desire to work at similar events. At no time did she complain, indicate, or imply that the Governor had acted improperly. (Pennington Aff. ¶¶10-11; Pennington Tr. at 63-64, 68-69).
- No one from the Governor's office, including Governor Clinton, ever requested that Ms. Pennington take any job action with respect to Ms. Jones, adverse or otherwise, or affect in any way her ability to be promoted or advance within the agency. (Pennington Aff ¶13; Pennington Tr. at 61-62).
- No one at AIDC ever asked Ms. Pennington to take any adverse action against plaintiff. (Pennington Aff. ¶13; Pennington Tr. at 62, 72). . . .

2. Plaintiff Suffered No Tangible Job Detriment

The concept of "tangible job detriment" in quid pro quo cases corresponds to that of "adverse employment action" in retaliation cases; both require a showing that plaintiff suffered a "materially adverse employment action." *Bryson v. Chicago State Univ.*, 96 F.3d 912, 916 (7th Cir. 1996). "Tangible" thus requires some concrete, negative change in working conditions. Numerous cases, moreover, have rejected harms that were based on plaintiffs' perceptions of detriment, rather than economic or other objective, material disadvantages. Under these standards, plaintiff's official employment records and the testimony of her supervisors, confirmed by plaintiff's own testimony, demonstrate beyond dispute that she suffered no tangible detriment.

Nonetheless, plaintiff makes three allegations that she claims rise to the level of material adverse job actions: (1) her treatment upon her return from maternity leave some 17 months after the alleged incident at the Excelsior Hotel; (2) her allegation that she was discouraged from seeking better positions at AIDC; and (3) her feelings that her supervisors treated her with hostility. As a matter of law, these do not constitute "tangible job detriments."

a.   Plaintiff's Treatment Following Her Maternity Leave
      Does Not Constitute an Adverse Job Action

When she returned from maternity leave, Ms. Jones asserts, there were changes in her job. Initially, she testified that she was downgraded, (Jones Tr. at 381) then that she was "demoted," (*id.* at 76). Alternatively, she asserted that her job duties were eliminated and she was given little to do:

A: [W]hen I came back, I no longer was at my desk. They had moved me completely to sit right outside Clydine's office, so she could watch me at all times. I was sitting right out front. And I didn't have any work to do. My work had been gone. I was sitting there doing nothing. . . .

Q: [N]ow, Mrs. Jones, isn't it a fact that when you came back, there was no change in your salary, was there?
A: No, there was not.

Q: There was no change in your supervisor, was there?
A: No. But I would just wonder why they would.

Q: There was no change in your title, was there?
A: —move me. . . .

A: Yeah, there was. I don't know what I was called. Probably a nobody sitting out front of Clydine's office. . . .

(Jones Tr. at 53-54). Upon further questioning, Ms. Jones also acknowledged that she continued to perform the same function of inputting data, only that the nature of the data she was inputting changed from purchasing information to personnel information. (*Id.* at 55.) In fact, as demonstrated by her employment records, Ms. Jones's statement that she was "demoted" or downgraded upon her return from maternity leave is erroneous. As Ms. Jones affirmed, there was no change in her pay or grade following her return.

In any event, claims such as this—which would amount at most to an immaterial alteration in job responsibilities—are insufficient to establish a tangible job detriment. In *Harlston v. McDonnell Douglas Corp.*, 37 F.3d 379 (8th Cir. 1994), the plaintiff also complained that her job duties had been changed in disadvantageous ways. The Eighth Circuit rejected plaintiff's assertion that this constituted an adverse job action:

[Plaintiff] was reassigned but suffered no diminution in her title, salary, or benefits. The substance of [her] complaint is that the job to which she was reassigned involved fewer secretarial duties and was more stressful. . . . This describes "nothing more disruptive than mere inconvenience or an alteration of job responsibilities." [citation omitted] Changes in duties or working conditions that cause no materially significant disadvantage, such as [the plaintiff's] reassignment, are insufficient to establish the adverse conduct required to make a prima facie case.

Id. at 382.

b. Ms. Jones's Unsubstantiated Allegation That She Was Discouraged From Applying for Unspecified Positions at AIDC Does Not Constitute a Tangible Job Detriment

Plaintiff asserts that she sought different jobs within AIDC, but was discouraged by Ms. Pennington from pursuing them. However, plaintiff could not specify a single job which she desired, but for which she had been discouraged from applying, could not say when these discussions with Ms. Pennington took place, and could not even identify the specific skills the purported jobs called for. Then plaintiff contradicted herself, saying she was not discouraged from pursuing another job, but rather from seeking a higher grade. (Jones Tr. at 35-38).

Needless to say, Ms. Jones's employment file does not support either assertion. There is no record of her ever applying for another job in the agency, and Ms. Pennington has testified that Ms. Jones never discussed that with her. (Pennington Aff. ¶13). Moreover, consistent with plaintiff's testimony that Ms. Pennington told her she liked plaintiff, (see Jones Tr. at 39), plaintiff's job reviews were all satisfactory. (See Exs. B-4, 5, 6). And, as she subsequently acknowledged, Ms. Jones did receive a step up to the next grade (Jones Tr. at 40); two months after her alleged encounter with Governor Clinton, in fact, she was elevated to Secretary I (Grade II), with an accompanying pay increase, because of some improvement in her data processing skills, notwithstanding that she still did not satisfy the objective requirements for a Secretary I position. (See Pennington Aff. at ¶6; Payroll Data Form, Ex. B-7).

A plaintiff's unsubstantiated and conflicting assertions cannot create an issue of fact to overcome overwhelming evidence to the contrary. And even if Ms. Jones's self-serving generalities are credited in this instance, courts have rejected claims, premised as plaintiff's is here, on allegations that she was discouraged from applying for promotion because of her belief that it would be futile—especially where there is no evidence that plaintiff sought an identifiable position, or did in fact apply for one.

c. Plaintiff's Allegations That Her Supervisors Were Rude Cannot Support a Finding of Adverse Action

Finally, Ms. Jones asserts that her supervisors were hostile and gave her the cold shoulder. When asked for specifics, Ms. Jones again responded with vague generalities: "Just every day when I went there, it just seemed like there was a lot of smoke in the air, just cloudy, you know, the way my supervisor treated me," and stated that Ms. Duckett would only say "hi" to plaintiff, and not engage in further banter. (Jones

Tr. at 70-71). The only specific act of rudeness to which plaintiff pointed was that she did not receive flowers on Secretary's Day in April 1992, nearly one year after the purported incident. She testified, however, that none of her supervisors told her, nor did she proffer any evidence, that this omission was the result of her alleged refusal of the Governor's alleged sexual advances in May 1991. (*Id.* at 71-73).

Claims such as this, that amount to nothing more than alleged hostility or personal animus directed toward the plaintiff, simply do not constitute adverse employment action.

3.   Any Job Action Plaintiff Experienced Was Not the Result of an Alleged Encounter with Governor Clinton

It would be insufficient, of course, for plaintiff merely to prove she suffered a tangible job detriment; it is plaintiff's burden also to prove that any adverse job action was taken as a result of her refusing to submit to an employer's advances. Here, there is a total failure of proof on the issue of causation.

There is nothing in this record to suggest that any change in plaintiff's working conditions could be attributed to Governor Clinton or plaintiff's alleged rejection of his purported sexual advances. Plaintiff's counsel never even asked the President—in their nearly five hours on the record deposing him—if he caused anyone at AIDC to take any adverse action against plaintiff. Nonetheless, we know clearly that he did not, because all three witnesses who were in plaintiff's chain of command at AIDC, and who would have been in a position to make decisions about her employment conditions, uniformly testified that he did not.

Specifically, plaintiff's three supervisors stated that they never discussed plaintiff with the Governor or anyone from his office; were unaware of the alleged incident until plaintiff made public allegations about it in 1994; and that neither the Governor nor anyone in his office ever asked them to take any job action with respect to plaintiff. (Pennington Aff. ¶¶11, 13, 15; Pennington Tr. at 61-64, 68-69, 72; Harrington Tr. at 55-60; Duckett Aff. ¶¶4-6). And by plaintiff's own testimony, none of her supervisors ever told her they were aware of her purported encounter with Governor Clinton or that they were treating her differently because of it, and she never told any of them about it or had any reason to believe they knew about it. (Jones Tr. at 44-45).

When, as here, the alleged harasser is uninvolved in employment decisions concerning the plaintiff, there can be no causal connection between a plaintiff's refusal of sexual advances and any detrimental job action that follows.

The undisputed record, moreover, negates any argument that causation should be inferred here from the sequence of alleged events. First, defendant was not plaintiff's direct supervisor. Second, many months—indeed more than a year in several instances—elapsed between the alleged incident at the hotel and the purported job actions

claimed by plaintiff. Finally, plaintiff testified that the Governor never condi-
tioned the receipt of job benefits or threatened her with concrete job detriments in connection with his alleged sexual advances. These circumstances, coupled with the testimony from plaintiff's supervisors, demonstrate
that there cannot be even an inference of causation on this record.

For all the foregoing reasons, plaintiff has not met her burden
of showing (1) a tangible job detriment (2) that resulted from her alleged
rebuff of Governor Clinton. Accordingly, she has failed to make out a
prima facie case of quid pro quo harassment.

Has President Clinton met his burden of production under *Celotex*? What must
plaintiff do?

PLAINTIFF'S MEMORANDUM IN OPPOSITION TO MOTION
FOR SUMMARY JUDGMENT

. . . C. SUBSTANTIAL EVIDENCE PROVES EVERY ELEMENT
OF PLAINTIFF'S QUID PRO QUO CLAIM, INCLUDING,
IF NECESSARY, TANGIBLE JOB DETRIMENT

With respect to Plaintiff's claim of quid pro quo sexual harassment in violation of her equal protection rights, Mr. Clinton argues that
Plaintiff's proof "falls" on two points . . . : (1) a tangible job detriment,
and (2) a link of causation between Plaintiff's refusal to submit to Mr.
Clinton's sexual demands and the tangible job detriment. To the contrary, the evidence tendered by Plaintiff is more than sufficient to prove
both points . . .

1. Tangible Job Detriment Is Proven

Ample evidence of tangible job detriments is presented here-
with. That evidence proves that after Plaintiff resisted Mr. Clinton's advances on May 8, 1991, the following occurred:

- Plaintiff was discouraged from applying for more attractive
  jobs and seeking reclassification at a higher pay grade within
  the AIDC.
- Plaintiff's job was changed to one with fewer responsibilities,
  less attractive duties, and less potential for advancement—
  and the reason given for the change proved to be untrue.
- Plaintiff was effectively denied access to grievance procedures that would otherwise have been available to victims of
  sexual harassment.
- Plaintiff was mistreated in ways having tangible manifesta-
  tions, such as isolating Plaintiff physically, making her sit in a
  location from which she was constantly watched, singling her
  out as the only female employee not to be given flowers on
  Secretaries Day, and making her sit at her workstation with
  no work to do. . . .

Opportunities for Advancement Denied. On two occasions Plaintiff informed her immediate supervisor, Ms. Clydine Pennington, that Plaintiff was interested in transferring to other Departments at the AIDC where higher-grade jobs were available. Jones Dep. at 35, lines 13-18; 37, lines 19. Because these jobs sought by Plaintiff were at a higher "grade," Plaintiff would have received more compensation. Jones Dep. at 37, lines 16-19. See AIDC "Employee Salary Changes" record. Plaintiff sought those positions not only because they would have entitled her to higher pay, but also because she believed that they would "broaden [her] skills" and "help [her] grow." Jones Dep. at 37.

Nevertheless, Ms. Pennington's response was to insist that Plaintiff stay where she was and to deter her from applying for the other jobs by assuring her that she would "grow" in that Department. Jones Dep. at 39. In fact, Plaintiff's responsibilities were reduced, even though she consistently received positive ratings in her formal performance reviews. Jones Dep. at 38, lines 1-2; Jones Performance Evaluations.

Responsibilities Reduced. Plaintiff's job responsibilities were changed. Jones Dep. at 5-7 lines 5-7; 55, lines 4-19. Her duties as a "purchasing assistant," involved in preparing purchase orders used by the agency, were taken away, and she was given the tedious task of putting applications for employment into a database. *Id.* at 55, lines 4-19. She was no longer dealing with the purchasing Department. *Id.* at 56, lines 7-8. Much of the time she "didn't have any work to do." Jones Dep. 53, line 22. These significant changes were made without discussing the move with her and in the absence of any request by her that she be moved. *Id.* at 56, lines 8-10. A jury could reasonably find that the removal of plaintiff's responsibilities impaired her potential for promotion. Like the plaintiff in *Bryson v. Chicago State University,* 96 F.3d at 916, Paula Jones was denied the "building blocks" of career advancement. . . .

Denial of Right to Invoke Grievance Procedure. By Executive Order No. 86-1, every agency of the State of Arkansas, including the AIDC, was required to have a formal grievance procedure. See Executive Order 86-01 (signed by Governor Clinton). A Uniform Grievance Procedure was issued by the agencies. See Memorandum dated July 16, 1985 from Artee Williams, Administrator, Office of Personnel Management, with attached procedure. The AIDC eventually developed a Grievance Procedure closely following the Uniform Grievance Procedure. See AIDC Grievance Procedure. Both the AIDC Grievance Procedure and the Uniform Grievance Procedure state that "[i]t is the policy of this agency that all employees be given the opportunity, through established steps and procedures, to resolve in a timely manner complaints or grievances they believe adversely affect their employment or working conditions."

In these policies, the definition of "grievance" determines for what matters the procedure may be invoked. "Grievance" is defined to include a complaint by an employee "regarding an aspect of his or her employment: including, but not limited to, . . . promotion, demotion, . . . discrimination or any other work-related problem except compensation and conditions that are beyond the control of agency management or are mandated by law." AIDC Grievance Procedure at 6.2. The meaning of the term "discrimination" is clarified thus: "Discrimination is on the basis of race, color, sex, age, national origin, religion, or disability." *Id.*

Mr. Clinton's conduct toward Plaintiff, and his threat to Plaintiff, caused a tangible job detriment in that they effectively denied Plaintiff her right to invoke the grievance procedure to seek redress for gender-based discrimination, including Mr. Clinton's own unwelcome sexual advances and sexual assault of Plaintiff, as well as the ensuing treatment of Plaintiff at the AIDC. Plaintiff was aware of the grievance procedure, but was afraid to take advantage of it. Jones Dep. at 62, lines 17-21. Mr. Clinton's threatening words and actions toward Plaintiff were said and done when he was Governor, the highest authority in the Executive Branch of the state government, and while he was attending an official state function. Plaintiff was subjected to the threatening words and actions when she was at work as an AIDC employee, and performing her job functions, so it was natural for her to conclude that invoking the grievance procedure would be futile and perhaps worse. The grievance procedure was a benefit available to all other employees. The deprivation of that benefit was a tangible job detriment to Plaintiff.

Hostile Treatment Having Tangible Effects. Plaintiff has tendered evidence—which the Court is obliged to accept as true—that following her rejection of Mr. Clinton's advances, the attitude of her supervisors toward her changed and became quite negative. Jones Decl. ¶Jones Dep. at 35, lines 10-25; p. 45, lines 15-20. Plaintiff testified that "there was a lot of hostility it seemed like between Cherry Duckett and I. She never would speak to me. . . . I would try to talk to her." *Id.* at 35, lines 18-19. And Clydine Pennington was "not as friendly as she used to have been." *Id.* at 45, lines 17-20. This change of attitude manifested itself in physical actions that directly and adversely affected Plaintiff's enjoyment of her job; in other words, there were tangible job detriments. The location of Plaintiff's work station was moved so that she had to sit directly outside Ms. Pennington's office, where she could be watched constantly. Jones Dep. at 53, lines 19-21. On Secretaries Day, Plaintiff was the only female in the office who did not receive flowers. Jones Dep. at 72, lines 12-16. There were times when Plaintiff literally was given no work to do and she suffered the embarrassment of having to sit at her work station doing nothing. *Id.* at 53, lines 22-23. In determining that similar actions constituted tangible job detriments, the court in Collins v. State of Illinois made the following observation: "One does not have to be an employment expert to know that an employer can make an employee's job undesirable or even unbearable without money or benefits even entering into the picture." Collins v. State of Ill., 830 F.2d at 703. . . .

Is this sentence a correct statement of the standard for evaluating plaintiff's evidence? What inferences does she seek? Are they reasonable?

In summary judgment proceedings, the evidence adduced by the nonmovant must be accepted as true, all reasonable inferences from the evidence must be drawn in favor of the nonmovant, and all conflicting evidence must be disregarded. Application of this standard leaves no doubt: there is substantial evidence of tangible job detriments, and Mr. Clinton is not entitled to summary judgment.

2.   Causation Is Proven

Substantial evidence supports the inference that Mr. Clinton caused Plaintiff to suffer the tangible job detriments enumerated above. Plaintiff was not treated badly by her supervisors at the AIDC until after her refusal to submit to Mr. Clinton's sexual demands. Jones Decl. ¶31. He had the power to control the terms and conditions of Plaintiff's employment, and he admitted that he was willing to use that power, specifically with reference to Plaintiff, for illegitimate reasons.

On May 8, 1991, Mr. Clinton was, as Governor, the highest ranking officer of the entire Executive Branch of the government of the State of Arkansas. President Clinton's Responses to Plaintiff's First Set of Requests For Admissions, Admission Nos. 1-2. The AIDC was an agency of state government, and was part of the executive branch controlled by Mr. Clinton. Admission Nos. 3, 4. David Harrington was the Director of the AIDC and served under Governor Clinton, Admission Nos. 5, 6. Mr. Harrington was Mr. Clinton's friend. Admission No. 7.

Note the use of Requests for Admissions.

Most importantly, while he was with Plaintiff in the hotel suite on May 8, 1991, Mr. Clinton told Plaintiff that if she got into trouble with Mr. Harrington for leaving the registration desk, Plaintiff was to have Mr. Harrington call Mr. Clinton "immediately" and Mr. Clinton would "take care of it." Jones Decl. ¶17. This statement by Mr. Clinton is a critical admission that: (a) Mr. Clinton had control over Mr. Harrington's decisions concerning both deployment and discipline of employees at the AIDC; (b) Mr. Clinton was willing to exercise that control to influence Mr. Harrington's decisions about employees based on illegitimate criteria wholly unrelated to the proper functioning of the AIDC; and (c) Mr. Harrington would in fact comply with Mr. Clinton's directives concerning treatment of employees, even if those directives were patently based on improper motives and served no legitimate interests of the AIDC. . . .

Counsel for Mr. Clinton makes much of the fact that several months elapsed between the incident at the Excelsior Hotel and some of the tangible detriments incurred by Plaintiff. This argument fails to recognize that the sexual advances to Plaintiff were not confined to May 8, 1991, but continued throughout Plaintiff's employment. As outlined in the Statement of Material Facts, Plaintiff encountered Mr. Clinton or his personal bodyguard, Trooper Ferguson, on at least four other occasions while Plaintiff was still employed at the AIDC. Moreover, Mr. Clinton's ability to control decisions about Plaintiff's employment remained in effect for as long as she was employed at the AIDC. . . .

From the evidence described above, a jury could reasonably draw the inference that Mr. Clinton caused Plaintiff to suffer adverse employment action as a result of her resistance to his sexual advances. "Viewing the facts in the light most favorable to the plaintiff and giving [her] the benefit of all reasonable factual inferences," the evidence that Mr. Clinton caused Plaintiff to suffer tangible job detriments is more than sufficient to preclude summary judgment. . . .

JUDGE WRIGHT'S RULING

Jones v. Clinton
990 F. Supp. 657 (E.D. Ark. 1998)

. . . Summary judgment is appropriate when "the pleadings, depositions, answers to interrogatories, and admissions on file, together with the affidavits, if any, show that there is no genuine issue as to any material fact and that the moving party is entitled to a judgment as a matter of law." Fed. R. Civ. P. 56(c). As a prerequisite to summary judgment, a moving party must demonstrate "an absence of evidence to support the nonmoving party's case." *Celotex Corp. v. Catrett,* 477 U.S. 317, 325 (1986). Once the moving party has properly supported its motion for summary judgment, the nonmoving party must "do more than simply show there is some metaphysical doubt as to the material facts." *Matsushita Elec. Indus. Co. v. Zenith Radio,* 475 U.S. 574, 586 (1986). The nonmoving party may not rest on mere allegations or denials of his pleading, but must "come forward with 'specific facts showing that there is a *genuine issue for trial.'*" *Id.* at 587 (quoting Fed. R. Civ. P. 56(e) and adding emphasis). See also *Anderson v. Liberty Lobby, Inc.,* 477 U.S. 242, 256 (1986). The inferences to be drawn from the underlying facts must be viewed in the light most favorable to the party opposing the motion. *Matsushita Elec. Indus. Co.,* 475 U.S. at 587 (citations omitted). However, "[w]here the record taken as a whole could not lead a rational trier of fact to find for the nonmoving party, there is no 'genuine issue for trial.'" *Id.* . . .

1.

To make a prima facie case of quid pro quo sexual harassment, this plaintiff must show, among other things, that her refusal to submit to unwelcome sexual advances or requests for sexual favors resulted in a tangible job detriment. "[A] supervisor's mere threat or promise of job-related harm or benefits in exchange for sexual favors does not constitute quid pro quo harassment. . . ." *Gary v. Long,* 59 F.3d 1391, 1396 (D.C. Cir. 1995). . . .

. . . The Court has carefully reviewed the record in this case and finds nothing in plaintiff's employment records, her own testimony, or the testimony of her supervisors showing that plaintiff's reaction to Governor Clinton's alleged advances affected tangible aspects of her compensation, terms, conditions, or privileges of employment.

Plaintiff's claim that she was discouraged from applying for more attractive jobs and seeking reclassification at a higher pay grade within the AIDC does not demonstrate any "tangible" job detriment as she has not identified a single specific job which she desired or applied for at AIDC but which she had been discouraged from seeking. Pl.'s Depo. at 37-40. When asked for such specific information, plaintiff merely testified that the unidentified jobs she sought were "a grade higher" but that her supervisor "would always discourage me and make me believe that I could grow within the administrative services, which in fact I didn't. I got degrade—downgraded." *Id.* at 38, 42. She further states that those "few" times that she would talk to her supervisor and receive discourage-

> Note Judge Wright's detailed references to the discovery record. These are usually edited out in casebook excerpts of decisions; they are included here to illustrate the specificity of the linkages required for summary judgment.

ment, she "would go ahead and fill out an application maybe or something." *Id.* at 41. There is no record of plaintiff ever applying for another job within AIDC, however, and the record shows that not only was plaintiff never downgraded, her position was reclassified upward from a Grade 9 classification to a Grade 11 classification, thereby increasing her annual salary. Pennington Aff. ¶6; Arkansas Human Resources Management System Payroll Data Form for P.R. Jones, Ex. B-7. Indeed, it is undisputed that plaintiff received every merit increase and cost-of-living allowance for which she was eligible during her nearly two-year tenure with the AIDC and consistently received satisfactory job evaluations. See *id.* Specifically, on July 1, 1991, less than two months after the alleged incident that is the subject of this lawsuit, plaintiff received a cost-of-living increase and her position was reclassified from Grade 9 to Grade 11; on August 28, 1991, plaintiff received a satisfactory job evaluation from her supervisor, Clydine Pennington; on March 11, 1992, the one-year anniversary of her hire date with AIDC, plaintiff received another satisfactory evaluation from Pennington and Cherry Duckett, Deputy Director of AIDC, which entitled her to a merit raise. *Id.* In addition, plaintiff was given a satisfactory job review in an evaluation covering the period of March 1992 until her voluntary departure from the AIDC in February 1993. Ex. B-6. Plaintiff signed this review on February 16, 1993, see *id.*, and would have received another merit increase one month later in accordance with this review had she elected to continue her employment at AIDC. Pennington Aff. ¶8.

It is plaintiff's burden to come forward with "specific facts" showing that there is a genuine issue for trial, see *Matsushita,* 475 U.S. at 587, and the Court finds that her testimony on this point, being of a most general and nonspecific nature (and in some cases contradictory to the record), simply does not suffice to create a genuine issue of fact regarding any tangible job detriment as a result of her having allegedly been discouraged from seeking more attractive jobs and reclassification.

Equally without merit is plaintiff's assertion that following her return from maternity leave in September 1992, she suffered a tangible job detriment when her job was changed to one with fewer responsibilities, less attractive duties, and less potential for advancement. These matters do not constitute a tangible job detriment as it is undisputed that there was no diminution in plaintiff's salary or change in her job classification following her return from maternity leave and, further, that her last review at AIDC following her return was positive and would have entitled her to another merit increase had she not resigned her position in order to move to California with her husband. Changes in duties or working conditions that cause no materially significant disadvantage, such as diminution in title, salary, or benefits, are insufficient to establish the adverse conduct required to make a prima facie case.

Isn't the last sentence in this paragraph a ruling as a matter of law that certain factors don't amount to a detriment? Should it have come earlier in the case? Can you argue why or why not?

Although plaintiff states that her job title upon returning from maternity leave was no longer that of purchasing assistant and that this change in title impaired her potential for promotion, her job duties prior to taking maternity leave and her job duties upon returning to work both involved data input; the difference being that instead of responsibility for data entry of AIDC purchase orders and driving records, she was assigned data entry responsibilities for employment applications. Pl.'s Depo. at 56; Pennington Aff. ¶16. That being so, plaintiff cannot establish a tangible job detriment. A transfer that does not involve a demotion in form or substance and involves only minor changes in working conditions, with no reduction in pay or benefits, will not constitute an adverse employment action, "[o]therwise every trivial personnel action that an irritable . . . employee did not like would form the basis of a discrimination suit." [citation omitted] Whether or not the reasons given for the change were untrue, plaintiff's allegations describe nothing 'more disruptive than a mere inconvenience or an alteration of job responsibilities. . . .

Finally, the Court rejects plaintiff's claim that she was subjected to hostile treatment having tangible effects when she was isolated physically, made to sit in a location from which she was constantly watched, made to sit at her work station with no work to do, and singled out as the only female employee not to be given flowers on Secretaries Day. Plaintiff may well have perceived hostility and animus on the part of her supervisors, but these perceptions are merely conclusory in nature and do not, without more, constitute a tangible job detriment. Absent evidence of some more tangible change in duties or working conditions that constitute a material employment disadvantage, of which the Court has already determined does not exist, general allegations of hostility and personal animus are not sufficient to demonstrate any adverse employment action that constitutes the sort of ultimate decision intended to be actionable under Title VII.

Similarly, plaintiff's allegations regarding her work station being moved so that she had to sit directly outside Pennington's office and, at times, not having work to do, describe nothing more than minor or *de minimis* personnel matters which, again without more, are insufficient to constitute a tangible job detriment or adverse employment action.

Although it is not clear why plaintiff failed to receive flowers on Secretaries Day in 1992, such an omission does not give rise to a federal cause of action in the absence of evidence of some more tangible change in duties or working conditions that constitute a material employment disadvantage. . . .

2.

The Court now turns to plaintiff's hostile work environment claim. Unlike quid pro quo sexual harassment, hostile work environment harassment arises when "sexual conduct has the purpose or effect of unreasonably interfering with an individual's work performance or creating an intimidating, hostile, or offensive working environment." [citation omitted] To prevail on a hostile work environment cause of action, a plaintiff must establish, among other things, that she was subjected to unwelcome sexual harassment based upon her sex that affected a term, condition, or privilege of employment. The behavior creating the hostile working environment need not be overtly sexual in nature, but it must be " 'unwelcome' in the sense that the employee did not solicit or invite it, and the employee regarded the conduct as undesirable or offensive." [citation omitted] The harassment must also be sufficiently severe or pervasive "to alter the conditions of employment and create an abusive working environment." [citation omitted] . . .

In assessing the hostility of an environment, a court must look to the totality of the circumstances. Circumstances to be considered include "the frequency of the discriminatory conduct; its severity; whether it is physically threatening or humiliating, or a mere offensive utterance; and whether it unreasonably interferes with an employee's work performance." No single factor is determinative, see *id.*, and the court "should not carve the work environment into a series of discrete incidents and then measure the harm occurring in each episode." [citation omitted]

First, the Court finds plaintiff's reliance on her assertions of tangible job detriment as establishing a hostile work environment to be misplaced. In its [decision on the Rule 12(c) motion], the Court noted that although the President's argument for outright dismissal of plaintiff's hostile work environment claim had "some force," further development of the record was nevertheless necessary. The Court based this conclusion in large part on plaintiff's representations that her rejection of the President's alleged advances caused her to suffer adverse employment actions, including being transferred to a position that had no responsible duties for which she could be adequately evaluated to earn advancement and failing to receive raises and merit increases. In this regard, the Court determined that the "totality" of the allegations alleged in this case were such that they could be said to have altered the conditions of plaintiff's employment and created an abusive work environment. However, development of the record has now established that plaintiff's allegations of adverse employment actions are without merit, with her claim of failing to receive cost-of-living increases apparently having even been abandoned. Plaintiff received every merit increase and cost-of-living allowance for which she was eligible during her nearly two-year tenure with the AIDC, her job was upgraded from Grade 9 to Grade 11 (thereby increasing her salary), she consistently received satisfactory job evaluations, and her job responsibilities upon her return from maternity leave were not significantly different from prior to her taking leave and did not cause her any materially significant disadvantage. These facts are clearly established by the record and dispel the notion that she was subjected to a hostile work environment.

Plaintiff certainly has not shown under the totality of the circumstances that the alleged incident in the hotel and her additional encounters with Ferguson and the Governor were so severe or pervasive that it created an abusive working environment. She admits that she never missed a day of work following the alleged incident in the hotel, she continued to work at AIDC another nineteen months (leaving only because of her husband's job transfer), she continued to go on a daily basis to the Governor's Office to deliver items and never asked to be relieved of that duty, she never filed a formal complaint or told her supervisors of the incident while at AIDC, and she never consulted a psychiatrist, psychologist, or incurred medical bills as a result of the alleged incident. Pl.'s Depo. at 44-45, 48, 62, 121-123. In addition, plaintiff has not shown how Ferguson's alleged comments, whether considered alone or in conjunction with the other alleged conduct in this case, interfered with her work, and she acknowledges that the Governor's statement about him and her looking like "beauty and the beast" was made "in a light vein" and that his patting her on the shoulder and asking her how she was doing was done in a "friendly fashion." Pl.'s Dep. at 243, 245.

While the alleged incident in the hotel, if true, was certainly boorish and offensive, . . . the Governor's alleged conduct does not constitute sexual assault. This is thus not one of those exceptional cases in which a single incident of sexual harassment, such as an assault, was deemed sufficient to state a claim of hostile work environment sexual harassment.

Considering the totality of the circumstances, it simply cannot be said that the conduct to which plaintiff was allegedly subjected was frequent, severe, or physically threatening, and the Court finds that defendants' actions as shown by the record do not constitute the kind of sustained and nontrivial conduct necessary for a claim of hostile work environment.

> Shouldn't a jury decide "the totality of the circumstances"?

In sum, the Court finds that the record does not demonstrate conduct that was so severe or pervasive that it can be said to have altered the conditions of plaintiff's employment and created an abusive working environment. Accordingly, the President is entitled to summary judgment on plaintiff's claim of hostile work environment sexual harassment. . . .

3.

Finally, the Court addresses plaintiff's state law claim of intentional infliction of emotional distress or outrage. Arkansas recognizes a claim of intentional infliction of emotional distress based on sexual harassment. To establish a claim of intentional infliction of emotional distress, a plaintiff must prove that: (1) the defendant intended to inflict emotional distress or knew or should have known that emotional distress was the likely result of his conduct; (2) the conduct was extreme and outrageous and utterly intolerable in a civilized community; (3) the defendant's conduct was the cause of the plaintiff's distress; and (4) the plaintiff's emotional distress was so severe in nature that no reasonable person could be expected to endure it. . . .

One is subject to liability for the tort of outrage or intentional infliction of emotional distress if he or she willfully or wantonly causes severe emotional distress to another by extreme and outrageous conduct. In *M.B.M. Co. v. Counce,* 596 S.W.2d 681, 687 (Ark. 1980), the Arkansas Supreme Court stated that "[b]y extreme and outrageous conduct, we mean conduct that is so outrageous in character, and so extreme in degree, as to go beyond all possible bounds of decency, and to be regarded as atrocious, and utterly intolerable in civilized society." Whether conduct is "extreme and outrageous" is determined by looking at "the conduct at issue; the period of time over which the conduct took place; the relation between plaintiff and defendant; and defendant's knowledge that plaintiff is particularly susceptible to emotional distress by reason of some physical or mental peculiarity." The tort is clearly not intended to provide legal redress for every slight insult or indignity that one must endure. The Arkansas courts take a strict approach and give a narrow view to claims of outrage, and merely describing conduct as outrageous does not make it so.

Plaintiff seems to base her claim of outrage on her erroneous belief that the allegations she has presented are sufficient to constitute criminal sexual assault. She states that "Mr. Clinton's outrageous conduct includes offensive language, an offensive proposition, offensive touching (constituting sexual assault under both federal and state definitions), and actual exposure of an intimate private body part," and that "[t]here are few more outrageous acts than a criminal sexual assault followed by unwanted exposure, coupled with a demand for oral sex by the most powerful man in the state against a very young, low-level employee."

While the Court will certainly agree that plaintiff's allegations describe offensive conduct, the Court, as previously noted, has found that the Governor's alleged conduct does not constitute sexual assault. Rather, the conduct as alleged by plaintiff describes a mere sexual proposition or encounter, albeit an odious one, that was relatively brief in duration, did not involve any coercion or threats of reprisal, and was abandoned as soon as plaintiff made clear that the advance was not welcome. The Court is not aware of any authority holding that such a sexual encounter or proposition of the type alleged in this case, without more, gives rise to a claim of outrage.

Moreover, notwithstanding the offensive nature of the Governor's alleged conduct, plaintiff admits that she never missed a day of work following the alleged incident, she continued to work at AIDC another nineteen months (leaving only because of her husband's job transfer), she continued to go on a daily basis to the Governor's Office to deliver items and never asked to be relieved of that duty, she never filed a formal complaint or told her supervisors of the incident while at AIDC, she never consulted a psychiatrist, psychologist, or incurred medical bills as a result of the alleged incident, and she acknowledges that her two subsequent contacts with the Governor involved comments made "in a light vein" and nonsexual contact that was done in a "friendly fashion." Further, despite earlier claiming that she suffered marital discord and humiliation, plaintiff stated in her deposition that she was not claiming damages to her marriage as a result of the Governor's alleged conduct, see Pl.'s Depo. at 122, and she acknowledged the request to drop her claim of injury to reputation by stating, "I didn't really care if it was dropped or not personally." *Id.* at 261-262. Plaintiff's actions and statements in this case do not portray someone who experienced emotional distress so severe in nature that no reasonable person could be expected to endure it.

Nevertheless, plaintiff submits a declaration from a purported expert with a Ph.D. in education and counseling, Patrick J. Carnes, who, after a 3.5-hour meeting with plaintiff and her husband a mere four days prior to the filing of President Clinton's motion for summary judgment, opines that her alleged encounter with Governor Clinton in 1991, "and the ensuing events," have caused plaintiff to suffer severe emotional distress and "consequent sexual aversion." The Court does not credit this declaration. . . .

Aside from other deficiencies with the Carnes declaration (including the fact that the substance of this declaration apparently was not disclosed in accordance with rules governing pre-trial discovery), the opinions stated therein are vague and conclusory and . . . do not suffice to overcome plaintiff's failure of proof on her claim of outrage.

In sum, plaintiff's allegations fall far short of the rigorous standards for establishing a claim of outrage under Arkansas law and the Court therefore grants the President's motion for summary judgment on this claim.

One final matter concerns alleged . . . pattern and practice evidence. Whatever relevance such evidence may have to prove other elements of plaintiff's case, it does not have anything to do with the issues presented by the President's and Ferguson's motions for summary judgment, i.e., whether plaintiff herself was the victim of alleged quid pro quo or hostile work environment sexual harassment, whether the President and Ferguson conspired to deprive her of her civil rights, or whether she suffered emotional distress so severe in nature that no reasonable per-

Plaintiff has argued that evidence of other relationships between the President and employees should be considered. Why does the judge reject that?

son could be expected to endure it. Whether other women may have been subjected to workplace harassment, and whether such evidence has allegedly been suppressed, does not change the fact that plaintiff has failed to demonstrate that she has a case worthy of submitting to a jury. Reduced to its essence, the record taken as a whole could not lead a rational trier of fact to find for the nonmoving party and the Court therefore finds that there are no genuine issues for trial in this case.

For the foregoing reasons, the Court finds that the President's and Ferguson's motions for summary judgment should both be and hereby are granted. There being no remaining issues, the Court will enter judgment dismissing this case.

NOTES AND COMMENTS

1. Compare to the motion to dismiss.   On either a Rule 12(b)(6) or a 12(c) motion, the standard for dismissal is whether the party opposing the motion (usually the plaintiff) has failed to state a claim upon which relief can be granted. The judge must assume all facts pled by the claimant to be true, and cannot look beyond the pleadings to other assertions of fact. (If she finds it necessary to do so, she can treat a Rule 12 motion as a motion for summary judgment. *See* Rule 12(b) and (c).) On a summary judgment motion, the judge *must* look beyond the pleadings as to factual issues; Rule 56(e) specifies that reliance on pleadings alone cannot suffice. The standard for summary judgment is whether there is a "genuine" issue of "material" fact. In *Jones v. Clinton,* compare Judge Wright's earlier ruling in Chapter 2 with the summary judgment ruling in this chapter. What has changed? Read the portions of each ruling that address the tangible job detriment and hostile environment issues. Can you pinpoint the difference? Do you agree that there is a difference? What about the intentional infliction of emotional distress claim?

2. What is a "material" fact?   How does the court identify which facts are material? Both parties refer to a multitude of facts (and in the full set of documents, a multitude more than you have read in the excerpts). On which does the judge focus? Which does she disregard? For example, on the quid pro quo sexual harassment claim, there is no question that the facts about whether Jones was treated badly at her office after the alleged encounter with Clinton are in dispute. If they were material, Judge Wright would have to deny summary judgment. Why aren't they material?

3. Why are some facts not "genuinely" in issue?   Returning to the tangible job detriment issue, Jones asserts not just rudeness, but that she was discouraged from applying for better, higher-paying jobs. Her supervisor denies having discouraged her. Such discouragement comes much closer than rudeness to satisfying the requirement that plaintiff show material detriment. How should the court treat this conflict in testimony? The problem has two dimensions. First, there is the credibility question: Was Jones lying? This is often the paradigmatic example of a question that should go to the jury. Second, if one assumes that she is telling the truth, there is still the question: What are the reasonable inferences that can be drawn from these facts?

Judge Wright cites *Matsushita* for two central points: for the requirement that the party opposing summary judgment produce specific facts to support a claim, and for the standard that a court should determine whether "the record taken as a whole" could not lead a rational fact finder to find for that party. Has Judge Wright crossed the line from assessing whether a "genuine" issue exists to simply weighing the evidence?

   4. Element(ary) analysis.   *Jones v. Clinton* is a classic he-said, she-said contest. How could such a case be decided on summary judgment? Put another way, does the summary judgment litigation resolve anything as to who told the truth about what happened on May 8, 1991? No. Indeed, other than an aside at the beginning of the President's brief (which might have been there primarily for the press and public), the briefs do not even discuss whether those acts occurred. Why is that fundamental question irrelevant to the motion for summary judgment?

Exercise 15—*Celotex* and Summary Judgment

Why is the Supreme Court's decision in *Celotex* key to the President's strategy on this motion? The law prior to *Celotex* followed the rule of *Adickes v. S.H. Kress & Co.*, 398 U.S. 144, 157 (1970), which imposed on the movant "the burden of showing the absence of a genuine issue as to any material fact." In *Adickes,* the Supreme Court ruled that summary judgment had been wrongly granted because of defendant's "failure to foreclose the possibility" that a policeman had been in the Kress store prior to plaintiff's arrest and had colluded with store employees to arrest her because she was seeking to integrate the store. Analyze how much difference it made to the outcome in *Jones v. Clinton* that the *Celotex* rule had superseded *Adickes*.

   5. Pretrial or quasi-trial?   As is obvious from the wealth of detail in both the briefs and in Judge Wright's opinion, the litigation of a summary judgment motion can amount to what seems like a trial in writing, or in slow motion. In addition to their briefs, parties also submit material facts statements, which are required by the local rules in most districts. For example, the Local Rules for the Eastern District of Arkansas provided:

Local Rule 56.1—Summary Judgment Motion

   (a) Any party moving for summary judgment pursuant to Rule 56 of the Federal Rules of Civil Procedure, shall annex to the notice of motion a separate, short and concise statement of the material facts as to which it contends there is no genuine issue to be tried.

   (b) If the non-moving party opposes the motion, it shall file, in addition to any response and brief, a separate, short and concise statement of the material facts as to which it contends a genuine issue exists to be tried.

   (c) All material facts set forth in the statement filed by the moving party pursuant to paragraph (a) shall be deemed admitted unless controverted by the statement filed by the non-moving party under paragraph (b).

Appended to these statements of material fact are copies of each page of the record cited—excerpts from deposition transcripts, interrogatory answers, etc. As you can imagine, the volume of paper involved in litigating a summary judgment motion can be quite large. The judge and/or her clerk must track through the supporting documents and analyze each assertion. At least in some cases, there might not be a great deal of difference between the number of hours expended in litigating and deciding a summary judgment motion and the time expended in trial. Why might summary judgment motions still be encouraged?

6. Power struggle.   In this kind of case, one federal judge wrote, "We must first ask not 'What is sexual harassment?' but 'Who gets to decide?' " Shira A. Scheindlin [a judge on the Court of Appeals for the Second Circuit] and John Elofson, Judge, Juries and Sexual Harassment, 17 Yale L. & Pol'y Rev. 813, 815 (1999). One notable aspect of Jones's brief and her statement of material facts was that, overwhelmingly, the citations to the record were to her own testimony, either at her deposition or in an affidavit prepared for the summary judgment motion. In other words, as outlined in Note 3 *supra,* her case turned in large part on her own credibility and on the reasonableness of the inferences from it that she asked the court to draw. Shouldn't the case have gone to a jury? A mountain of legal scholarship has attacked the three 1986 Supreme Court decisions cited by President Clinton's lawyers—*Celotex, Matsushita,* and *Liberty Lobby*—as draining too much power away from the jury, arguably the society's most democratic and representative governmental decision-making body, and shifting it to judges, to the general benefit of defendants.[1] Do you agree that summary judgment is too easy? How would that critique apply in *Jones v. Clinton?*

7. The risk of bias in summary judgment.   When the case involves a claim of discrimination, should there be a stronger hesitancy to decide it by summary judgment; that is, without permitting resolution by the "fair cross-section of the community" that is embodied (or should be) in a jury? 28 U.S.C. §1861. That question triggered a lively debate among federal judges in the Second Circuit. In *Gallagher v. Delaney,* 139 F.3d 388, 342 (2d Cir. 1998), another sexual harassment case, the court reversed the trial judge's grant of summary judgment, reasoning in part that:

> Characterizing behavior as sexually harassing can only be accomplished in a specific context. . . . The answer often depends upon perceptions of the circumstances. A federal judge is not in the best position to define the current sexual tenor of American cultures in their many manifestations. . . . Today, while gender relations in the workplace are rapidly evolving, and views of what is appropriate behavior are diverse and shifting, a jury made up of a cross-section of our heterogeneous communities provides the appropriate institution for deciding whether borderline situations should be characterized as sexual harassment and retaliation.

The *Gallagher* opinion sparked the article cited in Note 6 co-authored by Judge Scheindlin. Judge Scheindlin took the opposite position, arguing that the current confusion about what behavior constitutes harassment will be worse if judges defer to juries. "Unless judges take a more active role in deciding harassment cases, there is little possibility that an adequate definition of 'hostile work environment' will de-

---

1. For an excellent description of the impact of those and subsequent Supreme Court decisions, from the perspective of a D.C. Circuit Court judge, *see* Patricia M. Wald, Summary Judgment at Sixty, 76 Tex. L. Rev. 1897 (1998).

velop. Although juries undoubtedly have an important part to play, allowing them the authority to define the term on a case-by-case basis, as some recommend, will guarantee continued confusion." 17 Yale L. & Pol'y Rev. at 817. Which is the better position?

Moreover, the issues raised in *Jones* and other sexual harassment cases are profoundly complicated by sexuality and gender, two arenas in which rationality is notoriously porous. Feminist scholars have argued that women's assertions of facts and of harms, especially those related to sexuality, are systematically undercredited in the courts.[2] As you might surmise from the dates of the articles and cases cited in this Note, much of the debate over summary judgment in sexual harassment cases was triggered by reactions to the litigation of *Jones v. Clinton.*

8. Revisiting Rule 11.   Judge Wright's decision contains numerous references to the absence of evidence to support certain elements of Jones's claims. Reread Rule 11(b)(3). Would President Clinton have grounds for a Rule 11 motion on this basis? Even if he did, could he initiate that process now?

---

2. *See, e.g.,* Theresa M. Beiner, The Misuse of Summary Judgment in Hostile Environment Cases, 34 Wake Forest L. Rev. 71 (1999); Amy D. Ronner, The Cassandra Curse: The Stereotype of the Female Liar Resurfaces in *Jones v. Clinton,* 31 U.C. Davis L. Rev. 123 (1997).

CHAPTER ELEVEN

Settlement and Default

[I]t will remain one of history's great understatements that the President should have settled the case earlier.

—Jeffrey Toobin, *A Vast Conspiracy:*
The Real Story of the Sex Scandal That Nearly Brought Down a President

INTRODUCTION

There was no shortage of advice to the President to settle *Jones v. Clinton*. Lloyd Cutler, his White House Counsel in 1994, when the case was filed, advised him to settle. Numerous lawyers commenting on the case in the press as it was being litigated opined that he should settle. Even Monica Lewinsky, during one of her last conversations with the President in late 1997, told him that he should settle the case. And, indeed, the President's lawyers tried to settle the case, although perhaps not hard enough.

As you read the recounting of each that follows, ask yourself what your bargaining position would have been and why, at that point in the lawsuit, had you represented either Jones or Clinton. Note the shifting value of the case, both in financial terms and as to the other points that were important to one side or the other.

The first moment of near settlement occurred shortly before the case was filed. The deal fell apart because the President refused to waive his statute of limitations defense for six months. The terms of the proposed agreement were that Jones would receive no money, but the President would personally and publicly read a statement in which he said that he "had no recollection" of having met her, but that he "[did] not challenge the claim that we met there and I may very well have met her in the past." (See Introduction to Chapter 1.)

From then on, settlement negotiations were episodic. In 1996, while the issue of whether private civil suits against incumbent presidents should be suspended until after they left office was still being litigated, Jones's lawyers offered to settle for $1.6 million. Bennett rejected that figure immediately, and Jones's lawyers then offered to settle for $1.2 million, which Bennett (and presumably his client) also refused.

Then the Supreme Court ruled against President Clinton on the suspension issue, and settlement discussions once again became more serious.

Bennett had concluded that any amount less than a million dollars would not sound like an admission of guilt. Both sides were facing the prospect of harsh and expensive discovery efforts. Davis and Cammarata indicated to Bennett that they would consider a six-figure amount. In August, 1997, after intense negotiation, the lawyers believed that they had succeeded in settling the case: Clinton agreed to pay Jones $700,000, the full amount sought in the Complaint, and to issue a statement expressing regret, but not apologizing or admitting that the events had occurred. The statement read in part:

> the parties agree that Paula Corbin Jones did not engage in any improper or sexual conduct on May 8, 1991, and that the allegations and inferences about her published in the *American Spectator* are false and their adverse effects on her character and reputation are regrettable.

Jones, however, refused to accept the settlement, a decision that led her attorneys to withdraw from the case. (See Introduction to Chapter 5.)

Eventually, agreement was reached. Settlement occurred on November 13, 1998. Seven and a half months earlier, Judge Wright had granted President Clinton's summary judgment motion. Jones then filed an appeal with the U.S. Court of Appeals for the Eighth Circuit, which kept the lawsuit alive and created at least some possibility that summary judgment would be reversed, if only partially.[1] Moreover, the story of the Clinton-Lewinsky affair had broken in the media, and the House Judiciary Committee was preparing to submit articles of impeachment to the full House of Representatives. On both sides, hundreds of thousands of dollars' worth of lawyer time had been expended.

TEXT OF SETTLEMENT

The settlement terms were as follows:

> Whereas it is the desire of all the parties to end the above-captioned litigation for all purposes, it is hereby stipulated and agreed as follows:

---

1. On appeal, Jones raised two issues of significance. One was whether Judge Wright had erred in ordering Jones's lawyers not to pursue discovery concerning Monica Lewinsky, on the grounds that the Office of Independent Counsel needed to ensure that its criminal investigation would not be hampered. You will read more about this issue in the next chapter, because Lewinsky's attorneys attempted to appeal the discovery termination order as soon as it was issued, before the final summary judgment decision had been made. They failed, and so the issue became part of the overall appeal after the final judgment.

The second issue was whether Judge Wright had erred in ruling that sexual harassment could not be actionable absent a tangible job detriment. In two cases decided shortly after Judge Wright's summary judgment ruling, the Supreme Court ruled that sexual harassment could be actionable without evidence of tangible job detriment. *Faragher v. City of Boca Raton*, 524 U.S. 775 (1998) and *Burlington Industries, Inc. v. Ellerth*, 524 U.S. 742 (1998). For an argument that the Eighth Circuit would have reversed Judge Wright's decision, *see* Moira McAndrew, Note, How the Supreme Court's Reiteration of Sexual Harassment Standards Affirmed in *Faragher* and *Ellerth* Would Have Led to Jones' Survival in *Jones v. Clinton*, 47 Clev. St. L. Rev. 231 (1999). Other commentators disagreed, arguing that *Faragher* and *Ellerth* were

1. The Plaintiff, Paula Corbin Jones, will receive and accept a total payment of $850,000 . . . in full satisfaction of all claims for damages, including but not limited to any physical and personal injury, civil rights violations, emotional distress and any fees and expenses incurred in connection with this litigation of the facts and circumstances underlying it;

2. William Jefferson Clinton will cause said sum to be paid to the plaintiff within 60 . . . days of execution of this agreement;

3. The parties . . . hereby unconditionally release each other and their representatives in connection with any claims which have or could be made in or in connection with the litigation or the facts and circumstances underlying it;

4. Upon the execution of this agreement, the parties will jointly file a motion with the U.S. Court of Appeals for the Eighth Circuit, seeking voluntary dismissal of appeal No. 98-2161 EALR, each party to bear his or her own costs;

5. Nothing in this agreement shall be construed to be an admission of liability or wrongdoing by any party;

6. It is understood and agreed that this is the entire and only agreement between the parties and that it will be filed in open Court;

7. It is understood and agreed by the parties that the agreement of each of them to this stipulation for Settlement and Release is not subject to any conditions, and that the consideration recited herein is the sole consideration for the parties' agreement to this Stipulation;

8. It is understood and agreed that the parties have designated their counsel to execute this agreement on their behalf.

NOTES AND COMMENTS

1. Analyzing the terms of settlement.

(A) *"A total payment of $850,000"*—Why would President Clinton agree to pay more than the amount sought on the face of the complaint? Note that Paragraph 1 specifies that this amount includes "any fees and expenses incurred in connection with this litigation of the facts and circumstances underlying it." The nature of the lead claim (a constitutional violation) created the possibility that Jones could have been awarded attorneys' fees in addition to damages had she prevailed at trial.[2] By settling in this way, the question of how much plaintiff's attorneys will be paid is shifted to the plaintiff.

Therefore, on the Jones side of the lawsuit, a further agreement was reached as to the division of the $850,000. Jones received $200,000. The remainder was divided among her attorneys: $283,000 to Rader, Campbell, Fisher and Pyke, the firm that had become lead counsel in October 1997; $266,000 to Davis and Cammarata, her original attorneys; and $100,000 to The Rutherford Institute, the legal advocacy

---

distinguishable from *Jones* because the harassment in each of those cases continued over a long period of time, rather than consisting of a single alleged incident. *See* Marcia Coyle and Harvey Berkman, "Politics, Not Law, Is Behind Jones Settlement: Experts Say Recent Supreme Court Rulings Do Little to Bolster Her Appeal," National Law Journal, Oct. 12, 1998, at A1.

2. See 42 U.S.C. §1988.

group that worked as co-counsel with the Rader firm. Depending on the full amount of the Davis and Cammarata fees (one imagines that the amount they ultimately received was less than that), it is possible that Jones herself would have received more money had she settled for $700,000 in the summer of 1997.

(B) "*Unconditionally release each other . . . in connection with any claims which have or could be made in or in connection with the litigation or the facts and circumstances underlying it*"—This language clearly bars Jones from suing Clinton again based on any aspect of the alleged May 1991 incident or based on any events or facts related to her claims. If you have studied preclusion, you will appreciate even more the importance to defendants of such broad language.

(C) "*A motion seeking voluntary dismissal of [the] appeal*"—It is typical that a joint motion to dismiss would be filed to terminate the appeal, as described in the agreement. The settlement also specifies that there is no possibility of plaintiff seeking attorneys' fees for the appeal ("*each party to bear its own costs*").

(D) "*Nothing . . . shall be construed to be an admission of liability or wrongdoing*"—This was obviously important to President Clinton for political reasons. Why might it have been important for legal reasons as well, even with the total release language quoted above? Again, the law of preclusion is significant here.

(E) "*The entire and only agreement . . . will be filed in open Court*"—Including a provision that specifies whether the settlement will be publicly disclosed is common, although in most cases, the agreement is to keep the terms confidential. Insuring that the terms will be public is unusual. Both parties here probably had reasons to want there to be no questions about the terms on which they settled.

Can you think of any other issues that might have been, but were not, covered in the settlement?

2. Settlement-related remedies.   What if after the settlement agreement had been signed, one party had reneged? How would one enforce a settlement agreement? Unless the terms of a settlement agreement are incorporated into a judgment of the court (which was not done in *Jones v. Clinton*), the agreement is treated as an ordinary contract. Thus, one would have a remedy in contract law for failure to perform. If the contract is incorporated into judgment, what possible remedies would one have? Would there be other ways to raise the violation of a settlement agreement in the underlying lawsuit?

A strange variation on settlement law arose after the end of *Jones v. Clinton*. Abraham Hirschfeld, a wealthy New York real estate developer, had promised in 1998 that he would pay Paula Jones $1 million if she settled her case against President Clinton, saying that settlement was needed for the good of the country. He appeared at a press conference holding a check for that amount made payable to her and her lawyers. He and Jones entered into a formal contract, but he never made payment. In August 2001, Jones sued for breach of contract in the U.S. District Court for the Southern District of New York. Meanwhile, Hirschfeld, who was then 81, had been convicted of seeking (unsuccessfully) to arrange for the murder of a former business partner and was serving a one- to three-year sentence.

3. Default as an alternative scenario.   One of the lesser-known satellite controversies surrounding *Jones v. Clinton* arose when Harvard Law School Professor Alan Dershowitz attacked Robert Bennett, President Clinton's lawyer, for not having defaulted the case. Dershowitz argued that Bennett never should have permitted Clinton to be deposed regarding his sexual history. In 1997, Dershowitz wrote that Clinton should have deposited the full amount prayed for in the complaint with the court and taken a default under Rule 55, rather than respond to the questions from Jones's lawyers.

The Dershowitz default option became a topic of debate in legal periodicals. Some commentators derided the suggestion. Lawyer-journalist Jeffrey Toobin wrote that it "did have an elegant simplicity. It was also completely insane."[3] Other lawyers agreed that, at least in hindsight, the President's lawyers should have given greater consideration to default.[4] At what point in the case would that option have made the most sense?

4. Analyzing Rule 55.   Consider the Dershowitz proposal. Would President Clinton have been assured of avoiding potentially embarrassing questions? First, outline the steps in the process that would have occurred. What is the difference between default, entry of default, and entry of a default judgment? Would Jones's lawyers have had an opportunity to seek further information from him at any of those points? Why or why not?

5. The judicial role in default.   If President Clinton had defaulted, would the clerk of court have been authorized to enter judgment for Jones in the amount she prayed for in her complaint? If not, what process would have ensued? Could Jones's lawyers have sought a greater amount than they asked for in the complaint?

---

3. Toobin, A Vast Conspiracy: The Real Story of the Sex Scandal That Nearly Brought Down a President 50 (1999).

4. Roderick MacLeish, Jr., "No, Dershowitz Argument Is Sound," National Law Journal, Feb. 22, 1999, at A27 ("Letters"); David Rosenberg, "Default Would Have Shielded Clinton's Past," National Law Journal, Feb. 22, 1999, at A27 ("Letters").

CHAPTER TWELVE

Appeal

INTRODUCTION

As you have seen throughout this book, Judge Wright issued many decisions—including those on the motion to suspend the case, the motion to dismiss, a motion to amend, summary judgment, intervention, and multiple aspects of discovery—during the course of the lawsuit. The court's docket lists 65 separate orders by Judge Wright before the case ended (not counting scheduling orders). As each ruling issued, could the party who lost have appealed it? Generally, no. The law discourages piecemeal appeals; by statute, the jurisdiction of the courts of appeals is limited to appeals from "final decisions of the district courts."[1]

Under this principle, known as the final judgment rule, rulings on pre-trial motions are immediately appealable only if they are final, dispositive adjudications of the claims and relief sought in the case.[2] Judge Wright's decision granting summary judgment on all claims would be an example of a final judgment. A trial court's formal entry of judgment is typically the signal that there has been a "final decision" and that an appeal would be timely. See Rules 54, 55, 56, and 58.

However, there are exceptions to the final judgment rule, which allow for what are called *interlocutory appeals*. The most commonly used are provided for in 28 U.S.C. §1292. In *Jones v. Clinton*, the only contested issue regarding an interlocutory appeal arose under §1292(b), which requires that the order being appealed from:

> involves a controlling question of law as to which there is substantial ground for difference of opinion and . . . an immediate appeal from the order may materially advance the ultimate termination of the litigation.

The ruling in question was Judge Wright's order excluding all evidence concerning Monica Lewinsky. After the Office of Independent Counsel (OIC) Kenneth Starr learned of the Clinton-Lewinsky affair, both the prosecutors and Jones's lawyers

---

1. 28 U.S.C. §1291.
2. Liberty Mutual Ins. Co. v. Wetzel, 424 U.S. 737 (1976).

were pursuing evidence about it. The OIC asked Judge Wright to curb the discovery efforts of Jones's lawyers, so that its investigation would be paramount. That request led to the following order:

Order of January 29, 1998

In seeking limited intervention and a stay of discovery, OIC states that counsel for the plaintiff, in a deliberate and calculated manner, are shadowing the grand jury's investigation of the Monica Lewinsky matter. OIC states that "the pending criminal investigation is of such gravity and paramount importance that this Court would do a disservice to the Nation if it were to permit the unfettered—and extraordinarily aggressive—discovery efforts currently underway to proceed unabated." OIC's motion comes with less than 48 hours left in the period for conducting discovery. . . . Given the timing of OIC's motion and the possible impact that this motion could have on the proceedings in this matter, the Court is required to rule at this time on the admissibility at trial of evidence concerning Monica Lewinsky.

Rule 403 of the Federal Rules of Evidence provides that evidence, although relevant, "may be excluded if its probative value is substantially outweighed by the danger of unfair prejudice, confusion of the issues, or misleading the jury, or by considerations of undue delay, waste of time, or needless presentation of cumulative evidence." This weighing process compels the conclusion that evidence concerning Monica Lewinsky should be excluded from the trial of this matter.

The Court acknowledges that evidence concerning Monica Lewinsky might be relevant to the issues in this case. This Court would await resolution of the criminal investigation currently underway if the Lewinsky evidence were essential to the plaintiff's case. The Court determines, however, that it is not essential to the core issues in this case. In fact, some of this evidence might even be inadmissible as extrinsic evidence under Rule 608(b) of the Federal Rules of Evidence. Admitting *any* evidence of the Lewinsky matter would frustrate the timely resolution of this case and would undoubtedly cause undue expense and delay.

This Court's ruling today does not preclude admission of any other evidence of alleged improper conduct occurring in the White House.

In addition, and perhaps more importantly, the substantial interests of the Presidency militate against any undue delay in this matter that would be occasioned by allowing plaintiff to pursue the Monica Lewinsky matter. Under the Supreme Court's ruling in *Clinton v. Jones,* 117 S. Ct. 1636, 1651 (1997), "[t]he high respect that is owed to the Office of the Chief Executive . . . is a matter that should inform the conduct of the entire proceeding, including the timing and scope of discovery." There can be no doubt that a speedy resolution of this case is in everyone's best interests, including that of the Office of the President, and the Court will therefore direct that the case stay on course.

One final basis for the Court's ruling is the integrity of the criminal investigation. This Court must consider the fact that the government's proceedings could be impaired and prejudiced were the Court to permit inquiry into the Lewinsky matter by the parties in this civil case. In that regard, it would not be proper for this Court, given that it must generally yield to the interests of an ongoing grand jury investigation, to give counsel for the plaintiff or the defendants access to witnesses' statements in the government's criminal investigation. That being so, and because this case can in any event proceed without evidence concerning Monica Lewinsky, the Court will exclude evidence concerning her from the trial of this matter. . . .

Ten days after Judge Wright issued the order excluding the Lewinsky evidence, Jones's lawyers sought an immediate appeal.

PLAINTIFF'S MEMORANDUM IN SUPPORT OF MOTION FOR SECTION 1292(b) CERTIFICATION

. . . I.   THE ADMISSIBILITY OF THE LEWINSKY EVIDENCE INVOLVES CONTROLLING ISSUES OF LAW

On January 29, 1998, *before* plaintiff was allowed to conduct most of her discovery aimed at the Lewinsky evidence, the Court ruled that the Lewinsky evidence is inadmissible in this civil action. Without knowing the substance of the evidence, the Court made the legal determination that the Lewinsky evidence—whatever it might have turned out to be—"is not essential to the core issues in this case." In making this ruling, the Court necessarily (but perhaps inadvertently) answered certain "controlling question[s] of law" within the meaning of Section 1292(b).

. . . [T]he discovery aborted by the Court was reasonably calculated to lead to admissible evidence. . . .

In sum, the Court erred by denying plaintiff access to very powerful evidence that goes directly to the "core issues" in this case. . . . [T]he Court should make the finding that the Order involves controlling questions of law for purposes of Section 1292(b). The notion that the evidence "is not essential to the core issues in this case," raises controlling issues of law regarding the fundamental elements of plaintiff's causes of action, including proof of Mr. Clinton's conduct toward plaintiff, proof of his intent to discriminate, proof of the object of his conspiracy with Trooper Ferguson, proof of perjury and obstruction of justice in this case, and proof of factors governing the amount of punitive damages.

II.   THERE ARE SUBSTANTIAL GROUNDS FOR A DIFFERENCE OF OPINION AS TO THE LEGAL VALIDITY OF THE ORDER

The issue here is not merely whether the Lewinsky evidence would have been *relevant*. Rather, the issue is whether the Court erred as a matter of law by ruling the evidence *inadmissible* under Fed. R. Evid. 403 at this stage of the proceeding. There are substantial grounds for concluding that the Court erred.

First of all, when the Order was issued, it was impossible for the Court to do the balancing required by Rule 403, because the evidence being excluded was simply not yet discovered and not before the court. In an earlier order, the Court had postponed the Lewinsky deposition indefinitely, so her testimony was not before the Court. The depositions of other witnesses (such as Linda Tripp, Betty Currie, Kenneth Bacon, and Leon Panetta) had been scheduled by plaintiff but, due to the Order, plaintiff was not allowed to take them. The evidence which plaintiff had been able to gather was not presented to the Court, because plaintiff had been given no notice that the Court would be doing a Rule 403 analysis or even considering any admissibility issue. Without knowing the substance of the evidence, the Court had no information to place on one side of the scale, and it was error to rule the unknown evidence inadmissible under Rule 403. The Court should have permitted the discovery and *then* weighed the probative value of the fruit of that discovery. . . .

Should Mr. Clinton or his counsel suggest to the jury that Mr. Clinton has never engaged in conduct of the sort alleged by plaintiff, they will "open the door" to the Lewinsky evidence. Its probative value cannot be measured at this juncture, and so plaintiff's discovery should not be barred.

A second substantial ground for disagreement with the Order is based on Rule 415 of the Federal Rules of Evidence. Rule 415 provides that evidence of another "offense of sexual assault"—as that term is broadly defined in Fed. R. Evid. 413(d)—is absolutely admissible in this civil case. If Rule 415 merely stated that such evidence is relevant, the evidence might be subject to exclusion under Rule 403 in some circumstances; but since Rule 415 specifically declares that such evidence is admissible, it is error as a matter of law to exclude it under Rule 403. . . .

Third, not a shred of evidence suggested that admission or discovery of the Lewinsky evidence would delay the trial of this case. Even assuming *arguendo* that the Court is legally required to stay discovery due to the pending criminal investigation, there was no evidence that the investigation would require a stay until the May 26, 1998, trial date. Nor did the OIC ask for a stay of that duration. A stay of one or two months might have been sufficient to allow the investigation to be completed, in which event there would still be enough time to complete discovery in this case without delaying the trial. The striking of plaintiff's evidence and discovery efforts was completely unnecessary.

Fourth, even if the OIC had been seeking a stay that would have delayed the trial, which it was not, punishing *plaintiff* by excluding very potent evidence would be unjustified. The investigation is focused on apparently criminal conduct by Defendant Clinton and his agents, not by plaintiff. To punish plaintiff because Defendant Clinton's conduct is of such a nature as to warrant criminal investigation is manifestly unjust. There *is no legal authority whatsoever* for the proposition that a pending criminal investigation against a defendant is a valid legal basis for excluding evidence which the plaintiff wishes to offer.

Fifth, Fed. R. Civ. P. 26(c) requires a showing of "good cause" before the Court may disallow discovery of information which "appears reasonably calculated to lead to the discovery of admissible evidence" within the meaning of Fed. R. Civ. P. 26(b)(1). As explained above, the Court's previous rulings in this case establish that plaintiff's discovery of the Lewinsky evidence is well within the scope of proper discovery under Rule 26(b)(1). The order disallowed that discovery in the absence of any demonstration of "good cause" to do so.

For these and other reasons, the Court should vacate the Order. At a minimum, the Court should find that there is a substantial basis for a difference of opinion as to whether the Order is legally correct.

III.   AN IMMEDIATE APPEAL WOULD MATERIALLY ADVANCE
THE ULTIMATE TERMINATION OF THIS LITIGATION

An interlocutory appeal would actually expedite the ultimate resolution of this civil action, and avoid needless and wasteful expenditures of judicial resources and those of the parties.

If the case proceeds to trial without the benefit of the Lewinsky evidence, and if plaintiff does not prevail (or if the actual or punitive damages award is insufficient), then plaintiff will appeal the Order. In *addition,* however, while that appeal is pending, plaintiff will also be entitled to move for relief from the judgment under Fed. R. Civ. P. 60(b), based on the misconduct of Defendant Clinton relating to Ms. Lewinsky and Ms. Tripp (perjury, subornation of perjury, obstruction of justice, and conspiracy to suborn perjury and obstruct justice) and perhaps also based on newly discovered evidence arising out of the ongoing investigations by the OIC and the news media. As a motion under Rule 60 "does not affect the finality of a judgment or suspend its operation," *see* Fed. R. Civ. P. 60(b), these proceedings under Rule 60 will take place even as the judgment itself is being appealed. Then, whichever party does not prevail on plaintiff's rule 60 motion will undoubtedly initiate *another appeal.*[3]

This multiplicity of litigation is avoidable. The Court need only allow the discovery to proceed, and reserve until the time of trial its ruling on admission of the evidence—in other words, do what is routinely done as a matter of course in every other civil action. . . .

PRESIDENT CLINTON'S OPPOSITION TO PLAINTIFF'S MOTION FOR
SECTION 1292(b) CERTIFICATION

. . . The Eighth Circuit has decided that Section 1292(b) "should and will be used only in exceptional cases where a decision on appeal may avoid protracted and expensive litigation." [citation omitted] Thus, the statute should be used "sparingly," and the burden on the movant is a heavy one to show that the case is an "exceptional" one in which immediate appeal is warranted. [The §1292(b)] criteria cannot be satisfied here.

Simply put, because the January 29 Order was one within the Court's discretion, it cannot as a matter of law constitute "a controlling question" for purposes of Section 1292(b). The Eighth Circuit has already decided that no controlling questions of law can arise from "the discretionary resolution of discovery issues." [citation omitted] Similarly, pre-trial rulings on admissibility also are not subject to certification under Section 1292(b).

[T]he Eighth Circuit [has] refused to consider a question certified by the district court pursuant to Section 1292(b) when the question was one of whether certain files should be produced in discovery:

---

3. Moreover, plaintiff will, if necessary, petition for mandamus relief from the Order and will seek a stay of this case pending the outcome of same. A stay might delay the entire case. This risk can be avoided simply by permitting the discovery. [Footnote 4 in the original document.]

> The issue presented by appellants is merely whether the district court
> abused its discretion in ordering production of the files. As appellants recog-
> nize, this discovery ruling is committed to the district court's discretion, and
> an allegation of abuse does not create a legal issue. . . . Because the discre-
> tionary resolution of discovery issues precludes the requisite controlling ques-
> tion of law, we hold that appellants' challenge to the district court's balanc-
> ing of interest involves no controlling questions of law.
>
> [citation omitted] Similarly, a pretrial ruling on the admissibility of evidence is never
> properly the subject of a Section 1282(b) interlocutory appeal.
>
> Nor is there no reason to believe that certification of the January 29 Order
> will "materially advance the ultimate termination of the litigation." [citation omitted]
> To the contrary, it will only delay it. Indeed, the January 29 Order is but one of
> many evidentiary rulings that will be made in the course of this action. If every time
> an evidentiary ruling is made, an appeal is taken, this litigation would not be (as
> plaintiff purportedly wishes) quickly drawn to a close, but would be reviewed piece-
> meal by the Eighth Circuit.
>
> B.   Plaintiff's Rule 60 Argument Is Both Premature and Unavailing
>
> Finally, Plaintiff prematurely threatens appeal of any judgment made on
> the basis of a trial Court proceeding that does not include the Lewinsky evidence.
> This threat is made to manufacture grounds for plaintiff's argument that a refusal
> to certify an appeal under Section 1292(b) would delay resolution of the litigation.
> Specifically, plaintiff argues that she must be permitted to introduce at trial evi-
> dence of "the misconduct of Defendant Clinton relating to Ms. Lewinsky and Ms.
> Tripp . . . and perhaps also based on newly discovered evidence arising out of the
> ongoing investigations by the OIC and by the media." Otherwise, she would be
> entitled to move for relief from judgment under Fed. R. Civ. P. 60(b).
>
> This argument is based on mere speculation that new evidence would
> emerge—and that it would be favorable to plaintiff. More importantly, it fails to take
> into account the law of the Eighth Circuit, wherein motions for relief from judgment
> on the basis of new evidence are disfavored, and relief from judgment is only per-
> mitted if the new evidence is material, rather than, as here, collateral. *See Mitchell
> v. Shalala,* 48 F.3d 1039, 1041-1042 (8th Cir. 1995). Thus under *Mitchell,* this argu-
> ment, even if it were not woefully premature, would be unavailing. . . .

Postscript: Judge Wright denied the motion to certify an interlocutory appeal
under §1292(b), largely on the grounds argued by the President. (Note that the statute requires that even if a district judge certifies an interlocutory appeal, the prospective appellant must also obtain permission to proceed with the appeal from the court
of appeals.)

NOTES AND COMMENTS

1. Section 1292(b) criteria.   How do you assess the weight of the parties' arguments on each of the necessary criteria for §1292(b) certification?

(A) whether the order involves a controlling question of law;

(B) whether there is a substantial ground for difference of opinion; and

(C) whether certification will materially advance the ultimate termination of the litigation.

2. Other bases for interlocutory appeal.   Even if plaintiff failed to satisfy the criteria for §1292(b), could she have appealed this under the collateral order doctrine? Why or why not? On a writ of mandamus?

Exercise 16—Interlocutory Appeal of a Discovery Order

Return to Judge Wright's order of December 11, 1997 in Chapter 7 establishing the scope of discovery for Jones's inquiries into President Clinton's past sexual relationships. Would that have been appealable under any of the doctrines allowing interlocutory appeal? Write a memorandum to Bennett advising him whether to seek immediate appeal and if so, how, and with what likely results. Are there other orders that you have read in previous chapters that might have been immediately appealable?

APPENDIX ONE

Articles of Impeachment

Following are the four articles of impeachment of President Clinton submitted by the Committee on the Judiciary of the House of Representatives to the full House. The first and third articles were passed by the House and became the charges upon which President Clinton was tried by the Senate.

Article I

Passed by the House of Representatives 228 to 206
Vote in the Senate: 45 guilty, 55 not guilty

In his conduct while president of the United States, William Jefferson Clinton, in violation of his constitutional oath faithfully to execute the office of president of the United States and, to the best of his ability, preserve, protect, and defend the Constitution of the United States, and in violation of his constitutional duty to take care that the laws be faithfully executed, has willfully corrupted and manipulated the judicial process of the United States for his personal gain and exoneration, impeding the administration of justice, in that:

On August 17, 1998, William Jefferson Clinton swore to tell the truth, the whole truth, and nothing but the truth before a Federal grand jury of the United States. Contrary to that oath, William Jefferson Clinton willfully provided perjurious, false, and misleading testimony to the grand jury concerning one or more of the following: (1) the nature and details of his relationship with a subordinate Government employee; (2) prior perjurious, false, and misleading testimony he gave in a Federal civil rights action brought against him; (3) prior false and misleading statements he allowed his attorney to make to a Federal judge in that civil rights action; and (4) his corrupt efforts to influence the testimony of witnesses and to impede the discovery of evidence in that civil rights action.

In doing this, William Jefferson Clinton has undermined the integrity of his office, has brought disrepute on the presidency, has betrayed his trust as president, and has acted in a manner subversive of the rule of law and justice, to the manifest injury of the people of the United States.

Wherefore, William Jefferson Clinton, by such conduct, warrants impeachment and trial, and removal from office and disqualification to hold and enjoy any office of honor, trust or profit under the United States.

[Note: The preceding two paragraphs are repeated at the end of each Article and are omitted for editing purposes from the text of the following Articles.]

Article II
Rejected by the House of Representatives 229 to 205

In his conduct while president of the United States, William Jefferson Clinton, in violation of his constitutional oath faithfully to execute the office of president of the United States and, to the best of his ability, preserve, protect, and defend the Constitution of the United States, and in violation of his constitutional duty to take care that the laws be faithfully executed, has willfully corrupted and manipulated the judicial process of the United States for his personal gain and exoneration, impeding the administration of justice, in that:

(1) On December 23, 1997, William Jefferson Clinton, in sworn answers to written questions asked as part of a Federal civil rights action brought against him, willfully provided perjurious, false, and misleading testimony in response to questions deemed relevant by a Federal judge concerning conduct and proposed conduct with subordinate employees.

(2) On January 17, 1998, William Jefferson Clinton swore under oath to tell the truth, the whole truth, and nothing but the truth in a deposition given as part of a Federal civil rights action brought against him. Contrary to that oath, William Jefferson Clinton willfully provided perjurious, false, and misleading testimony in response to questions deemed relevant by a Federal judge concerning the nature and details of his relationship with a subordinate Government employee, his knowledge of that employee's involvement and participation in the civil rights action brought against him, and his corrupt efforts to influence the testimony of that employee.

. . .

Article III
Passed by the House of Representatives 221 to 212
Vote in the Senate: 50 guilty, 50 not guilty

In his conduct while president of the United States, William Jefferson Clinton, in violation of his constitutional oath faithfully to execute the office of president of the United States and, to the best of his ability, preserve, protect, and defend the Constitution of the United States, and in violation of his constitutional duty to take care that the laws be faithfully executed, has prevented, obstructed, and impeded the administration of justice, and has to that end engaged personally, and through his subordinates and agents, in a course of conduct or scheme designed to delay, impede, cover up, and conceal the existence of evidence and testimony related to a Federal civil rights action brought against him in a duly instituted judicial proceeding.

The means used to implement this course of conduct or scheme included one or more of the following acts:

(1) On or about December 17, 1997, William Jefferson Clinton corruptly encouraged a witness in a Federal civil rights action brought against him to execute a sworn affidavit in that proceeding that he knew to be perjurious, false, and misleading.

(2) On or about December 17, 1997, William Jefferson Clinton corruptly encouraged a witness in a Federal civil rights action brought against him to give perjurious, false, and misleading testimony if and when called to testify personally in that proceeding.

(3) On or about December 28, 1997, William Jefferson Clinton corruptly engaged in, encouraged, or supported a scheme to conceal evidence that had been subpoenaed in a Federal civil rights action brought against him.

(4) Beginning on or about December 7, 1997, and continuing through and including January 14, 1998, William Jefferson Clinton intensified and succeeded in an effort to secure job assistance to a witness in a Federal civil rights action brought against him in order to corruptly prevent the truthful testimony of that witness in that proceeding at a time when the truthful testimony of that witness would have been harmful to him.

(5) On January 17, 1998, at his deposition in a Federal civil rights action brought against him, William Jefferson Clinton corruptly allowed his attorney to make false and misleading statements to a Federal judge characterizing an affidavit, in order to prevent questioning deemed relevant by the judge. Such false and misleading statements were subsequently acknowledged by his attorney in a communication to that judge.

(6) On or about January 18 and January 20-21, 1998, William Jefferson Clinton related a false and misleading account of events relevant to a Federal civil rights action brought against him to a potential witness in that proceeding, in order to corruptly influence the testimony of that witness.

(7) On or about January 21, 23, and 26, 1998, William Jefferson Clinton made false and misleading statements to potential witnesses in a Federal grand jury proceeding in order to corruptly influence the testimony of those witnesses. The false and misleading statements made by William Jefferson Clinton were repeated by the witnesses to the grand jury, causing the grand jury to receive false and misleading information.

. . .

Article IV
Rejected by the House of Representatives 285 to 148

Using the powers and influence of the office of president of the United States, William Jefferson Clinton, in violation of his constitutional oath faithfully to execute the office of president of the United States and, to the best of his ability, preserve, protect, and defend the Constitution of the United States, and in disregard of his constitutional duty to take care that the laws be faithfully executed, has engaged in conduct that resulted in misuse and abuse of his high office, impaired the due and proper administration of justice and the conduct of lawful inquiries, and contravened the authority of the legislative branch and the truth-seeking purpose of a coordinate investigative proceeding in that, as president, William Jefferson Clinton, refused and failed to respond to certain written requests for admission and willfully made perjurious, false, and misleading sworn statements in response to certain written requests for admission propounded to him as part of the impeachment inquiry authorized by the House of Representatives of the Congress of the United States.

William Jefferson Clinton, in refusing and failing to respond, and in making perjurious, false, and misleading statements, assumed to himself functions and judgments necessary to the exercise of the sole power of impeachment vested by the Constitution in the House of Representatives and exhibited contempt for the inquiry. . . .

Jones v. Clinton Chronology

Date	Event
May 8, 1991	Alleged incident occurs
Jan. 1, 1994	"His Cheatin' Heart" article publication date; Jones learns of it and calls Daniel Traylor, a solo practitioner in Little Rock
Feb. 11, 1994	Announcement of Jones's claim at C-PAC press conference
May 5, 1994	Attempt to negotiate a settlement fails
May 6, 1994	Complaint filed
June 16, 1994	First conference with Judge Wright
June 27, 1994	Motion by Clinton to set briefing schedule
July 21, 1994	Ruling on order of motions
Aug. 8, 1994	Clinton's motion to dismiss on immunity grounds
Oct. 21, 1994	Jones's opposition to Clinton's motion to dismiss
Dec. 28, 1994	Judge Wright's decision on Clinton's motion to dismiss, which Clinton appeals
Nov. 15, 1995	First sexual encounter between Clinton and Monica Lewinsky
Jan. 9, 1996	Decision of Eighth Circuit on Clinton's motion to dismiss, which Clinton appeals to the Supreme Court
Mar. 29, 1997	Last sexual encounter between Clinton and Lewinsky
May 27, 1997	Supreme Court decision in *Jones v. Clinton*
July 3, 1997	Clinton's answer filed
July 3, 1997	Clinton's motion for judgment on the pleadings
July 29, 1997	Jones's opposition to motion for judgment on the pleadings
Aug. 5-6, 1997	Opposing counsel reach tentative settlement, which Jones refuses
Aug. 22, 1997	Ruling on motion for judgment on the pleadings; trial date set for May 27, 1998
Sept. 9, 1997	Jones's first team of lawyers withdraws

Date	Event
Oct. 1, 1997	Jones's new team of lawyers enters the case
Oct. 28, 1997	Jones's motion for leave to file amended complaint
Oct. 30, 1997	Order mandating confidentiality of discovery materials
Nov. 5, 1997	Clinton's motion for protective order regarding portions of the discovery requests
Nov. 10, 1997	Clinton's opposition to motion for leave to file amended complaint
Nov. 12, 1997	Deposition of Jones
Nov. 18, 1997	Jones's lawyers learn of Clinton's affair with Lewinsky
Nov. 24, 1997	Ruling granting leave to file amended complaint
Dec. 5, 1997	Jones's lawyers fax witness list to Clinton's lawyers, with Lewinsky's name
Dec. 8, 1997	Jones's first amended complaint filed
Dec. 11, 1997	Order ruling that Clinton must answer interrogatories about sexual activities
Dec. 17, 1997	Clinton's answer to amended complaint filed; he calls Lewinsky
Dec. 18, 1997	Order ruling on deposition questions for Jane Does that concern sexual activities
Dec. 19, 1997	Lewinsky receives subpoena duces tecum instructing her to bring to the deposition "each and every gift" that she had received from Clinton, including "jewelry and/or hat pins"
Dec. 23, 1997	Clinton answers "none" to Interrogatories 10 and 11
Jan. 7, 1998	Lewinsky affidavit filed
Jan. 8, 1998	One of Jones's secret lawyers tells a lawyer on the Office of Independent Counsel (OIC) staff about the Clinton-Lewinsky affair
Jan. 9, 1998	Further ruling on deposition questions for Jane Does
Jan. 12, 1998	At a daylong hearing, Judge Wright asks each side to summarize their evidence and urges both sides to settle
Jan. 12, 1998	OIC staff send word to Linda Tripp that they want to hear what she knows; Tripp calls Jackie Bennett and he travels to her home to interview her
Jan. 14, 1998	Bennett requests that Judge Wright preside over the deposition
Jan. 15, 1998	Independent Counsel Kenneth Starr obtains authorization to broaden his inquiry to include whether there was perjury and/or obstruction of justice in *Jones v. Clinton*
Jan. 16, 1998	OIC staff question Lewinsky at Pentagon City Mall; one of Jones's lawyers interviews Tripp
Jan. 17, 1998	Deposition of Clinton
Jan. 19, 1998	The media report Clinton-Lewinsky affair

Date	Event
Jan. 29, 1998	Order excluding Lewinsky evidence and halting discovery
Feb. 4, 1998	Motion by coalition of media groups for "limited purpose" intervention
Feb. 10, 1998	Jones's motion for §1292(b) certification of immediate appeal of ruling on Lewinsky evidence and discovery
Feb. 17, 1998	Clinton's motion for summary judgment
Mar. 9, 1998	Order denying Jones's motion for §1292(b) certification
Mar. 9, 1998	Order denying motion to intervene by media groups
Mar. 13, 1998	Jones's opposition to summary judgment
Mar. 31, 1998	Clinton's reply to Jones's opposition
April 1, 1998	Decision granting summary judgment, which Jones appeals
Aug. 17, 1998	Clinton testifies before grand jury and later makes a televised apology to the nation
Sept. 9, 1998	Starr submits his report to Congress
Oct. 20, 1998	Oral arguments before Eighth Circuit on Jones's appeal
Nov. 13, 1998	Settlement
Dec. 19, 1998	The House of Representatives votes to impeach President Clinton on two articles: obstruction of justice in *Jones v. Clinton* and perjury before the grand jury regarding his deposition and his relationship with Lewinsky
Feb. 12, 1999	The Senate acquits President Clinton. The vote on the article alleging obstruction of justice in *Jones v. Clinton* is 50 to 50. The vote on the article alleging perjury in his grand jury testimony is 45 guilty, 55 not guilty.
April 12, 1999	Judge Wright holds President Clinton in contempt for false statements made during discovery.
Jan. 19, 2001	The Circuit Court of Pulaski County, Arkansas, enters a consent order suspending President Clinton's license to practice law in Arkansas for five years. The OIC announces that it will not prosecute any matters that had been under investigation.

APPENDIX THREE

Standard Forms

JS 44
(Rev. 07/89)

CIVIL COVER SHEET

The JS-44 civil cover sheet and the information contained herein neither replace nor supplement the filing and service of pleadings or other papers as required by law, except as provided by local rules of court. This form, approved by the Judicial Conference of the United States in September 1974, is required for the use of the Clerk of Court for the purpose of initiating the civil docket sheet. (SEE INSTRUCTIONS ON THE REVERSE OF THE FORM.)

I (a) PLAINTIFFS

PAULA CORBIN JONES

DEFENDANTS

WILLIAM JEFFERSON CLINTON
DANNY FERGUSON

(b) COUNTY OF RESIDENCE OF FIRST LISTED PLAINTIFF __Los Angeles__
(EXCEPT IN U.S. PLAINTIFF CASES)

COUNTY OF RESIDENCE OF FIRST LISTED DEFENDANT __Pulaski__
(IN U.S. PLAINTIFF CASES ONLY)
NOTE: IN LAND CONDEMNATION CASES, USE THE LOCATION OF THE TRACT OF LAND INVOLVED

(c) ATTORNEYS (FIRM NAME, ADDRESS, AND TELEPHONE NUMBER)

Gilbert K. Davis   (703) 352-3880
9516-C Lee Highway
Fairfax, Virginia 22031
Co-counsel: Joseph Cammarata (same address)

ATTORNEYS (IF KNOWN)

II. BASIS OF JURISDICTION (PLACE AN × IN ONE BOX ONLY)

☐ 1 U.S. Government Plaintiff
☒ 3 Federal Question (U.S. Government Not a Party)
☐ 2 U.S. Government Defendant
☐ 4 Diversity (Indicate Citizenship of Parties in Item III)

III. CITIZENSHIP OF PRINCIPAL PARTIES (PLACE AN × IN ONE BOX FOR PLAINTIFF AND ONE BOX FOR DEFENDANT)
(For Diversity Cases Only)

	PTF	DEF		PTF	DEF
Citizen of This State	☐ 1	☐ 1	Incorporated or Principal Place of Business in This State	☐ 4	☐ 4
Citizen of Another State	☐ 2	☐ 2	Incorporated and Principal Place of Business in Another State	☐ 5	☐ 5
Citizen or Subject of a Foreign Country	☐ 3	☐ 3	Foreign Nation	☐ 6	☐ 6

IV. CAUSE OF ACTION (CITE THE U.S. CIVIL STATUTE UNDER WHICH YOU ARE FILING AND WRITE A BRIEF STATEMENT OF CAUSE
DO NOT CITE JURISDICTIONAL STATUTES UNLESS DIVERSITY)

42 U.S.C 1983 and 1985; Civil Rights Violations and other wrongs

V. NATURE OF SUIT (PLACE AN × IN ONE BOX ONLY)

CONTRACT
☐ 110 Insurance
☐ 120 Marine
☐ 130 Miller Act
☐ 140 Negotiable Instrument
☐ 150 Recovery of Overpayment & Enforcement of Judgment
☐ 151 Medicare Act
☐ 152 Recovery of Defaulted Student Loans (Excl. Veterans)
☐ 153 Recovery of Overpayment of Veteran's Benefits
☐ 160 Stockholders' Suits
☐ 190 Other Contract
☐ 195 Contract Product Liability

REAL PROPERTY
☐ 210 Land Condemnation
☐ 220 Foreclosure
☐ 230 Rent Lease & Ejectment
☐ 240 Torts to Land
☐ 245 Tort Product Liability
☐ 290 All Other Real Property

TORTS
PERSONAL INJURY
☐ 310 Airplane
☐ 315 Airplane Product Liability
☐ 320 Assault, Libel & Slander
☐ 330 Federal Employers' Liability
☐ 340 Marine
☐ 345 Marine Product Liability
☐ 350 Motor Vehicle
☐ 355 Motor Vehicle Product Liability
☐ 360 Other Personal Injury

CIVIL RIGHTS
☐ 441 Voting
☐ 442 Employment
☐ 443 Housing/ Accommodations
☐ 444 Welfare
☒ 440 Other Civil Rights

PERSONAL INJURY
☐ 362 Personal Injury— Med Malpractice
☐ 365 Personal Injury— Product Liability
☐ 368 Asbestos Personal Injury Product Liability

PERSONAL PROPERTY
☐ 370 Other Fraud
☐ 371 Truth in Lending
☐ 380 Other Personal Property Damage
☐ 385 Property Damage Product Liability

PRISONER PETITIONS
☐ 510 Motions to Vacate Sentence
Habeas Corpus:
☐ 530 General
☐ 535 Death Penalty
☐ 540 Mandamus & Other
☐ 550 Other

FORFEITURE /PENALTY
☐ 610 Agriculture
☐ 620 Other Food & Drug
☐ 625 Drug Related Seizure of Property 21 USC 881
☐ 630 Liquor Laws
☐ 640 R.R & Truck
☐ 650 Airline Regs
☐ 660 Occupational Safety/Health
☐ 690 Other

LABOR
☐ 710 Fair Labor Standards Act
☐ 720 Labor/Mgmt. Relations
☐ 730 Labor/Mgmt. Reporting & Disclosure Act
☐ 740 Railway Labor Act
☐ 790 Other Labor Litigation
☐ 791 Empl. Ret. Inc Security Act

BANKRUPTCY
☐ 422 Appeal 28 USC 158
☐ 423 Withdrawal 28 USC 157

PROPERTY RIGHTS
☐ 820 Copyrights
☐ 830 Patent
☐ 840 Trademark

SOCIAL SECURITY
☐ 861 HIA (1395ff)
☐ 862 Black Lung (923)
☐ 863 DIWC/DIWW (405(g))
☐ 864 SSID Title XVI
☐ 865 RSI (405(g))

FEDERAL TAX SUITS
☐ 870 Taxes (U.S. Plaintiff or Defendant)
☐ 871 IRS—Third Party 26 USC 7609

OTHER STATUTES
☐ 400 State Reapportionment
☐ 410 Antitrust
☐ 430 Banks and Banking
☐ 450 Commerce/ICC Rates/etc.
☐ 460 Deportation
☐ 470 Racketeer Influenced and Corrupt Organizations
☐ 810 Selective Service
☐ 850 Securities/Commodities/ Exchange
☐ 875 Customer Challenge 12 USC 3410
☐ 891 Agricultural Acts
☐ 892 Economic Stabilization Act
☐ 893 Environmental Matters
☐ 894 Energy Allocation Act
☐ 895 Freedom of Information Act
☐ 900 Appeal of Fee Determination Under Equal Access to Justice
☐ 950 Constitutionality of State Statutes
☐ 890 Other Statutory Actions

VI. ORIGIN (PLACE AN × IN ONE BOX ONLY)

☒ 1 Original Proceeding
☐ 2 Removed from State Court
☐ 3 Remanded from Appellate Court
☐ 4 Reinstated or Reopened
☐ 5 Transferred from another district (specify)
☐ 6 Multidistrict Litigation
☐ 7 Appeal to District Judge from Magistrate Judgment

VII. REQUESTED IN COMPLAINT:

CHECK IF THIS IS A CLASS ACTION
☐ UNDER F.R.C.P. 23

DEMAND $ 75,000+

Check YES only if demanded in complaint:
JURY DEMAND: ☒ YES ☐ NO

VIII. RELATED CASE(S) IF ANY (See instructions):

JUDGE _____   DOCKET NUMBER _____

DATE
May 5, 1994

SIGNATURE OF ATTORNEY OF RECORD

UNITED STATES DISTRICT COURT

AO 300 (12/93)

FILED
U.S. DISTRICT COURT
EASTERN DISTRICT ARKANSAS

JUN 2 4 1994

JAMES W. McCORMACK, CLERK
By: _____
DEP CLERK

WAIVER OF SERVICE OF SUMMONS

TO: Robert S. Bennett , Esquire
      (NAME OF PLAINTIFF'S ATTORNEY OR UNREPRESENTED PLAINTIFF)

I acknowledge receipt of your request that I waive service of a summons in the action of

JONES v. CLINTON, et al.,   which is case number LR-C-94-290
            (CAPTION OF ACTION)   (DOCKET NUMBER)

in the United States District Court for the_____Eastern_____District of

_____ARKANSAS_____ } have also received a copy of the complaint in the
action, two copies of this instrument, and a means by which I can return the signed waiver to you without
cost to me.

I agree to save the cost of service of a summons and an additional copy of the complaint in this
lawsuit by not requiring that I (or the entity on whose behalf I am acting) be served with judicial process
in the manner provided by Rule 4.

I (or the entity on whose behalf I am acting) will retain all defenses or objections to the lawsuit
or to the jurisdiction or venue of the court except for objections based on a defect in the summons or
in the service of the summons.

I understand that a judgment may be entered against me (or the party on whose behalf I am acting

if an answer or motion under Rule 12 is not served upon you within 60 days after_May 16, 1994_
                                                                          (DATE REQUEST WAS SENT)

or within 90 days after that date if the request was sent outside the United States.

5/23/94
DATE

Robert S. Bennett
SIGNATURE

Printed/Typed Name: Robert S. Bennett   Esquire

As   Counsel   of William Jefferson Clinton

Duty to Avoid Unnecessary Costs of Service of Summons

Rule 4 of the Federal Rules of Civil Procedure requires certain parties to cooperate in saving unnecessary costs of service
of the summons and complaint. A defendant located in the United States who, after being notified of an action and asked by a plaintiff
located in the United States to waive service of a summons, fails to do so will be required to bear the cost of such service unless good
cause be shown for the failure to sign and return the waiver.
It is not good cause for a failure to waive service that a party believes that the complaint is unfounded or that the action has
been brought in an improper place or in a court that lacks jurisdiction over the subject matter of the action or over its person or
property. A party who waives service of the summons retains all defenses and objections (except any relating to the summons or to the
service of the summons), and may later object to the jurisdiction of the court or to the place where the action has been brought.
A defendant who waives service must within the time specified on the waiver form serve on the plaintiff's
unrepresented plaintiff) a response to the complaint and must also file a signed copy of the response with the court. If the
motion is not served within this time, a default judgment may be taken against the defendant. By waiving service, a defendant
more time to answer than if the summons had been actually served when the request for waiver of service was received.

8

AO 88 (Rev. 11/91) Subpoena in a Civil Case

United States District Court

_____ DISTRICT OF _____

V.

SUBPOENA IN A CIVIL CASE

CASE NUMBER:

TO:

☐ YOU ARE COMMANDED to appear in the United States District Court at the place, date, and time specified below to testify in the above case.

PLACE OF TESTIMONY	COURTROOM
	DATE AND TIME

☐ YOU ARE COMMANDED to appear at the place, date, and time specified below to testify at the taking of a deposition in the above case.

PLACE OF DEPOSITION	DATE AND TIME

☐ YOU ARE COMMANDED to produce and permit inspection and copying of the following documents or objects at the place, date, and time specified below (list documents or objects):

PLACE	DATE AND TIME

☐ YOU ARE COMMANDED to permit inspection of the following premises at the date and time specified below.

PREMISES	DATE AND TIME

Any organization not a party to this suit that is subpoenaed for the taking of a deposition shall designate one or more officers, directors, or managing agents, or other persons who consent to testify on its behalf, and may set forth, for each person designated, the matters on which the person will testify. Federal Rules of Civil Procedure, 30(b)(6).

ISSUING OFFICER SIGNATURE AND TITLE (INDICATE IF ATTORNEY FOR PLAINTIFF OR DEFENDANT)	DATE

ISSUING OFFICER'S NAME, ADDRESS AND PHONE NUMBER

(See Rule 45, Federal Rules of Civil Procedure, Parts C & D on Reverse)

AO 88 (Rev. 11/91) Subpoena in a Civil Case

PROOF OF SERVICE

	DATE		PLACE

SERVED

SERVED ON (PRINT NAME)		MANNER OF SERVICE

SERVED BY (PRINT NAME)		TITLE

DECLARATION OF SERVER

I declare under penalty of perjury under the laws of the United States of America that the foregoing information contained in the Proof of Service is true and correct.

Executed on _____
DATE

SIGNATURE OF SERVER

ADDRESS OF SERVER

Rule 45, Federal Rules of Civil Procedure, Parts C & D:

(c) PROTECTION OF PERSONS SUBJECT TO SUBPOENAS.

(1) A party or an attorney responsible for the issuance and service of a subpoena shall take reasonable steps to avoid imposing undue burden or expense on a person subject to that subpoena. The court on behalf of which the subpoena was issued shall enforce this duty and impose upon the party or attorney in breach of this duty an appropriate sanction, which may include, but is not limited to, lost earnings and a reasonable attorney's fee.

(2)(A) A person commanded to produce and permit inspection and copying of designated books, papers, documents or tangible things, or inspection of premises need not appear in person at the place of production or inspection unless commanded to appear for deposition, hearing or trial.

(B) Subject to paragraph (d)(2) of this rule, a person commanded to produce and permit inspection and copying may, within 14 days after service of the subpoena or before the time specified for compliance if such time is less than 14 days after service, serve upon the party or attorney designated in the subpoena written objection to inspection or copying of any or all of the designated materials or of the premises. If objection is made, the party serving the subpoena shall not be entitled to inspect and copy the materials or inspect the premises except pursuant to an order of the court by which the subpoena was issued. If objection has been made, the party serving the subpoena may, upon notice to the person commanded to produce, move at any time for an order to compel the production. Such an order to compel production shall protect any person who is not a party or an officer of a party from significant expense resulting from the inspection and copying commanded.

(3) (A) On timely motion, the court by which a subpoena was issued shall quash or modify the subpoena if it

(i) fails to allow reasonable time for compliance;
(ii) requires a person who is not a party or an officer of a party to travel to a place more than 100 miles from the place where that person resides, is employed or regularly transacts business in per-

son, except that, subject to the provisions of clause (c)(3)(B)(iii) of this rule, such a person may in order to attend trial be commanded to travel from any such place within the state in which the trial is held, or

(iii) requires disclosure of privileged or other protected matter and no exception or waiver applies, or

(iv) subjects a person to undue burden.

(B) If a subpoena

(i) requires disclosure of a trade secret or other confidential research, development, or commercial information, or

(ii) requires disclosure of an unretained expert's opinion or information not describing specific events or occurrences in dispute and resulting from the expert's study made not at the request of any party, or

(iii) requires a person who is not a party or an officer of a party to incur substantial expense to travel more than 100 miles to attend trial, the court may, to protect a person subject to or affected by the subpoena, quash or modify the subpoena or, if the party in whose behalf the subpoena is issued shows a substantial need for the testimony or material that cannot be otherwise met without undue hardship and assures that the person to whom the subpoena is addressed will be reasonably compensated, the court may order appearance or production only upon specified conditions.

(d) DUTIES IN RESPONDING TO SUBPOENA.

(1) A person responding to a subpoena to produce documents shall produce them as they are kept in the usual course of business or shall organize and label them to correspond with the categories in the demand.

(2) When information subject to a subpoena is withheld on a claim that it is privileged or subject to protection as trial preparation materials, the claim shall be made expressly and shall be supported by a description of the nature of the documents, communications, or things not produced that is sufficient to enable the demanding party to contest the claim.

Notes on Sources

Most frequently cited sources:

Peter Baker, The Breach: Inside the Impeachment and Trial of William Jefferson Clinton (2000) ("Baker").

Joe Conason and Gene Lyons, The Hunting of the President (2000) ("Conason and Lyons").

Michael Isikoff, Uncovering Clinton: A Reporter's Story (1999) ("Isikoff").

Howard Kurtz, Spin Cycle: How the White House and the Media Manipulate the News (1998) ("Kurtz").

Stuart Taylor, Jr., "Her Case Against Clinton," The American Lawyer, November 1996 ("Taylor 1996").

Stuart Taylor, Jr. with Timothy J. Burger, "Jones' Credibility," Legal Times, June 23, 1997 ("Taylor 1997").

Jeffrey Toobin, A Vast Conspiracy: The Real Story of the Sex Scandal That Nearly Brought Down a President (1999) ("Toobin").

John W. Whitehead, Slaying Dragons: The Truth Behind the Man Who Defended Paula Jones (1999) ("Whitehead").

Bob Woodward, Shadow: Five Presidents and the Legacy of Watergate (1999) ("Woodward").

Preface

Clinton on "the dragnet of discovery": Woodward at 438.

Chapter 1

Characterization of The American Spectator as conservative: Stephen Braun, et al., "Pathway to Peril: How Clinton and His Adversaries Endangered His Presidency," Los Angeles Times, Jan. 31, 1999 at A1; Sean Piccoli, "Standard Claims Success on Arrival, But Doubts Remain," The Washington Times, Dec. 26, 1995 at A4.

Jones's reaction to the article in The American Spectator, her conversation with Ferguson, her contacting Traylor, and Traylor's initial handling of the case: Isikoff at 1-29, 39-47, 48-51, 81-84, 87-88; Toobin at 3-5, 10-22, 24-28; Conason and Lyons at 121-122; and Taylor 1996.

The "elves" who secretly worked on Jones's behalf: Isikoff at 83, 109-110, 182; Woodward at 182-183; Conason and Lyons at 59, 99-115, 125-126, 260, 298-300; Toobin at 40-47, 104; Don van Natta Jr. and Jill Abramson, "Quietly, a Team of Lawyers Kept Paula Jones's Case Alive," New York Times, Jan. 24, 1999, at A1; Haynes Johnson, The Best of Times: America in the Clinton Years 260-265 (2001); Lisa Brennan, "Jones Case Work Causes Firm Flap," National Law Journal, February 8, 1999, at A6; Cynthia Cotts, "Lawyers' Tale Feeds Conspiracy Theory," National Law Journal, October 19, 1998, at A6.

Davis and Cammarata are contacted and begin work; the parties attempt settlement: Isikoff at 90-93, 106; Toobin at 40-47; Woodward at 256-257; Taylor 1996; Viveca Novak, "Attorneys in Harassment Lawsuit Against Clinton Emerged in Wake of Conservative Groups' Search," Wall Street Journal, May 12, 1994, at A16; and Ruth Shalit, "The President's Lawyer," New York Times Sunday Magazine, Oct. 2, 1994, p. 42.

Descriptions of Davis and Cammarata as moderate: Viveca Novak, "Attorneys in Harassment Lawsuit Against Clinton Emerged in Wake of Conservative Groups' Search," Wall Street Journal, May 12, 1994, at A16; Isikoff at 106; Toobin at 123, 136; and Conason and Lyons at 126, 261, 298-299.

Bennett's conversations with Clinton (at various points in the lawsuit): Toobin at 46, 166, 215-216; Woodward at 255, 258-259, 360-361, 370.

Lawyer interviewing of Jones: Isikoff at 93.

Note 11: Bennett's request of a twelve-person jury: Toobin at 127.

Chapter 2

Cutler to Bennett: "Nothing else matters": Toobin at 52-53.

Argument in Supreme Court: Toobin at 115-117; Conason and Lyons at 260-263.

Events concerning then-Professor Clinton and student Susan Webber: Toobin at 171-172; Whitehead at 95-96; and Harvey Berkman, "Student of Prof. Clinton Will Judge His Lawsuit," National Law Journal, June 6, 1994, at A12.

Chapter 3

President Clinton "beginning to pay a political price": Taylor 1996 (quoted in Chapter 6); Taylor 1997; Toobin at 52; "A Conversation with Bob Bennett: Bill Clinton's Lawyer Discusses Paula Jones Case," Nightline, June 4, 1997, available at 1997 WL 12826147.

Chapter 5

The second unsuccessful attempt at settlement and the Davis-Cammarata letter to Jones: Toobin at 115-121, 125-126; Conason and Lyons at 304-305; Woodward at 178-180.

Elves "terrified that Jones would settle": Isikoff at 183; Conason and Lyons at 302.

Jones's new lawyers: Toobin at 134-136; Woodward at 357-359; Isikoff at 186-188; Conason and Lyons at 319-321; Whitehead at 3-6; and Robert L. Jackson, "Conservatives Rally to Paula Jones Litigation," Los Angeles Times, Dec. 13, 1997, at A23.

Whitehead's interview of then-Professor Clinton: Whitehead at 95-103.

Chapter 6

Flawed subpoena duces tecum to Tripp: Conason and Lyons at 340 (citing Starr Report Supp. Part 3, p. 4331).

Deposition of Jones: Toobin at 160-162.

Deposition of Willey: Isikoff at 271-272.

Paula Jones Legal Fund: Toobin at 119; Conason and Lyons at 260-261, 321-322; Ellen Joan Pollock, "Jones Is Creating a Fund to Defray Costs of Clinton Suit," Wall Street Journal, June 1, 1994, at B5; and "Paying for Paula," Legal Times, Dec. 8, 1997.

Chapter 7

First and second set of interrogatories to Clinton: Taylor 1997; Toobin at 138-139.

"We've been waiting three years . . .": Toobin at 217-218; Isikoff at 216-218.

Paula Jones Legal Fund and First Amendment issues: Whitehead at 317-318.

Chapter 8

Impeachment: Alison Mitchell, "The President's Acquittal: The Overview," New York Times, Feb. 13, 1999, at A1; Alison Mitchell, "Impeachment: The Overview: Clinton Impeached," New York Times, Dec. 20, 1998, at A1; Richard A. Serrano and Marc Lacey, "Impeachment: Clinton Impeached," Los Angeles Times, Dec. 20, 1998, at A1.

Jones's lawyers learn of Lewinsky, include her name on witness list, and notify Office of Independent Counsel Starr: Toobin at 164-166, 181-182, 187-188, 193-195; Isikoff at 231, 235-236, 252, 256-257, 266-268, 270, 272, 277-280; Woodward at 360-361, 370-371; Conason and Lyons at 337-340, 349-351, 356-357; Don van Natta Jr. and Jill Abramson, "Quietly, a Team of Lawyers Kept Paula Jones's Case Alive," New York Times, Jan. 24, 1999, at A1; and Cynthia Cotts, "Lawyers' Tale Feeds Conspiracy Theory," National Law Journal, October 19, 1998, at A6.

President Clinton's deposition: Isikoff at 323, 325-327, 329-333, 335-336; Woodward at 377-385; Toobin at 207-208, 217-227; and Conason and Lyons at 362-365.

Bennett's letter to Judge Wright: The National Law Journal Web page: *www.nlj.com/1999/upcoming/0215e.html.*

Suspension of Clinton's license to practice law: Neil A. Lewis, "Exiting Job, Clinton Accepts Immunity Deal," New York Times, Jan. 20, 2001, at A1.

Chapter 10

Litigation of summary judgment motion: Toobin at 292-296; Harvey Berkman, "The Big Win," National Law Journal, April 27, 1998, at A1.

Chapter 11

Cutler's advice: Woodward at 254.

Lewinsky's advice: Toobin at 178.

Other lawyers opined: An astute example is Debra S. Katz, "One Round Too Many," Legal Times, Jan. 26, 1998.

Possibility that Eighth Circuit might reverse some part of Judge Wright's summary judgment decision: Woodward at 478; Baker at 108, 134; and Robert L. Jackson, "Lewinsky Could Reappear in Jones Appeal Courts," Los Angeles Times, Oct. 21, 1998, at A18.

Settlement negotiations just before complaint was filed: see source notes for Chapter 1.

Settlement negotiations before Supreme Court decision: Toobin at 119.

Settlement negotiations after Supreme Court decision: see source notes for Chapter 5.

Settlement discussion before Judge Wright: Toobin at 208-209.

Final settlement and division of proceeds: Toobin at 393-395; "Paula Jones Splits Clinton Payment," International Herald Tribune, Mar. 6, 1999, at 3.

The Bennett-Dershowitz disputes: Toobin at 49-50; Alan M. Dershowitz, Sexual McCarthyism: Clinton, Starr, and the Emerging Constitutional Crisis at 115-120 (1999); Peter Aronson, "Dershowitz Goes After Bennett," National Law Journal, Feb. 15, 1999, at A1; Alan Dershowitz, "Commentary: Leading the President Astray," Los Angeles Times, Jan. 25, 1999, at B-5; "William Jeffress Responds to Alan Dershowitz," National Law Journal, Jan. 29, 1999; "Alan Dershowitz Responds to William Jeffress," National Law Journal, Feb. 4, 1999.

Hirschfeld: Toobin at 394; Baker at 117, 134, 166; Michael A. Riccardi, "Paula Jones Hits Hirschfeld with Lawsuit," New York Law Journal, Aug. 16, 2001, at 1.

Chronology

The primary sources were the court's docket and The Office of the Independent Counsel, Referral to the U.S. House of Representatives, Appendix Vol. II, Tab C: "Procedural History and Background of Jones v. Clinton."

Index